GOLD

first

NEW EDITION
with 2015 exam specifications

teacher's book

Clementine Annabell
Rawdon Wyatt

C000225268

Rationale

Welcome to *Gold First New Edition*, an innovative and engaging course for students preparing to sit Cambridge English: First or working at B2 on the common European framework. *Gold First* follows the same identity and approach as *FCE Gold Plus*, but has been comprehensively updated to reflect the 2015 Cambridge English: First exam specifications. Rich authentic texts, carefully chosen to appeal to adults and older teenagers, provide the basis for lessons that will captivate the interest of both students and teachers alike.

A well-prepared student will enter the exam confident both of their English level and the best strategies to approach each task. Students will finish the *Gold First New Edition* course confident of what to expect in the exam from the detailed Exam Focus section and tips for every practice task. In addition, there is an extensive writing reference section with sample graded answers and comments, and useful language for each genre.

The *Gold First New Edition* package combines a suite of printed and digital components that can be used individually or in a multitude of combinations to suit the learner's needs and the technology available. The table on page 5 gives an overview of how the components available with *Gold First New Edition* fit together. The teaching notes include many ideas for how and when to integrate the different components to provide a seamlessly integrated and easy-to-use course package that both tech-savvy teachers and those using an interactive whiteboard for the first time will find invaluable.

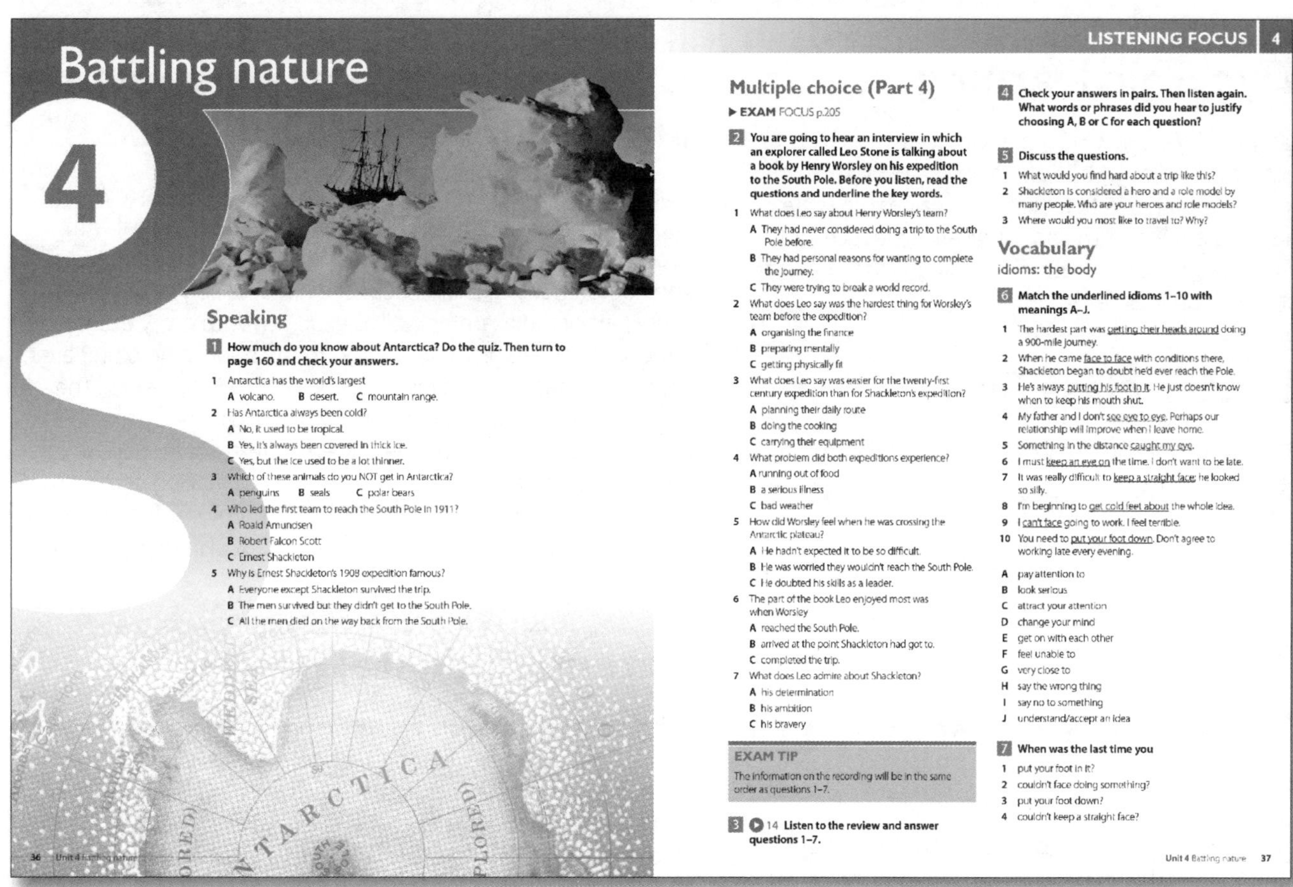

Battling nature

4

Speaking

1 How much do you know about Antarctica? Do the quiz. Then turn to page 160 and check your answers.

1 Antarctica has the world's largest
A volcano. **B** desert. **C** mountain range.

2 Has Antarctica always been cold?
A No, it used to be tropical.
B Yes, it's always been covered in thick ice.
C Yes, but the ice used to be a lot thinner.

3 Which of these animals do you NOT get in Antarctica?
A penguins **B** seals **C** polar bears

4 Who led the first team to reach the South Pole in 1911?
A Roald Amundsen
B Robert Falcon Scott
C Ernest Shackleton

5 Why is Ernest Shackleton's 1908 expedition famous?
A Everyone except Shackleton survived the trip.
B The men survived but they didn't get to the South Pole.
C All the men died on the way back from the South Pole.

36 Unit 4 Battling nature

LISTENING FOCUS | 4

Multiple choice (Part 4)

▶ **EXAM** FOCUS p.205

2 You are going to hear an interview in which an explorer called Leo Stone is talking about a book by Henry Worsley on his expedition to the South Pole. Before you listen, read the questions and underline the key words.

1 What does Leo say about Henry Worsley's team?
A They had never considered doing a trip to the South Pole before.
B They had personal reasons for wanting to complete the journey.
C They were trying to break a world record.

2 What does Leo say was the hardest thing for Worsley's team before the expedition?
A organising the finance
B preparing mentally
C getting physically fit

3 What does Leo say was easier for the twenty-first century expedition than for Shackleton's expedition?
A planning their daily route
B doing the cooking
C carrying their equipment

4 What problem did both expeditions experience?
A running out of food
B a serious illness
C bad weather

5 How did Worsley feel when he was crossing the Antarctic plateau?
A He hadn't expected it to be so difficult.
B He was worried they wouldn't reach the South Pole.
C He doubted his skills as a leader.

6 The part of the book Leo enjoyed most was when Worsley
A reached the South Pole.
B arrived at the point Shackleton had got to.
C completed the trip.

7 What does Leo admire about Shackleton?
A his determination
B his ambition
C his bravery

EXAM TIP
The information on the recording will be in the same order as questions 1–7.

3 14 **Listen to the review and answer questions 1–7.**

4 Check your answers in pairs. Then listen again. What words or phrases did you hear to justify choosing A, B or C for each question?

5 Discuss the questions.

1 What would you find hard about a trip like this?
2 Shackleton is considered a hero and a role model by many people. Who are your heroes and role models?
3 Where would you most like to travel to? Why?

Vocabulary
idioms: the body

6 Match the underlined idioms 1–10 with meanings A–J.

1 The hardest part was getting their heads around doing a 900-mile journey.
2 When he came face to face with conditions there, Shackleton began to doubt he'd ever reach the Pole.
3 He's always putting his foot in it. He just doesn't know when to keep his mouth shut.
4 My father and I don't see eye to eye. Perhaps our relationship will improve when I leave home.
5 Something in the distance caught my eye.
6 I must keep an eye on the time. I don't want to be late.
7 It was really difficult to keep a straight face; he looked so silly.
8 I'm beginning to get cold feet about the whole idea.
9 I can't face going to work. I feel terrible.
10 You need to put your foot down. Don't agree to working late every evening.

A pay attention to
B look serious
C attract your attention
D change your mind
E get on with each other
F feel unable to
G very close to
H say the wrong thing
I say no to something
J understand/accept an idea

7 When was the last time you

1 put your foot in it?
2 couldn't face doing something?
3 put your foot down?
4 couldn't keep a straight face?

Unit 4 Battling nature 37

Main features of the course

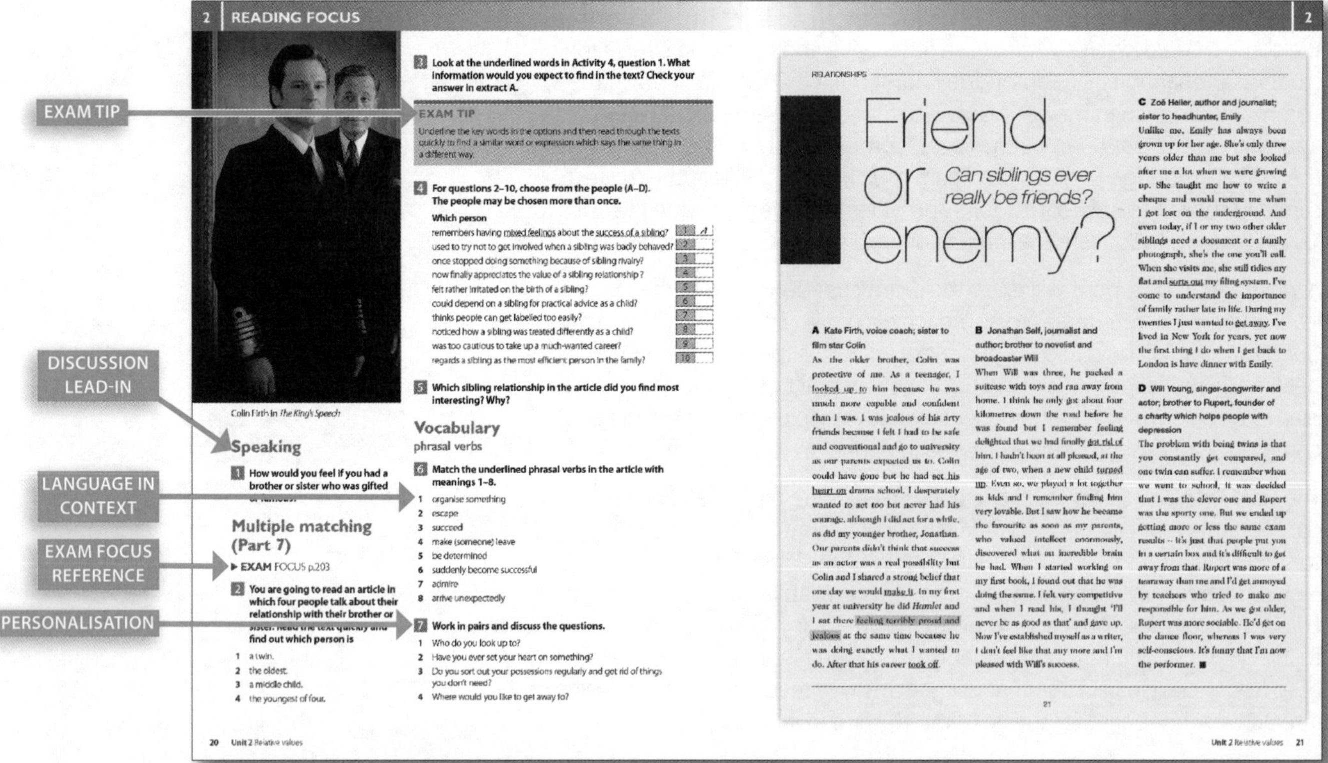

2 | READING FOCUS

Colin Firth in *The King's Speech*

Speaking

1 How would you feel if you had a brother or sister who was gifted

Multiple matching (Part 7)

▶ **EXAM** FOCUS p.203

2 You are going to read an article in which four people talk about their relationship with their brother or sister. Read the text quickly and find out which person is

1 a twin.
2 the oldest.
3 a middle child.
4 the youngest of four.

3 Look at the underlined words in Activity 4, question 1. What information would you expect to find in the text? Check your answer in extract A.

EXAM TIP

Underline the key words in the options and then read through the texts quickly to find a similar word or expression which says the same thing in a different way.

4 For questions 2–10, choose from the people (A–D). The people may be chosen more than once.

Which person

remembers having mixed feelings about the success of a sibling?	1	A
used to try not to get involved when a sibling was badly behaved?	2	
once stopped doing something because of sibling rivalry?	3	
now finally appreciates the value of a sibling relationship?	4	
felt rather irritated on the birth of a sibling?	5	
could depend on a sibling for practical advice as a child?	6	
thinks people can get labelled too easily?	7	
noticed how a sibling was treated differently as a child?	8	
was too cautious to take up a much-wanted career?	9	
regards a sibling as the most efficient person in the family?	10	

5 Which sibling relationship in the article did you find most interesting? Why?

Vocabulary
phrasal verbs

6 Match the underlined phrasal verbs in the article with meanings 1–8.

1 organise something
2 escape
3 succeed
4 make (someone) leave
5 be determined
6 suddenly become successful
7 admire
8 arrive unexpectedly

7 Work in pairs and discuss the questions.

1 Who do you look up to?
2 Have you ever set your heart on something?
3 Do you sort out your possessions regularly and get rid of things you don't need?
4 Where would you like to get away to?

20 Unit 2 Relative values

RELATIONSHIPS

Friend or enemy?

Can siblings ever really be friends?

A Kate Firth, voice coach; sister to film star Colin

As the older brother, Colin was protective of me. As a teenager, I looked up to him because he was much more capable and confident than I was. I was jealous of his arty friends because I felt I had to be safe and conventional and go to university as our parents expected us to. Colin could have gone but he had set his heart on drama school. I desperately wanted to act too but never had his courage, although I did act for a while, as did my younger brother, Jonathan. Our parents didn't think that success as an actor was a real possibility but Colin and I shared a strong belief that one day we would make it. In my first year at university he did *Hamlet* and I sat there feeling terribly proud and jealous at the same time because he was doing exactly what I wanted to do. After that his career took off.

B Jonathan Self, journalist and author; brother to novelist and broadcaster Will

When Will was three, he packed a suitcase with toys and ran away from home. I think he only got about four kilometres down the road before he was found but I remember feeling delighted that we had finally got rid of him. I hadn't been at all pleased, at the age of two, when a new child turned up. Even so, we played a lot together as kids and I remember finding him very lovable. But I saw how he became the favourite as soon as my parents, who valued intellect enormously, discovered what an incredible brain he had. When I started working on my first book, I found out that he was doing the same. I felt very competitive and when I read his, I thought 'I'll never be as good as that' and gave up. Now I've established myself as a writer, I don't feel like that any more and I'm pleased with Will's success.

C Zoë Heller, author and journalist; sister to headhunter, Emily

Unlike me, Emily has always been grown up for her age. She's only three years older than me but she looked after me a lot when we were growing up. She taught me how to write a cheque and would rescue me when I got lost on the underground. And even today, if I or my two other older siblings need a document or a family photograph, she's the one you'll call. When she visits me, she still tidies my flat and sorts out my filing system. I've come to understand the importance of family rather late in life. During my twenties I just wanted to get away. I've lived in New York for years, yet now the first thing I do when I get back to London is have dinner with Emily.

D Will Young, singer-songwriter and actor; brother to Rupert, founder of a charity which helps people with depression

The problem with being twins is that you constantly get compared, and one twin can suffer. I remember when we went to school, it was decided that I was the clever one and Rupert was the sporty one. But we ended up getting more or less the same exam results – it's just that people put you in a certain box and it's difficult to get away from that. Rupert was more of a tearaway than me and I'd get annoyed by teachers who tried to make me responsible for him. As we got older, Rupert was more sociable. He'd get on the dance floor, whereas I was very self-conscious. It's funny that I'm now the performer. ■

21

Unit 2 Relative values 21

Dynamic learning

Using *Gold First New Edition* makes it easy to teach light, fun classes with stimulating, discussion-rich lessons together with lots of personalisation. There is a strong emphasis on communicative practice and the development of natural speaking skills to develop student confidence.

Better class flow

Material in *Gold First New Edition* is divided into lessons on spreads or pages so that there is a natural progression through a variety of activities including individual, pair- and classwork. Each unit contains practice for all papers of the Cambridge English: First exam and every lesson includes an integrated range of skills with plenty of discussion.

Vocabulary presented in chunks

In *Gold First New Edition*, phrasal verbs, collocations, idioms and other vocabulary are presented and practised in context to help students understand and remember them better.

Comprehensive exam practice and support

Gold First New Edition ensures that both teachers and students know what to expect in the 2015 exam and how to deal with each part effectively, thanks to the carefully staged exam tasks and comprehensive Exam Focus section detailing strategies for every part of the exam, as well as extra tips with every exam task. Support levels are graduated through the book to help prepare students for tackling the tasks independently in the exam. The *Exam Maximiser* also provides plenty of revision, practice and extension, as well as a complete Practice Test, additional Use of English sections and advice on how to avoid making common exam errors. *MyEnglishLab: Cambridge First* provides further online practice of the skills students will need to excel in their exam as well as two full tests.

Extensive digital package

The *Gold First New Edition* digital components provide an easy-to-use solution for teachers and schools who wish to incorporate technology to a greater extent in their classes to provide a more engaging student experience. Components include *eText* for students, *eText IWB software* for teachers, *Online Testmaster* and *MyEnglishLab: Cambridge First*. You will find many ideas of how and when to use these included in the *Teacher's Book* along with other suggestions for incorporating technology, such as useful websites.

Gold First New Edition Package Components

Component	Technology Required	Description
Coursebook		• fourteen engaging units with authentic texts • exam-style practice and exam tips with every exam task • extensive reference section including Grammar Reference, Exam Focus and Writing Reference
Exam Maximiser	Internet connection for audio Download the Maximiser audio at **www.english.com/goldfirstne**	• additional practice of exam tasks and language points • activities follow on from but are not dependent on the *Coursebook* • plenty of extra listening practice, with audio available online • seven additional Use of English spreads and a complete Practice Test. • cross-references to *Exam Maximiser* tasks at the end of each lesson in the *Teacher's Book*
MyEnglishLab: Cambridge First	Computers with internet connection Students' unique access codes are on the inside front cover of their *Coursebook with MyEnglishLab*. Arrange your teacher's access code through your local Pearson office: **http://www.pearsonelt.com/worldwideoffices**	• designed to be used alongside the *Gold First* course • comprehensive training in the subskills and areas of language that underpin the exam • video presentations of each part of the exam • two full practice tests • automatic grading for most activities, giving students instant rich feedback and saving you time in the classroom • gradebook allows you to track students' progress as a group or individually • gradebook and Common Error Report help in identifying individuals or general areas for additional attention.
eText for students	Student netbooks/computers Students' unique access codes are printed on their eText Access Card.	• digital version of the coursebook • for use at home or on netbooks or computers in the classroom • includes interactive activities • students can listen as many times as they need to, and read along with the audio script.
Teacher's Book	Photocopier for photocopiables	• your complete guide to using all of the *Gold First New Edition* components in a blended classroom • lesson plans with answers, audio scripts and sample writing task answers • cross-references to all of the Gold components • supplementary ideas for warmers and extension activities • advice on using the digital components, and other ideas for a blended classroom, including useful websites • two photocopiable activities per unit
eText IWB software for teachers	Interactive Whiteboard/Projector	• can be used during class to display the course pages, play audio and do exercises • answers for all activities • video of a mock speaking test • essential IWB tools and ability to add notes, links and documents • games practising key grammar points or vocabulary from the unit.
Online Testmaster	Computer with internet connection Access the Testmaster through your local Pearson office: **http://www.pearsonelt.com/worldwideoffices**	• customisable tests in Word format • includes placement tests, a unit test for each unit, five progress tests and an exit test.
Class Audio	Internet connection or CD player Access the online audio through your local Pearson office: **http://www.pearsonelt.com/worldwideoffices**	• available online for teachers who choose not to use the IWB software • audio CDs are also available in some markets.

To place an order or for more information, go to **www.pearsonelt.com**.

Recommended with Gold First

Longman Exams Dictionary

With expert guidance on vocabulary building and writing skills, plus hours of interactive exam practice on the CD-ROM, the *Longman Exams Dictionary* is a must-have for students preparing for examinations.

- Covers key academic study areas
- 10,000 synonyms, antonyms and word families
- Over 1,000 Study Notes on vocabulary, grammar and common errors
- Academic Word List highlighted
- Topic Activator section focuses on vocabulary for common exam topics
- Essay Activator section focuses on key vocabulary for writing tasks

The *Longman Exams Coach CD-ROM* includes hours of interactive practice, with feedback including strategies to improve academic essay writing and listening practice.

Practice Tests Plus First 2 New Edition

The *Practice Tests Plus First 2 New Edition* offers comprehensive practice for each exam paper and includes:

- eight complete practice tests, two with exam guidance and question-specific tips
- audio and visual materials for students to practise for the speaking and listening papers at home
- a guide to the Cambridge English: First 2015 exam
- answer key and audio script to support teachers doing exam practice in class.

Practice Tests Plus First 2 New Edition includes online materials include:

- filmed examples of the speaking exam
- writing samples
- teaching tips and activity ideas.

Grammar and Vocabulary for Cambridge First

Grammar and Vocabulary for Cambridge First second edition offers integrated grammar and vocabulary practice for students preparing for the Cambridge First exam.

- Thorough review of key grammar points with thousands of corpus-based example sentences showing natural English in authentic contexts
- *Word Store* focusing on topics and lexical areas that are important for the exam
- Entry Tests to lead students to practice of specific language points
- Exam Practice every two units

Teaching strategies

The *Gold First New Edition Online Testmaster* includes an entry test which may be used as an aid to establish whether a student is at an appropriate level for the *Gold First New Edition* course. Even if two students were to attain an identical numerical score, no two learners are exactly the same and consequently it is natural that every teacher has to manage a degree of diversity in their class due to variation in prior knowledge, learning pace and style and motivation.

A key aspect to successfully teaching a multi-level class is to know your learners.

Ideas to help you know your learners:

Student reflection

Ask students to reflect on and describe their own goals, strengths and weaknesses in their personal English-learning journey. This works well as an initial writing assignment for the first day's homework on the course.

Test to help you teach

The *Gold First New Edition Online Testmaster* includes a range of assessment resources including entry and exit tests, fourteen unit tests and five progress tests. Using these tests can help you focus your classes more precisely to your students' needs.

Make time to listen

During group discussions and pairwork, take the opportunity to circulate and listen. Make notes on what you hear, especially any areas that require targeted development to deal with later in the lesson or at a future point.

Read student writing regularly

Each *Gold First New Edition* unit includes a writing assignment. By giving individualised feedback, you will learn a lot about each student as a writer. Make sure you keep in mind what you notice to include in future teaching.

Tutorials

Some teachers find meeting with students individually in a tutorial beneficial for monitoring and discussing progress. You could allow 15 minutes once a month for this.

Record-keeping

Records could be as simple as a page for each student in the class register binder, or could be kept electronically in a document or spreadsheet. Having a place to keep notes on each student including goals, test scores and writing feedback makes it easier to remember the details of individuals as well as to write reports.

Manage multi-level classes

Plenty of pairwork

Working in pairs and small groups gives students the opportunity to learn reciprocally. Discussing reasons for their answers in an activity can be particularly useful by providing both the challenge of articulating a reason effectively and the support of having someone else's thought process explained. The lesson plans in the *Gold First Teacher's Book* include pairwork in every lesson.

Mix them up

The more diverse your class, the more important it is to change partners regularly to ensure students get a range of practice with people with different strengths. This is particularly important for preparation for the speaking paper of Cambridge First, where students will be paired with someone who may have a different level than themselves. Repeating an exercise with a new partner is a strategy that is often used in the *Gold First Teacher's Book*, which gives students of all abilities the opportunity to improve their first performance.

Offer choices

Many students respond well to choices that help them make a decision about their own learning. For example: 'Okay, I'm going to offer you a choice here. For those who would like to look at the third conditional in more detail, I'm going to work through the Grammar Reference now. If you feel you are already familiar with the third conditional, you can start the third conditional activity on p.X.'

Have a plan for fast finishers

If your class is particularly diverse, there may be a significant variation in the time it takes for students to complete an exercise, especially during timed tests or writing activities. One option is to write the day's homework on the board before class, and let students know that if they finish class exercises early they can begin working on their homework. Another option for fast finishers is for them to design a few extra questions/exercises on the lesson topic. You could also have a basket of English newspapers/magazines/readers available.

Provide extra support

Some additional suggestions for students who are finding the course very challenging include:

- giving students the opportunity to rehearse before discussion activities, e.g. 'You're going to speak with your partner about the photos on p.X. Take a minute now to look at them and think about what you're going to say. I'll let you know when to begin.'
- for writing activities, eliciting starters on the board which students may choose to use
- encouraging students to listen to the audio again after class on *ActiveBook*.

See page 6 for some recommended additional resources.

Teaching with MyEnglishLab

MyEnglishLab: Cambridge First complements *Gold First* and allows you to provide students with a blended learning experience. Focusing on the subskills that underpin the Cambridge English: First exam, *MyEnglishLab: Cambridge First* includes interactive practice activities, video introductions to each part of the exam, and two full practice tests. You and your students can access these materials wherever there is an internet connection.

Using *MyEnglishLab: Cambridge First* allows you to spend less time marking exercises in class, which frees up classroom time for more communicative activities, project work, and so on, and students receive instant detailed feedback which is relevant to the answer they gave.

Introduce MyEnglishLab to your students

After you have registered and created your course, students can register using the unique access code from their Coursebook and your Teacher's course code. Students will feel more confident about accessing their online course activities if you demonstrate how in class.

Introducing the purpose of MyEnglishLab to your class is essential. You can discuss how you intend to use it and why it is beneficial: students can work in a digital format – perhaps they'll like this for variety and a sense of independence, or perhaps they are preparing for the computer-based test; they'll have access to additional practice of the key skills they'll need to excel in the exam; they can get instant feedback on their answers; they can track their progress very easily with the onscreen indicators.

Assign work regularly

You can make all of the material available for students to work through in their own time, or assign specific activities as you go through your course. Suggestions for activities to assign with Gold First are made in the Additional Practice sections of these teacher's notes. You can assign tasks to the whole class, to groups of students with different needs, or to individual students.

Make the most of the gradebook

Check the gradebook regularly to see how your students are doing. If students are not completing activities, you can email them to find out why. You can export the gradebook as an Excel file to make life easy when you need to write student reports.

The Common Error report shows the frequency and types of errors students have made on an exercise. This makes it easy for you to identify areas for further remedial teaching.

Messages

MyEnglishLab: Cambridge First enables you to send and keep track of messages to your students outside class. You can remind students about their homework, offer guidance, and have one-to-one exchanges with individual students. There is also a folder where you can upload documents for the class such as reading material, sample answers or notices.

Bands and fans

Speaking focus ▶ p.6

Speaking

Aim

- to introduce the topic of music and free time, and to give spoken practice

Warmer: A song that reminds you of something

Ask students to think of a song or a piece of music that reminds them of something, such as a person or a period of their life. It might be the first piece of music they bought for themselves, a song from a concert they attended, or a song a family member used to sing during their childhood. Give students a few minutes to think of a song and what it reminds them of. You could tell the class about a song you like and briefly what it reminds you of as an example. Ask students to move around the room speaking to as many people as possible to find out whether anyone has chosen similar or different memories. If students do not know each other, remind them to introduce themselves to each person before asking about the song they have chosen. Include yourself in the discussion. Allow about ten minutes for students to mingle. Finish the activity by eliciting any similarities students noticed between songs or memories that they chose.

1 Focus students on the photo, and elicit some descriptions. Ensure students understand the words *live* (a performance in person) and *gig* (a performance by a musician or a group of musicians playing modern popular music or a performance by a comedian). Put students into pairs to discuss the questions. Elicit a few answers to each question.

Answers

1 Students' own answers

Additional activity

Ask students what kinds of music styles they like and write them on the board. Elicit any other music styles students can think of, then get students to brainstorm words and phrases to describe the music with a partner. Add these words to the board.

Example styles: *jazz, country, pop, rock, soul, classical, R&B, hip hop*

Example descriptions: *rhythmic, loud, slow, has a strong beat, relaxing, catchy*

Vocabulary

free time activities: verb/noun collocations

Aim

- to review and expand students' knowledge of collocations related to free time activities

2 Students match the verbs in A with the activities in B. Ask students to compare their answers in pairs, then elicit responses as a class.

3 Elicit some additional free time activities and verbs that collocate. If students find this difficult, try eliciting activities that go with each verb in 2A, for example, *play football: What other sports could you play?* (*play tennis, play rugby,* etc.)

Answers

2 **do** yoga; **go** running, shopping; **go to** a film, a gig, the theatre; **go out for** a pizza; **go on** the computer; **have** friends round, a pizza; **play** computer games, football, the guitar; **watch** a DVD, a film, football, television.

3 Students' own answers

Sample answers
go rockclimbing, clubbing; go out for a meal; play basketball; have a nap; do an aerobics class

ADDITIONAL PRACTICE | **Maximiser** p.6, Vocabulary 1–2

Listening and speaking

asking and answering questions

Aim

- to practise asking and answering questions and to practise using phrases related to free time activities

4 Ask students to read the questions. Make sure they understand *underline* by demonstrating it on eText or the board. Play the recording of the first sentence and elicit the stressed words from the class. Play the rest of the recording and ask students to underline the stressed words. Elicit the answers, replaying with pauses as necessary. Drill the pronunciation by asking students to repeat each question after it is played on the recording. Pause and replay any questions that students find difficult.

5 Play the recording and ask students to complete the gaps. Play the recording a second time if necessary. Ask students to check their answers in pairs and then replay the recording with pauses to check as a class. Ask students to read the **Language Tip**. Write some example sentences on the board and elicit ways adverbs of frequency/longer adverbials could fit into the sentences. For example: *I watch a DVD on Friday nights. I usually/hardly ever/sometimes watch a DVD on Friday nights. I go to a yoga class. I go to a yoga class from time to time.* Then ask students to turn to the **Grammar Reference** on page 162 and go through it with them, displaying it on eText if you are using it.

6 Leave the **Grammar Reference** on eText as a reference and put students into pairs to ask and answer the questions. If time allows, put students into new pairs to repeat the exercise to increase confidence. Circulate, noting any issues with adverb placement for later practice.

Answers

4 1 How do you usually <u>relax</u> when you have some <u>free time</u>?

2 What do you <u>do</u> when you <u>stay in</u>? Where do you <u>go</u> when you <u>go out</u>?

3 Do you like being in a <u>large group</u> or would you rather be with a few <u>close friends</u>?

5 1 watching TV; my mood 2 stay in; have friends round 3 Playing the guitar 4 Doing yoga 5 computer games 6 for a pizza

6 Students' own answers

Additional activity

If students find adverb placement difficult, write up a simple sentence on the board, e.g. *I play tennis on Mondays,* and elicit different ways to customise the sentence with different adverbs and adverbials, e.g:

I usually/never play tennis on Mondays.

From time to time, I play tennis on Mondays.

I play tennis on Mondays from time to time.

Interview (Part 1)

listening to and answering questions

Aim

- to introduce an exam-style speaking task (Speaking, Part 1) and to practise giving personal information and opinions in an exam-style discussion

Refer students to the **Exam Focus** on page 206 and turn to it on eText if you are using it. Tell them that this is the first speaking part of the exam and consists of giving personal information and opinions. These are also very useful skills in everyday conversations. Read through the **Exam Focus** with students, making sure they understand everything. In strategy section 2, elicit some ways to sound interested and interesting (e.g. vary tone, body language, use a range of language). You could replay the recording for Activity 5 and notice if the speakers sound interested. In point 5 of the strategy, elicit some phrases for asking someone to repeat something, e.g. *Could you repeat that, please? Would you mind saying that again, please?*

7 Give students a few minutes to match the questions and topics, then compare their answers in pairs before you check as a class.

8 Put students into pairs and ask them to write two more questions for each topic (A–E) using the prompts. Elicit questions from some students and check that question formation is accurate.

9 Give students two minutes to read the questions and then play the recording. Ask students to discuss their answers in pairs and then play the recording again. Elicit answers, replaying or referring to the recording as necessary.

10 Put students in pairs and ask them to take turns asking and answering questions. Read the **Exam Tip** aloud. Circulate, providing feedback and encouraging students to provide full answers. Students can repeat the activity with a new partner, asking and answering different questions for more practice.

Answers

7 1 D 2 A 3 B 4 C 5 E 6 D/E 7 A

8 Students' own answers

9 1 Julia: 2 and 6; Stefan: 7 and 3.
2 Julia: not enough detail in first question; Stefan: yes
3 Julia was a bit flat.
4 I'm sorry. Would you repeat the question, please?

10 Students' own answers

Additional activity: Recording

Students recording themselves can provide a useful measure of their progress in speaking later in the course. If you have facilities to record students, such as a language lab or student mobile phones, ask students to repeat Activity 10, recording themselves and saving it with the date. Make sure that they know that the recording is for their own reference only and will not be shared.

ADDITIONAL PRACTICE | Maximiser p.6, Speaking 1 | **Teacher's Book** p.136/158, Photocopiable 1A *If this is the answer, what's the question?* | **MyEnglishLab: Cambridge First**, Speaking 1a *Part 1 Appropriate answers: What's the best response?*; Speaking 1b *Part 1 Appropriate answers: Practice*; Speaking 2 *Part 1 Detailed answers: What's missing?*

MyEnglishLab tip
Video introductions

There are video introductions to all of the exam papers in MyEnglishLab which students may find useful to watch for homework.

Reading focus ▶ p.8

Speaking

Aim

- to introduce vocabulary to prepare for the music 'tribes' reading text and to provide spoken practice

1 Put students into pairs and ask them to discuss the questions in pairs. Check students understand *be into something* (to like something a lot). Remind students to focus on avoiding one word answers. Elicit a few ideas for each question. (*Photo 1: 1960s, bike rally; Photo 2: 1990s, breakdancing, hip hop; Photo 3: 1980s, punk rock, tattoo, mohawk*)

Answers

1 Students' own answers

Gapped text (Part 6)

Aim

- to complete an exam-style gapped text activity (Reading and Use of English, Part 6)

Refer students to the **Exam Focus** on page 202 and turn to it on eText if you are using it. Read through it with students, making sure they understand everything. Leave it displayed on eText as a reference, so students can follow the strategy when they do the task.

2 Ask students not to read the article yet. Write on the board the title 'Are Music Tribes a thing of the past?'. Check students understand *tribes* (a group of people with the same interests). Ask students to predict what they think the answer will be. Give students one minute to skim the text quickly to find out the author's view. Emphasise that students need to skim quickly and not worry about unknown vocabulary at this stage. Compare answers with student predictions and elicit where in the text they found the answer.

3 Ask students to read the first two paragraphs again and answer the questions. Ask them not to use a dictionary, but instead to guess the meaning of unknown vocabulary through the context as it will be dealt with later in the lesson. Ask students to compare their answers in pairs before you check with the class.

4 Tell students that they are going to complete an exam-style question where sentences need to be fitted into the gaps in the article. Point out the **Exam Tip** to use words and phrases before and after each gap as a clue. Focus on the example. Ask students to read the sentence before the gap. Elicit the subject (young people) and the topic (buying music in the past). Focus on the example answer, E, and point out the pronoun *they* and the similar topic of buying music in the past. Ask a student to read out loud the sentence before the gap and then sentence E, and ask if it makes sense. Do the same with the second gap. Ask students to read the sentence before and after the gap. Elicit the topic (ways of buying music in the past and present). Point out the noun *excitement* in the sentence before, and point out the phrase *in any case*, after the gap, which suggests a contrast. Refer students to sentences A–G and elicit the correct answer C. Point out the word *However,* which suggests a contrast, and the words *that feeling,* which refer back to the noun *excitement.*

Ask students to work through the remainder of the activity and then prompt them to do **Exam Focus** strategy points 7–8.

5 Put students in pairs to compare their answers and then check as a class, eliciting reasons for each choice. If there are some answers that students are unsure of as you go through, ask students to read out the sentence before and after each gap with one or two alternative answers to help them learn to 'feel' which answer is correct.

6 Students discuss the questions in small groups of three or four. Remind students to focus on providing full answers.

Answers

2 No, but tribes now are different – they're broader and more inclusive.

3 1 *these impressions*: people's reactions to the groups of young people

they: the young people

2 *tracks, radio* and *cassette* link back to *records, stream, download.*

Neither adds more (negative) information about how young people these days are different; *They* refers back to young people.

4 1 E **2** C **3** G **4** A **5** B **6** D F is extra.

5–6 Students' own answers

Vocabulary

deducing words in context

Aim

- to practise using context to deduce unknown vocabulary

7 Explain that using context to guess the meaning of unknown words is a useful skill in both conversation and the Cambridge First exam. Complete the example with the class, finding *roam around* in the text and then asking what students think it means, using *scooter* and *all day* as clues. Emphasise that understanding the general idea is more important than getting the meaning exactly right. Ask students to complete the remaining words. Get students to compare their answers in pairs, then check as a class.

Answers

7 1 B **2** A **3** B **4** A **5** A **6** B

ADDITIONAL PRACTICE | **Maximiser** p.7–8, Reading 1–7 | **eText IWB**
Extra activity **MyEnglishLab: Cambridge First**, Reading 14 *Text structure – sequencing: Put the story in order*

Grammar focus ▶ p.10

Present simple and continuous

Aim

- to revise the use of present simple and continuous forms

1 Check students understand the meaning of *overtime* (time that you spend working in your job in addition to your normal working hours) and *sick leave* (time that you are allowed to spend away from work because you are ill). Put students in pairs and ask them to discuss whether each verb should be in the present simple or continuous form. Elicit answers from the class and discuss the reasons for the answers.

2 Ask students to match the uses listed with the examples in Activity 1. Go through the answers as a class, checking the reasons and examples. Read the **Language Tip** aloud. Ask students to turn to **Grammar Reference** on page 176 and read through it with the class (on eText if using it), checking that students understand everything. Leave it displayed on the IWB for students to refer to during Activities 3–5.

3 Ask students to complete the activity in pairs, then check as a class.

4 Elicit the answer to the first sentence as an example, then give students about ten minutes to complete the remainder of the activity. Students check their answers in pairs, then check as a class.

5 Give students about five minutes to write their sentences. Circulate and note any errors in the form or use of present simple or continuous and correct these with the class before students compare their sentences.

6 Put students into pairs to share their sentences and find out if they have anything in common. Elicit a few responses from individual students on how much they had in common with their partner.

Answers

1 1 's always downloading **2** 'm working **3** 's playing **4** comes **5** 'm getting **6** take

2 1 F **2** D **3** C **4** B **5** E **6** A

3 1 A) have = own/possess (stative verb) B) having = taking (activity happening at this moment)
2 A) appears = seems (stative verb) B) appearing = playing at (scheduled event in the future)
3 A) at this moment B) in general
4 A) thinking = considering B) it's my opinion
5 A) it's affected by B) depend on = rely on
6 A) has a good taste (stative verb) B) tasting = trying (happening at the moment of speaking)

4 1 don't like **2** is appearing **3** are saying **4** think **5** 's always checking **6** is getting **7** often go **8** 're being

5–6 Students' own answers

Alternative activity: Who's who? game

Ask students to write their sentences on an unnamed piece of paper. Collect them and number each one. Stick them up on the walls of the classroom. Give students ten minutes to walk around the class, reading the sentences and noting down their guesses about which student wrote each. When students are seated again, redistribute the papers (randomly) and ask each student to read aloud the paper they have been given. Ask for guesses as to which student wrote the sentences, before the student finally reveals who they are.

Additional activity: Writing questions

If students need extra practice of present simple and continuous forms, ask each student to write three questions using the present simple and three using the present continuous. Elicit a few questions to check the form selected is correct and the question formation accurate, then students ask and answer their questions in pairs.

Alternative activity: Online forum

Set up a forum on your learning management system for students to post their sentences. Encourage students to reply to posts where they have something in common. If you do not have a learning management system, you could create your own dedicated forum for your class using a blogging tool such as Wordpress.

ADDITIONAL PRACTICE | **Maximiser** p.8, Grammar 1

Use of English focus

▶ p.11

Vocabulary

phrasal verbs with *take*

Aim

- to review phrasal verbs with *take*

Warmer: Who do you take after?

Write on the board *Do you take after anyone in your family? If so, who?* Elicit the meaning of *take after* (have similar characteristics to an older relative). You may like to give a personal example, e.g. *I take after my mother in personality – we are both friendly and outgoing, but I take after my father in looks – people always comment that I look like him!* Give students a few minutes to discuss the question in pairs, then elicit a few responses.

Explain that in English there are lots of phrasal verbs (combinations of a verb and a preposition or adverb) which have many different meanings, often not literal at all, such as *to take after*. Tell students that some other languages, such as German, also have phrasal verbs and ask students if there are phrasal verbs in their first language.

1 Ask students to match the phrasal verbs 1–5 with the meanings A–E. Let students compare their answers in pairs, then check as a class.

Answers

1 1 E **2** A **3** C **4** B **5** D

Additional activity: Recording vocabulary

Ask students *What strategies do you use to record and learn new vocabulary? A notebook? Flashcards? What do you think would be the most effective way for you to learn vocabulary?* Give students a few minutes to discuss their answers in small groups and then elicit some responses. If students have smartphones, they may be interested in apps such as *Flashcards* which allow the user to create flashcards easily for practice – anywhere, anytime. Encourage students to begin using some kind of system for learning vocabulary.

ADDITIONAL PRACTICE | **eText Game**: Noughts and crosses | **eText IWB** Extra activity |

Multiple-choice cloze (Part 1)

Aim

- to practise using the strategy of elimination to complete an exam-style cloze (Reading and Use of English, Part 1)

Refer students to the **Exam Focus** on page 200 and turn to it on eText if you are using it. Read through it with students, making sure they understand everything.

2 Emphasise that the students should read the text quickly to find the answer to the question without worrying about the gaps or unknown vocabulary at this stage. Allow two minutes for this activity.

3 Tell students that elimination is a very useful technique when answering a multiple-choice cloze. Ask students to discuss the question in pairs, then elicit the answers.

4 Point out to students that this question is aligned with strategy 4 in the **Exam Focus**: *Check the words on either side of the gap.* Complete this question as a class.

5 Read the **Exam Tip** to students. Ask students to cover the answers, then focus on the second gap. Elicit what the missing word might be, then ask students to look at the four options for the gap. Read out the sentence with each of the options in turn and discuss as a class which fits best with the meaning. Elicit that the correct answer is *released* because it collocates with *album*. Then ask students to complete the activity.

6 Ask students to compare their answers in pairs, especially discussing 4 and 8. Before you check the answers as a class, give students a few minutes to complete strategy 5 of the **Exam Focus**: *Read the whole text again to make sure the options you have chosen make sense.* As you check the answers, elicit reasons for each choice.

7 Students discuss the questions in small groups of 3–4.

Answers

2 Students' own answers

3 A and B are wrong because you use these verbs to describe the location of things rather than people. D is wrong because it would need to be 'who lives in'.

4 1 C heard and D known **2** C heard (It's not possible to use *know* in this way in the present perfect.)

5 1 C **2** A **3** D **4** C **5** A **6** C **7** B **8** D

6 to take off (to suddenly start being successful); to take up (to accept the offer)

7 Students' own answers

ADDITIONAL PRACTICE | **Maximiser** p.9, Use of English 1–2 | **MyEnglishLab: Cambridge First**, Use of English 8 *Phrasal Verbs: Rewriting with phrasal verbs*

Listening focus ▶ p.12

Multiple matching (Part 3)

Aim

- to complete an exam-style listening exercise (Listening, Part 3)

Refer students to the **Exam Focus** on page 205 and turn to it on eText if you are using it. Read through it with students, making sure they understand everything.

1 Check that students understand what Facebook and Twitter are. Ask students to complete the activity, then put them into pairs to compare their answers. Elicit a few responses and check students have understood the vocabulary.

2 Give students time to read the question, then play the recording.

3 Tell the students that one of the extracts (1–4) has a similar meaning to one of the statements A–H in Activity 1. Ask students to read the statements and then elicit the response.

4 Tell students that they are going to listen to the remaining speakers and they need to choose a statement in Activity 1 that matches what each speaker says. Read the **Exam Tip** with the class. Ask students to identify the key words in the statements, then elicit some synonyms or alternative ways of saying things, e.g. B: *I only download music that's free = music that I don't have to pay for, that doesn't cost anything,* etc. Then play the recording.

5 Put students into pairs to compare answers, then play the recording again, pausing after each speaker to check the answers.

Answers

1 Students' own answers
2 Twitter, taste in music, new bands
3 3 G
4 2 A **3** B **4** E **5** D

Speaking

Aim

- to practise expressing opinions and reporting someone else's opinion

6 Put students into pairs for the discussion. On the board, revise some useful expressions for comparing and contrasting, e.g. *I'm similar to (speaker A) because we both …; (Speaker B) …, whereas I …; I agree with (Speaker C) because ….* If you have a small class, elicit responses from each pair. If you have a large class, put students into new pairs to report on their discussion.

ADDITIONAL PRACTICE | **Maximiser** p.9, Listening 1 | **MyEnglishLab: Cambridge First**, Listening 3 *Listening for paraphrasing: Holiday views*

Grammar focus ▸ p.13

Habit in the past

used to/would

Aim

- to review *would* and *used to* to express habit in the past and to provide spoken practice

1 Put students into pairs to answer the questions. Check as a class, then read the **Language Tip**. You may like to share another example, such as: *I am used to getting up early (I'm accustomed to)/I used to get up early (it's no longer true).*

Additional activity: *used to* – mill drill

Ask students to each think of 2–3 activities that they enjoyed doing as children, e.g. climbing trees, reading books, jumping on the trampoline. Write on the board:

Did you enjoy …… as a child?

I used to like …… but I don't anymore/I've outgrown it.

I still like …… actually!

I'm afraid I never liked …… .

Model the activity by asking one of the students to ask you the question, inserting one of the activities they thought of and then responding using the structures above. Tell students to move around the room asking and answering the questions. Finish by eliciting a few similarities or differences that students discovered.

Ask students to turn to the **Grammar Reference** on page 168 and read through it with the class (on eText if using it), checking students understand everything.

2 Put students into pairs to discuss the sentences. Remind students that *would* can be used to talk about past habits and repeated actions but NOT about past states (**Grammar Reference** 8.2). Elicit answers, giving feedback on the use of *used to* and *would*. *Would* is more formal than *used to* and is typically used in writing.

3 Ask students to look at the picture and elicit the time period they think it is from (the 1980s). Tell students that punk was very popular in Britain in the 1980s and this is an extract about an insurance broker reminiscing. Give students about ten minutes to complete the gap fill, and then put them into pairs to compare their answers before you check with the class.

Answers

1 1 no 2 yes 3 used to 4 would 5 used to
2 1 yes 2 yes 3 no 4 no
3 1 used to be 2 smile 3 used to go/would go 4 used to meet/would meet 5 used to just walk around/would just walk around 6 work/am working 7 am getting 8 love 9 am discovering 10 am enjoying

ADDITIONAL PRACTICE | **Maximiser** p.10, Grammar 1–2 | **Teacher's Book** Photocopiable 1B *Over to you* p.136/159 | **eText IWB** Extra activity

Speaking

Aim

- to provide spoken practice, especially of expressing habit in the past

4 Put students into new pairs for the discussion. Encourage students to respond to their partner with follow-up questions.

Writing focus ▶ p.14

Informal email (Part 2)

using informal language

Aim

- to review useful phrases for informal emails and to practise writing an exam-style informal email (Writing, Part 2)

Remind students that the writing task for Cambridge First is in two parts: the first is a compulsory letter/email and for the second they will be given a choice. One of the choices will be to write an informal letter or email. Refer students to the **Exam Focus** on page 203 for more details.

1 Put students into pairs for the discussion. Elicit a few responses to the questions from the class.

2 Ask students to read the task and answer the questions. Ask students to turn to the **Exam Focus** on page 203, and go through it (on eText if using it), checking that they understand everything. Then ask students to turn to the **Writing Reference** on page 182. Display it on the IWB if you are using eText, and go through the task, modelling answers with students. Ask students to highlight useful phrases, then go through the Useful language box together.

3 Ask students to choose the correct alternatives to complete the email. Check answers as a class.

4 Elicit what style is used for an email to a friend (informal). Ask students to decide which expressions could be used in an email to Josh. Check answers as a class. Read the **Language Tip** aloud and explain that some elements of punctuation are more common in informal texts.

5 Ask students to look at the exam task and identify the two things Max is asking for (what there is for students to do in the evening and what things you most like doing). Students do the activity, then check their answers in pairs.

6 Ask students to do the activity in pairs. Elicit examples of formal and informal language.

7 Ask students to do the exam task in Activity 5. Put students into pairs to read their letters together and add or cut words as necessary.

Answers

1 Students' own answers

2 1 Josh 2 to give some information about where to see live music in my town 3 informal

3 1 there's a music festival every summer 2 you'll be able to see 3 enjoy going a lot 4 mainly interested in 5 – you won't be disappointed because there's something for everyone. (dashes are more informal than semi-colons and relative clauses are more common in more formal written texts) 6 But 7 If you like, I could 8 Let me know what you think.

4 1 and 3

5 1, 2, 6

6 I: 2, 3, 4, 5 F: 1, 6

7 Students' own answers

ADDITIONAL PRACTICE | **Maximiser** p.11, Writing 1–4 | **eText IWB Game:** *Sheep out* | **MyEnglishLab: Cambridge First**, Writing 4 *Register in writing: keeping the style*; Writing 6 *Informal functions in writing: Matching them together*

Review ▶ p.15

Aim

- to revise structures and vocabulary covered in Unit 1

1–4 Ask students to complete the activities, circulating to provide assistance. Ask students to check in pairs before checking as a class. Alternatively, set as a homework activity.

Answers

1 1 used to enjoy 2 would always go 3 am used to performing 4 took off instantly 5 don't take after 6 am getting used to

2 1 don't like 2 are saying 3 don't think 4 is always doing 5 is getting 6 are playing

3 1 A 2 B 3 C 4 C

4 1 fans 2 collection 3 downloaded 4 once 5 released 6 available 7 tastes 8 concerts

ADDITIONAL PRACTICE | **Maximiser** p.10, Use of English 1 | **Online Testmaster** Unit 1 Test

Relative values

Use of English focus ▶ p.16

Speaking

Aim

- to give spoken practice and to review and extend vocabulary related to personality

Warmer: Personality brainstorm

Write *Personality* on the board. Divide students into four groups and give them three minutes to make a list of as many adjectives or phrases as they can think of to describe personality. On the board, draw three columns with the headings: *Positive, Negative* and *Positive or negative.* Choose three students, one for each column, to record the vocabulary on the board. Ask groups in turn to read out one of the words or phrases on their list. Decide together whether it is positive, negative or both and get the student assigned to the appropriate column to record it on the board. Ask students to check any unknown words, using dictionaries. Keep the words and phrases displayed on the board while students discuss the questions in Activity 1.

1 Students discuss the questions in pairs. Remind students of the phrasal verb *take after* (to share similar characteristics with an older relative). If you think students will find this activity difficult, consider writing on the board the following starters: *I think my friends would say I'm …; I have a reputation for being ….*

2 Ask students to complete the quiz by putting one tick in each row.

3 When students have finished the quiz, tell them to check their results on page 157 and then complete the sentences. Check that students understand the meaning of *tend to* (if something tends to happen, it happens often and is likely to happen again).

4 Put students in pairs to discuss the results. Remind students to focus on expanding their answers. Elicit a few responses to each question.

Answers

1 Sample answers

1 I think my friends would say I'm very ambitious because I work very hard to get what I want; My friends would probably say I make them laugh.

2 I take after my mum, we're both perfectionists; My brother and I have a lot in common, we're both very sociable and love a good argument.

2–4 Students' own answers

Additional activity: Useful websites

There are many websites offering personality tests that can be used to continue to develop students' vocabulary in this area, e.g.: **www.animalinyou.com, www.gotoquiz.com/personality_plus_1, www.quizrocket.com/career-personality-test.**

Vocabulary

formation of adjectives

Aim

- to practise adjective formation

5 Check students understand the nouns in the box. If necessary, explain *pessimist* (someone who always expects bad things to happen) and *harm* (damage, injury or trouble). Ask students to copy the table (make sure they leave enough space to fill it in), and copy it onto the board or bring it up on eText. Elicit the adjective *cautious* from *caution*, and elicit where to put it in the table. Ask students to complete the table then to compare their answers in pairs. Then check as a class on the board/eText. Point out the spelling change in *dramatic* and *sympathetic*.

6 Ask students to underline the stressed syllable in each word. Play the recording to check, then replay the recording, pausing for students to repeat the words.

7 Ask students to make a list of the negative forms of the words which use the suffix *-less* or prefix *un-*. Elicit additional words that use these prefixes or suffixes.

Answers

5

-able	*-ous*	*-ic*	*-al*	*-ful*
sociable	adventurous	realistic	practical	thoughtful
comfortable	cautious	dramatic	emotional	harmful
lovable	generous	pessimistic	personal	hopeful
predictable		sympathetic		meaningful
reliable				

6 sociable, comfortable, lovable, predictable, reliable, adventurous, cautious, generous, realistic, dramatic, pessimistic, sympathetic, practical, emotional, personal, thoughtful, harmful, hopeful, meaningful

Stress changes in: dramatic, generous, pessimistic, reliable, sympathetic

7 comfort*less*, love*less*, thought*less*, harm*less*, (hope*less*), meaning*less*; *un*sociable, *un*comfortable, *un*lovable, *un*predictable, *un*reliable, *un*adventurous, *un*generous, *un*realistic, *un*dramatic, *un*sympathetic, *un*emotional

Additional activity: More antonyms

Ask students to find the antonyms for the remaining adjectives in the table, using a dictionary (*practical – impractical, pessimistic – optimistic, cautious – incautious/impulsive, personable – disagreeable, dramatic – natural/dull, personal – public*). Put students into pairs to discuss the top three qualities they would look for in a new friend or life partner. Ask pairs to report back.

ADDITIONAL PRACTICE | **Maximiser** p.12, Vocabulary 1–3 | **Teacher's Book** p.137/160 Photocopiable 2A *Dialogue pairs*

Word formation (Part 3)

Aim

- to complete an exam-style word formation task (Reading and Use of English, Part 3)

Refer students to the **Exam Focus** on page 201 and turn to it on eText if you are using it.

Read through it with students, making sure they understand everything. Tell them that you are going to work through the strategy points together in the example.

8 Tell students that the text is about a problem with describing people's personalities. Ask them to complete strategy 1– to quickly skim the text to find out what the problem is without worrying about the gaps or unknown vocabulary at this stage.

9 Refer back to strategy 2 in the **Exam Focus**, and model this with the first gap (0) as an example by asking students *What part of speech is this?* (noun) and *How do we know it is a noun?* (it is preceded by a possessive apostrophe, and the sentence needs an object to make sense). Then get students to work in pairs to decide what part of speech the word in each remaining gap will be.

10 Refer back to strategy 3 in the **Exam Focus** and ask students to fill in the gaps using the words at the end of each line. Refer to strategy 4 and give students a few minutes to read the text again to make sure their answers make sense and the words are spelt correctly. Finally, students compare their answers in pairs before you check as a class.

Answers

8 Suggested answer: People behave differently in different situations.

9 Adjectives: 1, 2, 5, 6, 8; Nouns: 3 (singular), 4 (plural), 7 (plural)

10 1 hopeful 2 pessimistic 3 reality 4 characteristics 5 unpredictable 6 adventurous 7 differences 8 meaningless

Teaching tip

Checking in pairs

Encourage students to speak as much as possible when they check answers in pairs. Remind them that checking their answers together is valuable speaking practice.

ADDITIONAL PRACTICE | **Maximiser** p.13, Use of English 1 | **MyEnglishLab: Cambridge First** Use of English 1 *Word families: Which one is right here?*

Listening focus ▶ p.18

Multiple choice (Part 4)

Aim

- to complete an exam-style listening task (Listening, Part 4)

Warmer

Ask students to describe the pictures in pairs, then elicit the words *siblings, adopted* and *only child.*

1 Students discuss the questions in pairs. Encourage students to develop their answers as much as possible and avoid one word answers.

2 Refer students to the **Exam Focus** on page 205 and turn to it on eText if you are using it. Tell students they are going to complete an exam-style listening task, and refer them back to strategy 1 in the **Exam Focus**. Elicit what kind of recording it is (a radio interview) and the topic (birth order). Refer students to strategy 2 and ask them to underline the key words in the first question of Activity 4 only. If using eText, do this on the board.

Suggested answers

1 Students' own answers

2 Max says that people mistakenly believe that oldest children

A are likely to do well in the future.

B will be happier than their siblings.

C are often very independent at a young age.

3 Re-read strategy 3 aloud and play the first part of the discussion while students answer the questions. Then re-read strategy 4 aloud and play the first part of the recording again while students check their answers. Elicit answers to the questions.

4 Ask students to underline the key words in questions 2–7 before playing the remainder of the recording.

5 Ask students to check their answers in pairs, then play the recording again, pausing after each section to check answers. If you are using eText, display the audio script on the board and elicit the key words or phrases where the answers were found.

Answers

3 **1** mistakenly believe → isn't supported by any real facts A: to do well → leading happy, as well as successful, lives B: will be happier → have the best chance of leading happy … lives C: very independent → responsible and independent

4 **1** A **2** C **3** B **4** B **5** C **6** C **7** A

Key phrases in the audio script: **1** the vast majority of people believe that the oldest child's always the most successful **2** parents often encourage the oldest child to help their younger brothers and sisters to learn new skills **3** I do remember hating my younger brother and thinking that he was my parents' favourite, and this is something that's quite common in oldest children **4** imaginative and artistic **5** where there are either two boys, or two girls, the birth order effect is stronger **6** it'd be much easier for two third-born children **7** our relationships outside our family can have just as much influence

ADDITIONAL PRACTICE | **Maximiser** p.13, Listening 1 | **MyEnglishLab: Cambridge First** Listening 2 *Dealing with distraction: Choose the correct version*

Speaking

Aim

- to give spoken practice on the topic of families

6 Check that students understand *to get on with someone* (to like someone and have a friendly relationship with them). Students discuss the questions in pairs. Encourage them to focus on turn-taking and continuing discussion.

Additional activity: Writing

Ask students to write a short article of 140–190 words on one of these two topics: *What is the ideal number of children in a family? How do you think birth order has affected your family?*

You can use this task as an assessment for the Writing Focus in Unit 3, page 34, noting down any areas to focus on.

Grammar focus ▶ p.19

Adverbs

Aim

- to review the role of adverbs and practise using the adverbs *close/closely* and *hard/hardly* in context

Warmer: Adverb list

Elicit some examples of adverbs e.g. *slowly (He ran slowly); naturally (Naturally, we want you to come).*

Put students into pairs and give them three minutes to make a list of as many adverbs as they can. Ask students to put their lists aside until later in the lesson.

1 Ask students to underline the adverbs, then to answer the questions. Check the answers as a class.

2 Students choose the correct adverb then check their answers in pairs. Write the adverb pairs *close/closely, late/lately* and *hard/hardly* on the board and ask students to describe the difference between the adverbs in each pair. Refer students to the **Grammar Reference** on page 161 (and turn to it on eText if you are using it). Go through the notes and examples, and check the difference between the adverb pairs.

Additional activity: Warmer continuation

Ask students to re-form their pairs from the warmer activity and to use the Grammar Reference on page 161 to check that all of the words on their list are adverbs, not adjectives. Ask pairs to swap lists with another pair then to write an example sentence using each of the adverbs on the list they have been given. Elicit a few examples checking that the adverb use and placement is correct.

Answers

1 A hard B well C slowly D hardly
1 hard, well 2 hard, well

2 1 hardly 2 hard 3 lately 4 late 5 close
6 closely

ADDITIONAL PRACTICE | **Maximiser** p.14, Grammar 1

Vocabulary

extreme adjectives

Aim

- to use a range of adverbs with extreme adjectives

Warmer: Acting out extremes

Explain that in English 'extreme' adjectives are preceded by different adverbs to 'normal' adjectives. Write a list of extreme adjectives describing feelings on pieces of paper and distribute to students. Ask them in turn to act out their adjective and ask the class to guess it.

3 Students match the adjectives with the extreme versions. Students check their answers in pairs then check as a class. Elicit other extreme adjectives and write them on the board, e.g. *boiling* (very hot), *ridiculous* (very silly), *hilarious* (very funny).

4 Students work in pairs to choose the correct adverbs. Check the answers as a class.

5 Students choose the correct adverbs to form the rules. Get them to check their answers in pairs before checking as a class.

Answers

3 1 D 2 E 3 F 4 B 5 C 6 A

4 1 fairly 2 very 3 completely, absolutely 4 very
5 (an) absolutely 6 a bit, fairly

5 1 Really 2 Completely and absolutely 3 A bit

ADDITIONAL PRACTICE | **Maximiser** p.14, Grammar 2 | **eText IWB** Extra activity

Speaking

Aim

- to practise using adjectives with modifiers and to provide spoken practice of agreeing and disagreeing

6 Ask students to complete sentences 1–3 with phrases A–C. Students discuss their answers in pairs.

Reading focus ▶ p.20

Speaking

Aim

- to introduce the topic of sibling relationships in preparation for the reading activity

Warmer: Pelmanism

Write the following pairs of words individually on the board in a random order: *lovable/endearing; talented/gifted; suffer/hurt; sociable/friendly; self-conscious/nervous; annoyed/angry.* Put students in pairs to discuss which of the words on the board are synonyms. Then invite a student to come and cross off two synonyms and give a sentence using the words. Continue this way until all the pairs are matched.

1 Check students understand the word *gifted* (having a natural ability to do one or more things extremely well). Elicit the names of at least five people who are gifted or famous. Students discuss the question in pairs. Select a few students to give their answers.

Multiple matching (Part 7)

Aim

- to complete an exam-style multiple-matching task (Reading and Use of English, Part 7) and to practise the strategies of identifying key words in questions then scanning a text for the answers

Refer students to the **Exam Focus** on page 203 and turn to it on eText if you are using it. Read through it with students, making sure they understand everything.

2 Give students two minutes to skim the text to answer the questions. Emphasise that they are skimming the text because in the exam they will not have time to read in detail.

3 Read the **Exam Tip** with the class, then focus on the underlined words in Activity 4, question 1. Elicit what information students would expect to find and then ask students to check their answer in extract A. Ask students to underline the key words in Activity 4, question 2, then find a word or expression with a similar meaning in the text. This is a good opportunity to practise scanning for specific words.

4 Ask students to underline the remaining key words before they complete the rest of the task. Remind them to follow strategies 5 and 6 and highlight possible answers first, then go back and find the exact answer for each question. Allow around 15 minutes for students to complete the questions. Circulate while students are doing the activity and, if necessary, help by eliciting paraphrases for the key words in the options. Allow students to compare their answers in pairs, then check as a class. Elicit words or expressions in the text that helped students answer each question.

5 Students discuss the question in pairs. Elicit a few ideas from the class to finish.

Answers

1 Students' own answers

2 **1** Will Young **2** Jonathan Self **3** Kate Firth **4** Zoë Heller

3 Suggested answer: You would expect to find two conflicting emotions (highlighted in extract A).

4 (Key words and words/expressions in the text in brackets)

1 A (mixed feelings, successful sibling; feeling terribly proud and jealous) **2** D (not get involved, sibling behaved badly; get annoyed by teachers who tried to make me responsible for him) **3** B (stopped doing something; gave up) **4** C (appreciates the value of a sibling relationship; I've come to understand the importance of family rather late in life) **5** B (felt rather irritated, birth of a sibling; I hadn't been at all pleased … when a new child turned up) **6** C (depend on a sibling, practical advice as a child; she looked after me a lot when we were growing up, taught me how to write a cheque, would rescue me when I got lost) **7** D (people get labelled; people put you in a certain box and it's difficult to get away from that) **8** B (sibling was treated differently; I saw how he became the favourite) **9** A (too cautious, much wanted career; desperately wanted to act, never had his courage) **10** C (most efficient; if I … need a document or family photograph, she's the one you'll call)

5 Students' own answers

ADDITIONAL PRACTICE | **Maximiser** p.14–15, Reading 1–3 | **eText IWB** Extra activity | **MyEnglishLab: Cambridge First** Reading 19 *Paraphrasing: find the synonyms*; Reading 20 *Paraphrasing: find the opposites*

MyEnglishLab tip

Gradebook

The MyEnglishLab exercises are marked automatically so that students can have immediate feedback. Log on to and check the Gradebook to see their progress.

Vocabulary

phrasal verbs

Aim

- to expand vocabulary of phrasal verbs and use them in spoken practice

6 Ask students if they can remember any phrasal verbs from Unit 1 (*take off, take after*). Students match the eight underlined phrasal verbs in the text to their meanings. Students compare their answers in pairs, then check as a class.

7 Students discuss the questions in pairs. Elicit a few responses to each question, checking that students are using the phrasal verbs appropriately.

Answers

6 **1** sort out (para C) **2** get away (para C) **3** make it (para A) **4** get rid of (para B) **5** set your heart on (para A) **6** take off (para A) **7** look up to (para A) **8** turn up (para B)

7 Students' own answers

Additional activity

Ask students to work in pairs and write four questions using the four phrasal verbs *make it, take off, turn up, sort out*. Circulate, checking that question forms are accurate and that the phrasal verbs have been used appropriately. Ask pairs to join together into groups of four to ask and answer their questions.

Grammar focus ▶ p.22

Listening

Aim

- to complete an exam-style multiple-matching listening task (Listening, Part 3)

Warmer: Review of relations vocabulary

Have a class brainstorm of relations vocabulary and write the words on the board, e.g. *grandparents, (great) aunt, stepfather, mother-in-law, niece, nephew, half-brother*. Elicit the difference between *stepfather/father-in-law, half-sister/stepsister/sister-in-law, great niece/grandchild*.

1 Elicit the meaning of *to get on well with someone* (to like someone and have a friendly relationship with them). Students discuss the questions in pairs.

2 Ask students to read the comments A–E. Then play the recording while students match speakers 1–5 to the comments. Ask students to check their answers in pairs, then play the recording again, pausing after each speaker to elicit the answer.

Answers

1 Students' own answers

2 **1** C **2** B **3** D **4** A **5** E

Verb patterns with *-ing* and infinitive

Aim

- to review the use of verbs followed by the *-ing* or infinitive forms

3 Students match examples A–E to rules 1–5. Get them to compare answers in pairs before you check as a class. Read the **Language Tip** aloud and elicit further examples for each point, e.g. *I let her come with me; I made him tell me the truth*. Ask students to turn to the **Grammar Reference** on page 178 (and turn to it on eText if you are using it). Go through the notes and examples, checking students understand everything.

4 Students choose the correct answers, then compare answers in pairs. Go through the answers as a class, ensuring that students understand the difference between each pair.

5 Focus students' attention on the photo and elicit any information students know about Carly Simon and James Taylor. (They are both Grammy award-winning singer songwriters from the USA, popular from the 1970s. They have two children together, Ben and Sally, who are also both in the music industry.) Give students a few minutes to read the article, then elicit what Ben liked and disliked about having famous parents.

6 Students complete the text with the *-ing* or infinitive form of the verbs in brackets. Students compare their answers in pairs before you check as a class.

7 Ask students to think about the situation. Then give them a few minutes to discuss their ideas in pairs. Circulate, making sure that students are using the *-ing* and infinitive forms correctly after verbs.

Answers

3 **1** D (enjoy) **2** C (worried about) **3** B (a waste of time) **4** E (offered) **5** A (like someone to do something)

4 **1** A making B to make (*stop* + *-ing* = discontinue an activity, *stop* + infinitive = in order to) **2** A phoning B to phone (*try* + *-ing* = do something as an experiment, *try* + infinitive = make an effort to do something difficult) **3** A to buy B buying (*remember* + *-ing* = refers back to the past, *remember* + infinitive = refers forward in time) **4** A having B to have (*go on* + *-ing* = continue, *go on* + infinitive = a change of activity) **5** A to tell B telling (*regret* + *-ing* = refers to the past, something you are sorry about, *regret* + infinitive = used to give bad news)

5 liked: going on tour with his dad, sleeping on the tour bus; disliked: being introduced as Taylor and Simon's son

6 **1** going **2** sleeping **3** to travel **4** splitting up **5** having **6** introducing **7** playing/to play **8** to know **9** to teach **10** doing **11** to go **12** being/to be

7 Students' own answers

Additional activity: Video celebrity interviews

Students prepare a one-minute interview with a celebrity (either real or made up) for a show called 'Interview with the stars'. Divide the class into two groups: the 'interviewers' and the 'celebrities'. Students work in pairs within their group, with the interviewers preparing a list of questions and the celebrities planning their personalities and brief life story. To make this easier, you could give general roles first, e.g. pop star, sportsperson, politician, etc. Then match up each 'interviewer' with a 'celebrity' for the interviews. Compile the videos and show them using the interactive whiteboard.

Teaching tip

Student videos

- Set a time limit for the video (in this case 60 seconds).
- Put students into small groups of no more than three to ensure all participants are active.
- Encourage students to plan together before they begin filming.
- Give students notice to bring any props they need.
- Organise a quiet place where each group can film.

ADDITIONAL PRACTICE | Maximiser p.16, Grammar1–3 **| Teacher's Book** p.138/161 Photocopiable 2B *Hit or miss* **| eText IWB** Extra activity **| MyEnglishLab: Cambridge First**, Use of English 20: *to/-ing: What exactly did he say?*

Speaking focus ▶ p.23

Collaborative task (Part 3)

agreeing and disagreeing

Ask students to read the **Exam Focus** on page 207.

Aim

- to prepare for an exam-style collaborative task (Listening, Part 3)

1 Ask students to look at the photos and the exam task and discuss the question as a class.

2 Explain that students are going to listen to Alana and Federico completing the task. Play the recording. Ask students to discuss the answers in pairs, then play the recording a second time. Check answers.

3 Draw the table from the Coursebook on the board or display on eText and ask students to copy it and complete it with the phrases in the box. Check students know how to pronounce the expressions. Check answers and complete the table on the board/eText. Keep the table displayed on the board/eText for students to refer to while doing Activities 4 and 5.

4 Before doing the task, ask students to read the **Exam Tip**. Elicit a few more phrases to add to the *Asking opinions* column of the table, e.g. *What do you think? How about you?* Ask students to do the task slowly first, using at least five different expressions from the table. Then ask them to repeat the task with a new partner with a timer set for one minute. After the task, ask students if they used any phrases from the table. Students could repeat the task with a new partner for further practice.

5 Students discuss the questions in pairs.

Answers

1 Students' own answers

2 twin sister/brother (Alana thinks you would tell a twin sister everything; Federico is close to his brother); grandparents (you learn a lot from them; they are patient and kind); father/son relationships (you can share hobbies); teacher (teachers can have a huge effect; a friend of Alana's was encouraged to take up drama and become an actor).

3 Agreeing: So do I/Neither do I; That's very true; I hadn't thought of that; Exactly!; Good point; I suppose so
Disagreeing politely: I'm not convinced; I'm not sure about that; I see what you mean, but …; Well, actually …
Asking opinions: What about you?; What's your view …?
Expressions of agreement that are uncertain: I suppose so; OK, but …

4–5 Students' own answers

Additional activity

Ask students to find a new partner for the discussion in Activity 5 and repeat for extra practice.

ADDITIONAL PRACTICE | Maximiser p.16, Speaking 1 | **MyEnglishLab: Cambridge First** Speaking 13: *Part 3 Assessment: Read the examiner's comments*

Writing focus ▶ p.24

Essay (Part 1)

Using linkers for contrast

Aim

- to complete an exam-style task of writing a semi-formal letter (Writing, Part 1)

Remind students that the writing task for Cambridge First Certificate is in two parts. The first part is an essay and for the second they will have a choice (see the **Exam Focus** on page 203). Ask students to turn to the **Writing Reference** on page 180 and go through the example (on eText if you are using it).

1 Ask students to read the exam task, focusing on the question and prompts. Ask them to think of advantages and disadvantages of each situation. Share ideas as a class.

2 Put students in pairs to match the sentences. Check answers as a class. Students then discuss which statements they agree with.

3 Put students in pairs to answer the question and check as a class.

4 Ask students to read through the essay and underline where the three points from the notes in Activity 1 are mentioned. If you are using eText IWB, a student could do this on the board.

5 Put students in pairs to find the reasons for the student's point of view. Check answers as a class, then students decide whether they agree or disagree with them.

6 Students read the essay again and select the correct alternatives to complete the sentences. Read the **Language Tip** aloud and check students understand the correct position(s) of linking words in a sentence.

7 Ask students to turn to page 157. Read the exam task aloud. Put students in pairs to discuss their ideas. Elicit suggestions for a third point and write them on the board. Read the **Exam tip** aloud. Either set the writing task as homework, or ask students to complete it in class while you circulate.

Answers

1 Students' own ideas

2 1 C 2 B 3 F 4 A 5 E 6 D

3 1, 4, 6

4 Points 1, 2 and 3 in paragraph 2. Point 2 also in paragraph 3

5 This makes playing with other children outside the family easier; because they may be jealous of each other; because you don't have shared memories; so it's always possible to make friends with your sibling as adults

6 1 Even though 2 However 3 On the other hand 4 Despite

7 Sample answer

We may all have strong ideas about whether it is better to have parents that are older or parents that are younger. However, there are advantages and disadvantages to both situations.

If you have young parents, they will still be quite young when you are growing up, so you may have similar interests. They may remember more clearly what it is like to be a teenager or young adult.

Older parents might not have as much energy as younger parents. This could mean it is more difficult for them to deal with sleepless nights and the physical effort it takes to look after young children.

On the other hand, younger parents don't have the same experience of life as older parents. Older parents have been through many good and bad times before their children are born. This means that they might be more able to deal with unexpected problems.

While there are good and bad things about having older or younger parents, the most important thing is to enjoy being with them. After all, it isn't possible to make your parents any younger or older.

ADDITIONAL PRACTICE | **Maximiser** p.17, Writing 1–6 | **MyEnglishLab: Cambridge First**, Writing 2 *Understanding the question in Part 1: Have they got the right idea?*

Review ▶ p.25

Aim

- to revise structures and vocabulary covered in Unit 2

1–5 Ask students to complete the activities, then check in pairs before checking as a class on eText. Alternatively, set as a homework activity.

Answers

1 1 get rid of 2 looked up to 3 turned up 4 took off 5 make it 6 get away

2 1 ~~hardly~~ hard 2 ~~closely~~ close 3 ~~absolutely~~ very/really 4 ~~very~~ absolutely 5 ~~free~~ freely 6 ~~completely~~ very/really 7 ~~a bit~~ absolutely 8 ~~hardly~~ hard

3 1 confident 2 independent 3 practical 4 sociable 5 creative 6 cautious

4 1 reliable 2 imaginative 3 adventurous 4 realistic 5 hopeless 6 sympathetic

5 1 having 2 to work 3 running 4 to lock 5 to invite 6 working 7 finish 8 not to

ADDITIONAL PRACTICE | **Maximiser** p.18–19, Use of English | **Online Testmaster** Unit 2 Test

Things that matter

Reading focus ▶ p.26

Multiple choice (Part 5)

Aim

- to practise answering an exam-style multiple-choice reading task

1 Elicit the meaning of *matter* in the unit title (to be important, especially to be important to you, or to have an effect on what happens). Ask students to put the things in order of importance to them. Give them a few minutes to share their answers with a partner.

Refer students to the **Exam Focus** on page 202 and turn to it on eText if you are using it. Read through it with students, making sure they understand everything. Leave the strategy points displayed on eText for students to refer to as they do the next activities.

2 Refer to strategy 1 in the **Exam Focus**, and tell students that the title, picture and first paragraph provide useful clues to understanding the rest of the article. Ask them to look at these only and not to read the rest of the article yet. Elicit predictions of what the article will be about. (If you are using eText, display these on the board before students open their books.) Give students a few minutes to skim the article to check their predictions and get a general idea of what it is about.

3 Read the **Exam Tip** aloud, then read through strategies 3 and 4. If you are using eText, demonstrate on the board with the first question (highlight *writer's attitude towards football fans*) then elicit which part of the text answers the question (the last three lines of the first paragraph). Read through the four options for question 1 with the class. Refer to strategy 5, pointing out that the meaning will be the same but the language will be different. Refer to strategy 6 and elicit any options that students think are obviously wrong, then ask students to choose the correct option. Ask students to work through the remaining questions, following the steps in the strategy. Put students into pairs to compare their answers, then check as a class.

4 Students discuss the questions in pairs. Remind students that every discussion is an opportunity to practise for the speaking exam (turn-taking, variety of language, etc). For extra practice, students could discuss the questions again with a new partner.

Answers

1 Students' own answers

2 Suggested answers: passions/interests

3 (key phrases from the article in brackets)

1 D (enrich our lives and make us better people) **2** B **3** A (teaching you how to sob … how to sing with enthusiasm) **4** B (they do not happen every week) **5** C (Calm, controlled middle-aged women are suddenly prepared to …) **6** B (what defines us as human is … the ability to care about something)

4 Students' own answers

ADDITIONAL PRACTICE | **Maximiser** p.20–21, Reading 1–3 |
eText IWB Extra activity |

Vocabulary

-ed adjectives and prepositions

Aim

- to ensure that students understand the distinction between adjectives that end in *-ed* and *-ing* and to practise using them with the correct prepositions

5 Ask students to complete the questions with the correct prepositions, then check as a class. Read the **Language Tip** with the class. Share the following examples, eliciting the word in brackets: *I'm very interested in the lesson* and *the lesson is (interesting). Sky-diving is terrifying. I'm (terrified) of sky-diving.* Students ask and answer the questions in pairs. Finish by eliciting a few responses for each question, checking for accurate use of the adjectives and prepositions.

Answers

5 **1** in **2** of **3** about **4** by **5** by **6** about

Additional activity: Useful websites

The BBC English website has a podcast and online quiz: **www.bbc.co.uk/worldservice/learningenglish/radio/specials/934_gramchallenge3/**

There is also a photocopiable worksheet available at: **www.pearsonlongman.com/adult/pdf/Giving_opinions.pdf**

ADDITIONAL PRACTICE | **Maximiser** p.21, Vocabulary 1–2 | **eText Game:** Pelmanism | **MyEnglishLab: Cambridge First**, Speaking 5: *Part 2 Comparing pictures: What's the missing phrase?*; Speaking 12 *Describing and explaining pictures: Match the halves together*

MyEnglishLab tip

Preview

You can preview exercises on MyEnglishLab by clicking on 'Preview'.

Grammar focus ▶ p.28

Present perfect and past simple

Aim

- to review the structures and uses of present perfect and past simple and to use them correctly in written and spoken practice

Warmer

Ask: *What do you know about blogs? Do you follow any blogs? Do you blog, or do you know any bloggers personally?* Ask students to discuss the questions in pairs, then report back to the class.

1 Refer students to the picture of *Anna* and tell them that she is a new blogger. Ask them to read Anna's blog post and answer questions 1–5. Get students to compare answers in pairs, then check as a class.

2 Ask students to look at the underlined verb forms and decide which ones describe completed actions in the past and which ones describe past habits that are now finished. Check as a class.

3 If you are using eText, magnify Anna's blog. Ask students to look at the highlighted example and elicit the form (*have* + past participle). Ask students to find four more examples of the present perfect in the text. If you are using eText, ask a student to circle the examples on the board.

4 Ask students to match the examples with uses of the present perfect. Get them to check in pairs before you check as a class.

5 Elicit the difference between *for* and *since*. Ask students to turn to the **Grammar Reference** 21.3 on page 176 and read through it with the class (on eText if using it). Check that students understand everything.

6 Ask students to decide which time expressions are usually used with the past simple and which with the present perfect. Get students to compare their answers in pairs before you check as a class. Point out that *once* can be used with both forms (*I once met Johnny Depp; I've only met him once*).

Answers

1 **1** for most of her life **2** no **3** a month ago, when a colleague persuaded her to **4** for a month **5** four

2 **1** I left home; a colleague at work persuaded me
2 my friend and I used to help out; the owner would let us ride the ponies

3 I've (never) owned one; I haven't been back there (since); I've only had four (so far); I've (just) got my confidence back

4 **1** B **2** C **3** A

5 for = a period of time; since = a point in time

6 **1** past simple: in 2010, once, last month, ago, at lunchtime
2 present perfect: yet, so far, already, never, once, just, this month

present perfect simple or continuous?

7 Give students a couple of minutes to complete the questions and then elicit the answers.

8 Complete the first sentence together as an example, then give students time to complete the remaining sentences. Let students compare their answers in pairs, then check as a class. Ask students to read the **Grammar Reference** on page 176 for more information.

9 On the board, write *Have you ever …?* and *How long …?* and elicit a few possible ways to complete each question using vocabulary from question 8 or students' own ideas. Put students into pairs to think of more questions, then ask and answer them. Remind them that they should use the past simple when asking follow-up questions with *When? Why?*, etc. Circulate, providing feedback and vocabulary as required.

Answers

7 1 B 2 A

8 1 've ridden/been riding 2 once witnessed 3 lived 4 had 5 've never been 6 've just won

9 Students' own answers

ADDITIONAL PRACTICE | **Maximiser** p.22, Grammar 1–2 | **Teacher's Book** p.139/162 Photocopiable 3A *True or false?* | **eText IWB** Extra activity

Use of English focus

▶ p.29

Grammar

as and *like*

Aim

- to identify differences in use between *as* and *like* and to practise using them accurately in context

1 Tell students that in English there are some situations where *as* and *like* can be used interchangeably and others where only one is correct. Ask students to complete the sentences, then put them into pairs to compare answers before you check answers as a class. Go through the **Language Tip** with the class, eliciting further examples for each structure.

Ask students to turn to the **Grammar Reference** on page 164 and read through it with the class (on eText if using it), checking they understand everything.

Answers

1 1 like 2 as/like 3 as 4 like 5 as 6 as/like

Additional activity: Discussion questions

Write the following gapped questions on the board and ask students to discuss in pairs whether *as* or *like* fits in the gap. Elicit the answers, then tell the students to ask and answer each question with their partner.

Do you look …… other members of your family? (like)

What is your dream house …… ? (like)

What do you usually feel …… doing after class? (like)

…… a student, what do you find most difficult about learning English? (As)

Open cloze (Part 2)

Aim

- to complete an exam-style cloze task (Reading and Use of English, Part 2)

2 Elicit the difference between *depressed* (very unhappy) and *depressing* (making you feel very sad). Ask students to discuss the questions in pairs, then elicit a few answers from the class.

3 Refer students to the **Exam Focus** on page 201 and turn to it on eText if you are using it. Read through it with students, making sure they understand everything. Tell them that you are going to work through the strategy points together in the example. Magnify the strategy section on eText and tick off each strategy as students complete it. Refer to strategy 1 and the questions in Activity 3. Give students a few minutes to skim the text and underline three things that make Pixie happy. Ask students if they are like her and elicit a few responses.

4 Refer to strategy 2 and the **Exam Tip**. Ask students to look at the example (0) in the text. Ask *What kind of word is in the gap?* (a preposition), *How did you know it should be a preposition?* (it comes between a verb and a noun). Do question 1 together by reading the words that come before and after the gap and asking students what *kind* of word goes in the gap (a preposition). Put students into pairs to discuss what kind of word goes in each gap. Elicit answers.

5 Refer to strategy 3 and ask students to fill each gap with the most appropriate word. Remind students that only one word can fit each gap.

6 Refer to strategy 4 and ask students to re-read the whole text in pairs, comparing their answers, checking that the words they have added make sense and also checking spelling. Finally, check answers as a class.

Answers

2 Students' own answers

3 being on stage; writing music; listening to music

4 *on* is a preposition **1** preposition **2** preposition **3** preposition **4** relative pronoun **5** conjunction **6** auxiliary verb **7** adverb **8** verb

5 **1** like **2** about **3** as **4** which **5** when/while **6** have **7** more **8** does

6 Students' own answers

ADDITIONAL PRACTICE | **Maximiser** p.22 | Use of English 1–2, **MyEnglishLab: Cambridge First**, Use of English 10: *Word patterns: Put in the missing preposition*

Vocabulary and Listening focus ▶ p.30

Speaking and vocabulary

money

Aim

- to develop vocabulary related to money and to provide spoken practice

Warmer: Money brainstorm

On the board, draw the symbols $, £, € and ask students what currencies these represent and what the smallest unit is of each currency. Elicit some examples of where each currency is used. Then elicit other words or phrases students associate with money, writing them on the board in a mind map.

1 Tell students that the picture shows a website selling luxury items. Elicit the terms *grand piano, sports car, high heels.* Ask students to match the price tags with the items then compare their answers in pairs.

2 Give students a few minutes to match the two halves of the expressions. Check answers as a class, then elicit a few responses to the question of whether students have similar expressions in their language.

3 Ask students to complete the sentences, then compare their answers in pairs. Check answers with the class. Check that students understand all the sentences and ask them to put a tick next to the ones they agree with. Elicit a few phrases that can be used for agreeing and disagreeing politely, such as those listed in Activity 3 on page 23 of the Coursebook. If you are using eText, you could display the phrases from that page on the board for reference. Students discuss their answers to the questions in small groups.

Answers

1 designer shoes: £675 designer watch: €4,200 luxury sports car: $158,500 Picasso painting: $102.3 million grand piano: £35,000
1–3 Students' own answers

2 **1** H **2** D **3** G **4** E **5** A **6** C **7** B **8** F

3 **1** within **2** in **3** on **4** away **5** to **6** of

Additional activity: Useful website

BBC Learning English has an audio soap opera called *The Flatmates*. Each episode has a language point explanation and online quiz. Episode 7 includes a number of money idioms. **www.bbc.co.uk/worldservice/learningenglish/flatmates/episode07/index.shtml**

ADDITIONAL PRACTICE | **Maximiser** p.23, Vocabulary 1–2 | **eText Game:** Noughts and crosses (money)

Sentence completion (Part 2)

Aim

- to complete an exam-style listening task (Listening, Part 2)

Warmer: A class of multi-millionaires

Ask students to imagine that they are all multi-millionaires. Write the following questions on the board and ask students to ask and answer them in pairs:

How did you make your fortune? What is your attitude to money? What is a typical working day like for you? What do you spend your money on? Where do you live?

After a few minutes, bring the class together again and ask a volunteer the first question. When they have answered, they should ask another question to another student. Continue until all students have had a turn.

Refer students to the **Exam Focus** on page 204 and turn to it on eText if you are using it. Read through it with students, making sure they understand everything.

4 Focus attention on the picture and tell students this is a multi-millionnaire called Gavin Norris and they are going to hear about his life. Ask them to read the gapped sentences and put a tick next to the items A–E that they expect to hear about.

5 Play the recording and elicit the answer to Activity 4 from the class.

6 Refer students to strategy 1 of the **Exam Focus**. Ask students to look at the first gap and guess what information would fit in it (a noun, something that Gavin sold in a market to start his business career). Ask students to guess what that might have been, then put them into pairs to discuss and predict the kind of information that is missing from the remaining gaps. Elicit ideas from the class.

7 Read strategy 2 and 3 and the **Exam Tip** with the class. Play the recording again, while students complete the sentences.

8 Ask students to check their answers in pairs. Read strategy 4 and 5 with the class, then play the recording again, pausing after each gap for students to check their answers and spelling. Check as a class.

9 Check that students understand *inherit* (to receive money, property, etc from someone after they die). Put students into pairs to discuss the questions, then elicit a few responses from the class.

Answers

4 Students' own answers

5 Students' own answers (the text gives information about A, B and D)

6 Suggested answers: **1** (a number) 5
2 (a noun) 1, 2, 3, 4, 6, 7, 9, 10
3 (a plural form) 1, 2, 3, 4, 7
4 (only one word) 2, 3, 4, 6, 7, 8, 9, 10

7 **1** (sports) shoes **2** shops **3** children **4** farmers
5 100 **6** hospital **7** family **8** property
9 freedom **10** house

9 Students' own answers

ADDITIONAL PRACTICE | **Maximiser** p.23, Listening 1 | **MyEnglishLab**: **Cambridge First**, Listening 12 *Listening for detail: Complete the sentences*

Grammar focus ▶ p.32

comparing

Aim

- to review the use of comparatives, superlatives and modifiers when comparing items

Warmer

Focus attention on the picture and elicit the words *coins, change, money box, jar, pocket money, piggy bank.* Ask what money expressions students can remember from page 30. Elicit ideas and write them on the board, then ask students to check on page 30.

1 Ask students to complete the sentences, then play the recording for students to check.

2 Ask a student to read the first two sentences. Ask the class if the sentences have a similar or different meaning. Ask students to continue with the remaining sentences in pairs. Check answers.

3 Refer students to the **Grammar Reference** on page 165 (and turn to it on eText if you are using it). Go through the notes and examples. Leave the **Grammar Reference** on eText while students complete the sentences. Ask students to check answers in pairs then check with the class.

Answers

1 **1** not as interested as/less interested than
2 the most satisfying **3** much happier than

2 **1** different **2** similar **3** similar

3 **1** quite as high/good as **2** one of the most
3 much less **4** higher than
5 a bit wealthier/more wealthy than **6** not as easy

ADDITIONAL PRACTICE | **Maximiser** p.24, Grammar 1–3 | **eText IWB** Extra activity

Speaking

comparing quantities

Aim

- to practise comparing quantities using modifiers and to give spoken practice

4 Read through the table with the class and elicit some example sentences, e.g. *I don't spend much time exercising.* Ask students to write six sentences. If some students finish early, encourage them to add more detail.

5 Put students into groups of three to compare their sentences. Ask them to work as a group to write a paragraph about their time and money. Alternatively, set the writing activity individually as a homework task.

Answers

4 Students' own answers

5 Sample answer

The thing we spend most money on is clothes. The thing we spend least money on is travel. More than half of us spend quite a lot of money on eating out in restaurants. The thing we spend most time doing is studying. More than half of us study for more than 20 hours a week. The thing we spend the least time on is exercising. Less than half of us do exercise regularly.

Additional activity: Create an online survey

There are many websites where you can create a free online survey. For example, Survey Monkey **http://www.surveymonkey.com/**. You can create a survey, using up to ten questions and 100 responses. Make a short survey for your students about how they spend their time. Ask students to complete the survey and then put them into pairs to create their own five-question survey about how students spend their time.

Topics could include the amount of time students spend online, doing exercise or eating. Ask students to send you the links to their survey. Compile a list of the links and then email/post these to students for them to respond to. After students have replied to each others' surveys, ask each pair to prepare a short spoken report summarising their findings, using the language for comparing quantities on page 32.

Speaking focus ▶ p.33

Long turn (Part 2)

comparing

Aim

- to ensure that students know what is expected in Speaking, Part 2 and to practise an exam-style speaking task

Warmer: True or false?

Write the following sentences on the board and ask students to discuss in pairs whether they are true or false.

In Paper 5, Part 2 (individual long turn):

1 *The examiner gives you a series of photos to compare.*
2 *First you answer questions about the photos, then you compare them.*
3 *You have one minute to do both parts of the task.*
4 *When you have finished, your partner will be asked a question related to the topic.*

Then ask students to read the *What do you have to do?* section of the **Exam Focus** on page 206 to check. (Display the relevant information on eText if you are using it.) Elicit the answers to the questions, then go through the strategies in the **Exam Focus**, ensuring students understand everything.

Answers

1 False (the examiner gives you two photos)
2 False (you compare the photos first, then you will be asked a question) **3** True **4** True

1 Focus attention on the photos (magnify them on eText if using) and ask students to look at them and choose whether A or B best describes what the photos have in common.

2 Put students into small groups and give them five minutes to make lists of similarities and differences. Encourage them to think of at least three for each list. Elicit responses, annotating them on the board.

3 Read the question aloud, then play the recording for students to check. Compare answers as a class.

4 Give students a few minutes to complete the activity, then check answers as a class, discussing the questions. Refer students to the **Grammar Reference** on page 164 (and turn to it on eText if using). Go through the notes and examples, checking that students understand everything.

5 Read sentences A and B aloud. Then ask students to discuss the questions in pairs before eliciting responses.

6 Ask students to make sentences and compare with a partner before you elicit responses. Emphasise that these are useful constructions to use in the exam.

7 Tell students they are going to do an exam-style task. Refer students to the **Exam Focus** on page 206 and turn to it on eText if you are using it. Read through the notes with the class and ensure students understand everything. Focus on strategy 2 and tell students they can use *both, also* and *too* to talk about similarities, and *whereas* and *while* to talk about differences. Focus on strategy 3 and remind students of the phrases for speculating in Activity 4. Divide pairs into As and Bs, then tell As to turn to page 152 and Bs to turn to page 154. Read the **Exam Tip** aloud and ask students to think about the main similarities and differences for their pictures. After students have done the activity, elicit some phrases they used to compare the two photos. Write them on the board and check that students know how to use them correctly. Then ask students to repeat the activity, with As and Bs swapping. If there is time, students could change partners and repeat the activity for extra practice.

8 Give students a few minutes to discuss the question, then elicit a few responses to finish.

Answers

1 A

2–3 Students' own answers

4 1 like 2 like/as if/as though 3 like
4 like/as if/as though 5 like/as if/as though

You can only use *like* in **1** and **3** because it's followed by a noun. In the other sentences, *like, as if* and *as though* can all be used.

5 1 B 2 B 3 A

6 1 Both the pictures show an achievement./The pictures both show an achievement.

2 The man also looks happy./Also, the man looks happy.

3 The man seems to be enjoying himself, too.

7 Students' own answers

8 Students' own answers

Additional activity: Photo task sheets

Ask students to prepare a task sheet in pairs with two photos and a follow-up question related to the topic in the photos. Students could search for the photos online, or in magazines and newspapers, as a homework activity. Collect the task sheets and redistribute them to the pairs. The students look at the photos and Student A compares the two photos using some of the language on page 33, then asks Student B the follow-up question. After about five minutes, ask students to pass on the task sheet to the next pair. This time, Student B compares the photos and Student A answers the follow-up question. Repeat several times, circulating to listen for use of the target language. Note down some phrases as good examples to share with the class. To finish, ask each pair to choose which task sheet they thought was the best, and why.

ADDITIONAL PRACTICE | **Maximiser** p.24, Speaking 1–2 | **MyEnglishLab: Cambridge First**, Speaking 5 *Part 2 Comparing pictures: What's the missing phrase?*; Speaking 12 *Describing and explaining pictures: Match the halves together*

Writing focus ▶ p.34

Article (Part 2)

Aim

- to practise an exam-style writing task (Writing, Part 2)

Warmer: *I'd like to have …*

Write the starter on the board: *Three things I'd like to have are …* and ask students to complete it with physical or abstract things. Put students in small groups to compare and discuss their answers. Ask each group to summarise their discussion.

Ask students to turn to the **Writing Reference** on page 192 and read the task (magnify the task on eText if using it). Ask students to quickly skim the sample answers to find out what the student wants, and why (A: a computer to keep pictures of friends and keep in touch with friends and family; B: a lot of money so she could study in other countries, buy a house for her parents and help people in need). Give students time to re-read the sample answer and then to discuss in pairs the strengths and weaknesses of the answers. Elicit the following: Strengths: answers the question, relevant information, good range of language and structures, well-organised; Weaknesses: some inaccurate use of vocabulary and structures (see comments box on Coursebook page 192), a mix of informal and formal language.

1 Ask students to turn back to page 34 and read the task box aloud. Then elicit responses to questions 1 and 2.

2 Tell students that they are going to read two opening paragraphs and decide which is more effective, taking into account the listed criteria. Give students time to read the paragraphs and answer the questions, then discuss their answers in pairs. Elicit a few ideas from the class.

3 Put students into pairs to choose which paragraph to include the details in. Elicit answers.

4 Give students about 30 minutes to write their paragraphs in pairs, circulating to help as necessary.

5 Ask students to read the concluding sentences and decide which would have the most positive effect.

6 Give students a few minutes to make notes on their own response to the advert. Read the **Language Tip** aloud and elicit other extreme adjectives and adverbs, turning back to Activity 3 on page 19 of the Coursebook if necessary.

7 Students complete the writing task for homework, or alternatively allow about 30 minutes in class.

8 Put students into small groups to swap their articles, or photocopy students' articles and distribute them for reading. Alternatively, you could set up an online magazine as described in the *Additional activity*.

Answers

1 1 informal, because it's for young people 2 describe a possession and say why it's important to you

2 *A* and *B* both answer the question, but *Paragraph A* is most effective.

3 Suggested answers:
Paragraph two: B, C, F, G; Paragraph three: A, D, E, H

4 Sample answer

By simply looking at my computer, you wouldn't be able to see how important it is to me. It's an inexpensive Toshiba model and quite ordinary to look at. If you started it up, you'd find it user-friendly but not particularly high-tech as it is already two years old.

So, what makes it so special to me? Well, a great deal of its sentimental value comes from the fact that it was an eighteenth birthday gift from my parents. Since then, it has become increasingly important to me because of the hundreds of photos stored on it, along with all my friends' contact details.

5 B It is more interesting and less abrupt.

6 Students' own answers

7 Sample answer

My childhood was one of the happiest times of my life, so it's no surprise that one of my most treasured possessions is a special reminder of that time; my teddy bear, Bertie.

Bertie is a small grey bear who has shiny black buttons for eyes and wears a red velvet coat. His fur has worn off in a few places and one of his ears is slightly ripped, but I couldn't care less about that.

The reason Bertie has so much sentimental value to me is that he has been with me my entire life. I even have a picture of me as a newborn baby with Bertie right next to me in my cot.

One day, I hope to pass Bertie on to my children and see them enjoy a cuddle with my special bear.

8 Students' own answers

Additional activity: Online magazine

Set up an online magazine (a blog) where students can post their writing. You can do this on a site such as **www.wordpress.com** or **www.blogger.com**. These sites allow the students' work to be published to a wider audience (or they can be set up with private access) and also for comments to be added. (You can choose to moderate comments before they are posted.) Ensure students are happy for their work to be posted before you publish it, and ask if they would like a pseudonym to be used.

ADDITIONAL PRACTICE | **Maximiser** p.25, Writing 1–4 | **Teacher's Book** p.139/163 Photocopiable 3B *I couldn't live without …*

Review ▶ p.35

Aim

- to revise structures and vocabulary covered in Unit 3

1–4 Ask students to complete the activities, circulating to provide assistance. Ask students to check in pairs before checking as a class on eText. Alternatively, set as a homework activity.

Answers

1 1 D 2 B 3 A 4 C 5 D 6 B

2 1 has lived/been living here for 2 haven't seen Mike since 3 time (that) I have visited/been to 4 have already had 5 spend hardly any/hardly spend any 6 far more expensive than 7 just as friendly as 8 one of the most expensive

3 1 worried 2 interesting 3 exciting 4 embarrassed 5 frightening 6 relieved

4 1 about 2 like 3 much/far 4 as 5 by 6 as 7 been 8 both/each

ADDITIONAL PRACTICE | **Online Testmaster** Unit 3 Test, **eText**

Battling nature

Listening focus ▶ p.36

Speaking

Aim

- to introduce vocabulary for the listening activity and to give spoken practice

1 Focus attention on the pictures and elicit anything students already know about Antarctica. Put students into pairs and ask them to take turns to read the questions aloud and then discuss each answer. Refer students to page 160 to check their answers.

Answers

1 **1** B **2** A **3** C **4** A **5** C

Multiple choice (Part 4)

Aim

- to complete an exam-style listening task (Listening, Part 4)

2 Refer students to the **Exam Focus** on page 205 and turn to it on eText if you are using it. Read through the notes with students, making sure they understand everything. Read strategy 1 with the class and ask students to read the introduction. Elicit information about the listening (it is a book review about two journeys to the South Pole). Read strategy 2 with the class, then give students a few minutes to read through the questions and underline the key words. Before you play the recording, ask students the following questions: *Who do you think Leo is? What do we know already about the two journeys from the questions?* Elicit a range of answers.
Read the **Exam Tip** aloud, then read strategy 3 with the class. Focus on question 1 and elicit some possible paraphrases for the three options, e.g. A: *It was the first time they had considered …*; B: *It was important to him to …*; C: *They wanted to be the best/first to …* . Put students into pairs to think of paraphrases for the options in the remaining questions. Elicit some examples from the class.

3 Play the recording while students answer questions 1–7.

4 Read strategy 4 with the class. Put students into pairs to compare their answers, then play the recording again for them to check. Play the recording once more, pausing to elicit answers and words or phrases that justify the answers. If you are using eText, you could display the audio script on the board and highlight or underline the key phrases.

5 Put students into small groups to discuss the questions, eliciting a few responses to each one from the class to finish.

Answers

2 1 What does Leo say about Henry Worsley's team?
2 What does Leo say was the hardest thing for Worsley's team before the expedition?
3 What does Leo say was easier for the twenty-first century expedition than for Shackleton's expedition?
4 What problem did both expeditions experience?
5 How did Worsley feel when he was crossing the Antarctic plateau?
6 The part of the book Leo enjoyed most was when Worsley …
7 What does Leo admire about Shackleton?

3 See 4 below.

4 (key phrases in brackets)
1 B (all related to members of Shackleton's team)
2 B (mental challenge … struggled with most)
3 A (Shackleton travelling into the unknown while Worsley's team had a map and modern navigation equipment)
4 C (high winds … Shackleton also endured)
5 B (began to doubt he'd ever reach the Pole)
6 B (arrived at the place where Shackleton decided to turn back)
7 C (courage)

5 Students' own answers

Additional activity: Writing

Ask students to write a short article (120–150 words) describing a journey they would like to take. They should include reasons for their choice, problems they would anticipate and how they think they would feel at the end of the journey.

ADDITIONAL PRACTICE | **Maximiser** p.26, Listening 1 | **MyEnglishLab: Cambridge First**, Listening II *Dealing with distraction: What's the best answer?*

Vocabulary

idioms: the body

Aim

- to extend students' knowledge of body idioms

Warmer

Draw a stick figure on the board. Draw an arrow to the person's face and write *face*. Put students into pairs and ask them to draw a similar figure. Tell them that they have three minutes to label as many body parts as they can. After three minutes, ask students to count the number of body parts they have named. Get the pair with the most body parts to read aloud their list and tell other students to put a tick next to the parts they have that are read out. Students read out any additional parts they labelled.

6 Tell students there are many idioms that use parts of the body. Ask students to read the sentences aloud, then give students time to match the idioms. They can check their answers in pairs before you check as a class.

7 Elicit a few responses for each question from the class, then put students into small groups. Ask each group to write a sentence using each of the remaining six idioms from Activity 6: *get your head around something; face to face; see eye to eye; catch your eye; keep an eye on something; get cold feet about something*. Get students to find a partner from another group and to compare their sentences. Finish by eliciting a few sentences for each idiom, checking they are appropriate in form and use.

Answers

6 **1** J **2** G **3** H **4** E **5** C **6** A **7** B **8** D **9** F **10** I

7 Students' own answers

Additional activity

Ask students to compare the body idioms with any similar ones in their first language. Ask *Do they use the same body part? Are there any that are very different?* Discuss as a class.

ADDITIONAL PRACTICE | **Maximiser** p.26, Vocabulary 1–2

Grammar focus ▶ p.38

Narrative forms

past simple, past continuous and past perfect

Aim

- to review narrative verb forms

1 Check students understand *desert island* (a small tropical island that is far away from other places and has no people living on it), *shipwreck* (the destruction of a ship in an accident) and *to blow up* (to explode). Ask students to read Paragraph 1 and elicit predictions for what might happen next.

2 Ask students to read Paragraph 1 again and decide in pairs which of the underlined forms is an example of each structure. Check answers.

3 Ask students to discuss the questions in pairs, then elicit responses. Ask students to turn to the **Grammar Reference** on page 177 and read through 21.5, 21.6 and 21.7 with the class (on eText if using it), checking students understand everything.

4 Give students a couple of minutes to skim the rest of the story to check their predictions from Activity 1. Ask *How did the story end?* (Fishermen rescued Richards after three days.) *Were your predictions correct?*

5 As an example, focus on the first sentence (on eText if using it). Read the sentence aloud and ask students to choose the appropriate situation from Activity 3, i.e. *Does this refer to a finished event, a situation which happened before another past action or an action already in progress when something else happened?* (an action that was already in progress). Elicit the structure we use for this kind of situation (past continuous) and the form (*was missing*) and write it on eText if using. Ask students to fill the rest of the gaps with the correct form of the verb in brackets, referring back to Activity 3 or the **Grammar Reference** if they are unsure. Students can compare their answers in pairs before you do a class check.

Answers

1 Students' own answers

2 1 set off 2 was sailing 3 had planned

3 1 set off 2 had planned 3 was sailing

4 Students' own answers

5 1 was missing 2 had to 3 heard
4 had rescued 5 had floated
6 was starting/had started

past perfect simple and past perfect continuous

6 Tell students that past perfect can be used in a simple or continuous form. If necessary, elicit the form of the past perfect with the class (*had + been + -ing* form). Put students into pairs to complete the sentences and match them to the statements. Elicit the answers from the class.

7 Elicit the correct verb forms for the first sentence as an example. Students can then complete the remaining sentences, then compare with a partner. Remind students of the *Watch out!* note in the **Grammar Reference** – that the past perfect is not used very often and it is correct to revert to the past simple once the time sequence is established. Check answers with the class.

Answers

6 1 had been working (B), had never needed (A)
2 had been hurting (B) 3 had never seen (A)
4 hadn't heard (A)

7 1 hurt; had been hoping/had hoped
2 was recovering; studied/was studying
3 was swimming; cut
4 hadn't been feeling/hadn't felt; decided

ADDITIONAL PRACTICE | **Maximiser** p.27, Grammar 1–2 | **eText IWB** Extra activity | **eText Game:** Stepping Stones (narrative forms) | **MyEnglishLab: Cambridge First**, Use of English 14 *Past tenses: transform the verb*

Speaking focus ▶ p.39

Collaborative task (Part 3)

ranking

Aim

- to complete an exam-style speaking task (Part 3) and to equip students with useful expressions they can use to rank items in the collaborative task

Refer students to the **Exam Focus** on page 207 and turn to it on eText if you are using it. Read through it with students, making sure they understand everything.

1 Put students into pairs to do the task. Elicit the answers as a class, checking that students understand *raft* (flat structure used for floating on water made from pieces of wood tied together), pointing to the photograph as an illustration.

2 Before they begin, emphasise that students should talk about all the points in the exam task Refer students back to the **Exam Focus** on page 207. Focus on strategy 4 and elicit some phrases that are used for turn-taking and agreeing, e.g. *What do you think? Do you agree? Yes, I agree with you. Yes, I think so, too.* Focus on strategy 5 and point to parts of the picture. Elicit phrases for describing the things in different ways. Ask them to repeat the task with a new partner. If your class will find this easy, you can extend the task by adding a timer or asking students to record themselves and listen back.

3 Play the recording and check with the class what the students decide (making a fire and finding water). Ask whether students agree with the decision and if they have alternative suggestions.

4 Give students time to read the sentences before you play the recording. Play the recording while students fill in the gaps, pausing as necessary. Ask students to check their answers in pairs. Play the recording again, pausing to check after each item.

5 Ask students to read through the completed sentences in Activity 4 and elicit the opposites for each gap.

6 Explain that students are going to do a similar task to the one in Activity 3, but this time they are going to focus on the *least* useful skills. Read through the **Exam Tip** and Tell students you are going to time them while they do this activity. Then ask students if they found they had too much/too little time to do the activity. Discuss strategies for dealing with timing, e.g. not dismissing an idea immediately/bringing the discussion back to focus on the question.

Answers

1 How difficult it would be to learn these survival skills. Which two survival skills would be the most useful?
2 Students' own answers
3 Students' own answers
4 1 top, list 2 put, above 3 highest priority 4 out of these
5 1 bottom 2 below 3 lowest priority 4 least useful
6 Students' own answers

Discussion (Part 4)

Aim

- to practise discussing questions in an exam-style Speaking task (Part 4)

7 Remind students to make sure they take turns in their discussion and to use expressions for agreeing and disagreeing. Students discuss the questions in pairs.

Answers

7 Students' own answers

ADDITIONAL PRACTICE | **Maximiser** p.28, Speaking 1–2 | **MyEnglishLab: Cambridge First** Speaking 15 *Part 3: Linking ideas together: Type what you hear*

Reading focus ▶ p.40

Speaking

Aim

- to provide spoken practice and to introduce topic and vocabulary for the multiple matching activity

1 Focus attention on the photo and read out the paragraph headings. If using eText, ask students not to open their books yet. Put students into pairs and ask them to discuss the questions. If necessary, pre-teach *shock, frostbite, hypothermia.*

Answers

1 Students' own answers

Multiple matching (Part 7)

Aim

- to complete an exam-style multiple-matching task (Reading and Use of English, Part 7)

Refer students to the **Exam Focus** on page 203 and turn to it on eText if you are using it. Read through it with students, making sure they understand everything. Tell them that they have already done stategy 1 in the previous activity and that they are now going to work through the remaining strategies. If you are using eText, keep the strategies displayed for students to refer to while they complete the activities.

2 Read strategy 2 with the class and ask students to skim the article then elicit answers to the question.

3 Read strategy 3 with the class and focus attention on the underlined key word *panicking* in question 1. Elicit the key words in question 2 and underline them (*stay awake*). Give students a few minutes to underline the key words/phrases in the remaining questions.

4 Before students choose their answers, refer them to strategies 4 and 5. Model the strategies by asking students to scan for a situation where someone panicked (highlighted section in text A). Then focus on question 2 and ask students to scan the texts for someone who focused on staying awake. Elicit the section and underline it on eText (B – *I had to fight the desire to go to sleep).* Tell students to scan the texts to find information relevant to the remaining key words. Then refer students to strategies 6 and 7 and ask students to complete the task. Read the **Exam Tip** aloud and warn students that once they have found relevant information they must read it very carefully to make sure it is the correct answer. Circulate while students answer the questions. Put students into pairs to compare their answers. To finish, check the answers as a class.

5 Students discuss the questions in pairs. Elicit a few answers to each question from the class.

Answers

2 Yes, John Neidigh had concussion, a collapsed lung, cracked ribs and a shattered leg.

3 Shock: All of them Frostbite: A Hypothermia: A, B

4 (key words and expressions in the text in brackets)

1 A (panicking; started screaming, out of my mind)
2 B (stay awake; fight the desire to go to sleep)
3 D (in pain all over; needles stuck in every part of your body)
4 C (thrown up into the air; felt the entire trailer lift off the ground)
5 A (crying helped him to survive; tears running across face, realised …)
6 C (multiple injuries; concussion, collapsed lung)
7 A (a long wait; fourteen hours)
8 D (deafness; couldn't hear anything)
9 B (difficult to relate; feeling disconnected)
10 D (variations in body temperature; frozen, boiling)

5 Students' own answers

Additional activity: More on the text

Put students in pairs and assign each pair one of the four sections of the article. Ask them to select three interesting words or collocations from the text and write two comprehension questions and one opinion question about the text. Both students should write these down. Then put students into groups of four, with one person who has looked at each article in each group. (If you do not have the right number of students to form groups of four, there may be some groups of three.) Students take turns to share the vocabulary they chose, then ask their three questions to the group.

ADDITIONAL PRACTICE | **Maximiser** p.28–29, Reading 1–3 | **Teacher's Book** p.140/164 Photocopiable 4A *Four stories* | **eText IWB** Extra activity

Vocabulary

collocations and idioms: weather

Aim

- to review weather collocations and idioms

Warmer: Weather brainstorm

Elicit any words or phrases that students know related to weather and write them on the board. Encourage students to look back at sections A and B of the article for additional words/expressions related to weather, e.g. *a lovely July afternoon, drizzle, lightning bolt, twister.*

6 Put students into pairs to match the words in column A with their collocations in column B. Check answers as a class.

7 Students discuss the questions in pairs. Elicit answers.

8 Students discuss the questions in pairs. Elicit answers.

Answers

6 **1** D **2** E **3** A **4** B **5** C **6** J **7** I **8** F **9** G **10** H

7 Students' own answers

8 **1** afraid **2** angry **3** in a hurry **4** annoyed **5** disappointed/sad/worried **6** angry

ADDITIONAL PRACTICE | **Maximiser** p.29, Vocabulary 1 | **eText IWB Game:** Pelmanism (weather collocations) | **MyEnglishLab: Cambridge First**, Reading 9 *Understanding attitude and opinion in reading: Match the meaning*; Reading 11 *Understanding text purpose when reading: What type of text?*.

Grammar focus ▶ p.42

Articles

definite, indefinite and zero articles

Aim

- to review use of articles and to practise selecting the correct article in context

1 Students complete the rules then compare their answers in pairs before you check as a class.

2 Students match the rules with the examples from the text, then compare in pairs before you check as a class. Read the **Language Tip** aloud and share a few more examples, such as: *I hurt my leg (NOT the leg), I washed my hands (NOT the hands), I shook her hand (NOT the hand).* Ask students if this is the same or different in their own language. Refer students to the **Grammar Reference** on page 163 and read through it with the class (on eText if using it), checking that students understand everything.

3 Tell students they are going to read a story by a pilot. After students complete the gaps, check their answers in pairs before you check as a class. Refer back to the **Grammar Reference** if questions arise.

Answers

1 1 the 2 the 3 – 4 the 5 the 6 – 7 a/an 8 –

2 A 7 B 3 C 2 D 8 E 4 F 8

3 1 – 2 – 3 – 4 – 5 the 6 the 7 the 8 a 9 a 10 the 11 a 12 a 13 the 14 – 15 –

ADDITIONAL PRACTICE | **Maximiser** p.30, Grammar 1–2

Speaking

Aim

- to use vocabulary related to survival in spoken practice

4 Put students into small groups and ask them to go through the list, sharing any experiences they have had. Then, bring the class together and ask students to report the experiences of others in their group.

Use of English focus

▶ p.43

Vocabulary

negative prefixes

Aim

- to use negative prefixes to form antonyms

1 Model the activity by underlining the first prefix on the board, (<u>un</u>successful) then give students a few minutes to underline the remaining prefixes. Check as a class and if you are using eText, invite a student to underline the prefixes on the board.

2 Students complete this activity in pairs. Check answers as a class.

3 Students discuss the questions in pairs. For extra practice, students could swap partners and repeat.

Answers

1 1 <u>un</u>successful 2 <u>in</u>credible 3 <u>dis</u>couraged 4 <u>im</u>possible 5 <u>mis</u>understood 6 <u>ir</u>responsible

2 1 disadvantage 2 misread 3 unlikely 4 impatient 5 irregular 6 incapable

3 Students' own answers

Additional activity:
Dictionary work – story building

Put students into groups of three and give each group one of the negative prefixes above. If you have a large class, there will be more than one group with each prefix. Ask students to use dictionaries, either online or paper, to look for words using their prefix. Then, give each group 15 minutes to write a short story with as many different words using their prefix as possible. Ask each group to share their story and the group that used the most words with the prefix is the winning group.

Word formation (Part 3)

Aim

- to complete an exam-style word formation task (Reading and Use of English, Part 3)

Refer students to the **Exam Focus** on page 201 and turn to it on eText if you are using it. Read through it with students, making sure they understand everything.

4 If you have access to the internet, search for images of *Death Valley, California* and display them on the board. Ask students what kind of place it is and how they think it got its name.

5 Refer to the **Exam Focus** and remind students that it is an important strategy to decide what part of speech is missing before adding a word (see strategy 3). Ask students to predict as much as possible about each missing word, e.g. what part of speech it is, if it is singular or plural, positive or negative, etc. Elicit ideas from the class for each gap.

6 Ask students to complete the gap fill. Read the **Exam Tip** aloud and ask students to compare answers in pairs before you check as a class.

7 Put students into pairs and ask them to make a list of at least four pieces of advice for a very hot or cold climate. Then group each pair with another pair. The pairs then take turns to read their advice without mentioning whether it is for a hot or cold climate. The other pair has to say whether the advice is for a hot or a cold climate.

Answers

4 Students' own answers
5 adjective: 1, 3, 4, 5, 6 noun: 2, 7, 8
6 **1** lucky **2** visitors **3** dangerous **4** inexperienced **5** sensible **6** Warning **7** sickness **8** assistance
7 Students' own answers

Additional activity:
Bear Grylls Worst Case Scenario videos

On the IWB, go to: **http://dsc.discovery.com/videos/worst-case-scenario/**. Tell students that Bear Grylls is a popular adventurer, famous for his TV show where he shows people how to survive in worst case scenarios. Elicit any additional information that students know about Bear Grylls. If students are not familiar with Grylls, give them a few minutes to look at his profile page on the site and then elicit a few main points. If students have access to individual computers, put them into pairs and ask them to select a video that interests them. Otherwise, select a video to play on the IWB. Ask students to read the title and predict the advice. Play the video. Ask students to discuss their answers before you replay it. Ask each pair to share their responses to the video. Ask *What did you watch? What did you learn? Were you surprised by the advice?*

ADDITIONAL PRACTICE | **Maximiser** p.30, Use of English 1–3 | **MyEnglishLab: Cambridge First**, Use of English 2 *Similar words: Which is the right one?*

Writing focus ▶ p.44

Essay (Part 1)

Expressing and supporting ideas

Aim

- To complete an exams-style writing task (Writing, Part 1) practising expressing and supporting ideas in an essay.

1 Ask students to turn to the opening page of the unit (page 36) and look at the photo. How would they feel about visiting a place like this? Can they think of other places with extreme environments that they would like to visit (deserts, jungles, mountains)? Put students in pairs to discuss the questions, then invite them to share their ideas with the class.

2 Ask students to look at the essay task. Put students in pairs to decide whether they agree or disagree with the idea that 'adventure tourism' should be encouraged. Ask them to think of any examples they might have heard in the news or seen in documentaries.

3 Put students in pairs to do the activity. Check answers as a class. Ask which phrase is used to express a personal opinion (*In my view*) and a negative opinion (*The problem is*).

4 Remind students that in an essay it is important to support opinions with reasons. Ask them to think of the ideas they had in Activity 2. Can they find any of the same ideas in sentences A–D? Put students in pairs to do the activity and check answers as a class.

5 Ask students to do the activity individually, then they compare their ideas with another student. Read the **Exam Tip** aloud and ask students to turn to the **Writing Reference** on page 180. If you are using eText IWB, display this page on the board. Ask students to look at the topic sentences for each paragraph in the model answer.

6 Ask students to read through the suggestions in the box, then think of their own ideas for the third point. Ask them to compare their ideas with a partner.

7 Read through the task with the class and ask students to underline the key points. If you are using eText IWB, a student can do this on the board. Ask students to brainstorm ideas for the topic and think about what their third point could be. Give students a few minutes to make notes on the positive and negative points about living in the country. Remind them that there is no correct answer. They have to show that they can express their ideas and support them with reasons or examples. Students can complete the essay in class or it can be set for homework.

Answers

1 Students' own answers

2 Students' own answers

3 negative effects of tourism: 2 (disagree) and 3 (agree); personal risk 1 (agree) and 4 (disagree)

4 A 2 B 4 C 3 D 1

5 Students' own answers

6 Students' own answers

7 Sample answer

Does living in the countryside provide a better way of life?

TV programmes often show beautiful scenes in the countryside that feature the wildlife, fantastic landscapes and beautiful beaches, for example. They don't often show a lot of detail about what rural life is actually like. Is it really better to live in the countryside than in a city?

It is true that living in the countryside offers some obvious health benefits. The air is less polluted, and you may have more opportunities to spend time outdoors enjoying nature. This can be good for your mental health as well as physical health.

On the other hand, there are some clear advantages to living in a city. Public transport is often better and there are more facilities for education, leisure and entertainment.

However, people aren't always able to choose to live in the country, even if they want to. Some people have to move to cities to find employment as jobs are much more plentiful there.

I think that living in the countryside can provide a better way of life, but really this depends on your lifestyle and your personal situation.

Additional activity: Writing

Before class: Photocopy page 188 of the Coursebook, with one photocopy for each pair of students. Cut each sheet into five parts: the task, the two individual sample answers, and the two sets of comments.

In class: Put students into pairs and first give them the task. Ask them to brainstorm ideas for the essay. Elicit ideas from the class.

Hand out the two sample answers and two sets of comments. Ask students to read the two sample answers and match them to the comments. Check answers and ask students which story they prefer, and why.

Ask students to choose one of the sample answers to correct and improve. Pairs can compare their final versions with other pairs who have worked on the same essay.

ADDITIONAL PRACTICE | **Maximiser** p.31 Writing 1–5 | **Teacher's Book** p.141/166 Photocopiable 4B *A good start* | **MyEnglishLab: Cambridge First**, Writing 1 *Making a plan: Sort the plan out*

MyEnglishLab tip
Writing exercises

The MyEnglishLab writing exercises contain more useful language for exam tasks, so suggest students complete them before they do the task.

Review ▶ p.45

Aim

- to revise structures and vocabulary covered in Unit 4

1–4 Ask students to complete the activities, circulating to provide assistance. Ask students to check in pairs before checking as a class on eText. Alternatively, set as a homework activity and then go through the interactive activities on eText to check.

Answers

1 1 an 2 the 3 the 4 the 5 the 6 - 7 the 8 the 9 a 10 an 11 the 12 a 13 a 14 - 15 a 16 a

2 1 incapable 2 misunderstood 3 unreliable 4 impatient 5 irresponsible 6 dissatisfied

3 1 B 2 A 3 E 4 F 5 C 6 D

4 1 had been living 2 were walking for 3 had forgotten how to 4 hadn't/had not been

ADDITIONAL PRACTICE | **Maximiser** p.32–33, Use of English | **Online Testmaster** Unit 4 Test

Eat your heart out!

Grammar focus ▶ p.46

Speaking and vocabulary

Aim

- to introduce or revise a range of food vocabulary and to give spoken practice

1 Focus students on the photos and ask them to discuss the questions in pairs. Then elicit some responses to each question from the class.

2 Put students into pairs to discuss the questions.

3 Ask students to complete the phrases then compare their answers in pairs before you check as a class. Check that students understand the meaning of each phrase.

4 Ask students to discuss the diet in their country with their partner. If you have a mixed nationality class, you could extend this activity by asking students to prepare short presentations about the food of their country (with slides if you have a projector or interactive whiteboard).

Answers

1–2 Students' own answers

3 **1** fat **2** vegetarian **3** vitamins **4** balanced **5** low **6** free

4 Students' own answers

ADDITIONAL PRACTICE | **Maximiser** p.34, Vocabulary 1

Countable and uncountable nouns

Aim

- to review whether common foods are countable or uncountable

5 Write the three headings on the board (A *always uncountable*, B *always countable*, C *can be countable or uncountable*). Ask students to copy the headings and write the foods under the correct heading. Put students into pairs to check and then elicit answers as a class. Ask students to take turns to come up to the board and write up each answer.

6 Put students into pairs to discuss the questions, then elicit the answers. Focus students' attention on the first **Language Tip** and read through it together. Elicit some other questions or phrases using *rice*, e.g. *In my country, we eat several different types of rice regularly.* Point out that *pasta* is also uncountable in English but countable in many other languages. *Noodles* is countable and usually plural, however, e.g. *These noodles are delicious!*

Ask students to turn to the **Grammar Reference** on page 167 and read through it with the class (on eText if using it), checking they understand everything.

Answers

5 A fat, honey, rice, salt B egg, vegetable C cake, cheese, chicken, chocolate, coffee, curry, fruit, meat

6 1 A refers to one cake, B refers to several cakes

2 A refers to the meat, B refers to the animals

Expressions of quantity

Aim

- to review expressions of quantity and to contrast the meaning of *few/a few, little/a little*

7 Ask students to turn to page 160 and look at the table, which provides a useful summary of which expressions of quantity (listed across the top) can be used with different structures (listed down the side). Ask students to use the information in the table to choose the correct expressions of quantity in the sentences. Ask students to check their answers in pairs, then elicit responses. Ask students to write three sentences about their own eating habits using expressions of quantity from the table, then to share them in small groups.

8 Ask students to discuss the difference in meaning between the examples in pairs, then elicit responses. Ask students to turn to the **Grammar Reference** on page 168 and read through it with the class (on eText if using it), checking they understand everything.

9 Model the activity by asking a few questions using the sentences, e.g. *Do you eat much fruit? Are there many healthy snacks in your local shop?* With weaker classes, get students to prepare the questions in pairs first and check the questions for accuracy before students ask and answer them in pairs.

Answers

7 1 much 2 a lot of 3 very little 4 hardly any 5 a lot of 6 a few 7 any 8 some

8 1 A refers to a small number, B refers to hardly any

2 A refers to a small amount, B refers to hardly any

9 Students' own answers

ADDITIONAL PRACTICE | **Maximiser** p.34, Grammar 1–2 | **Teacher's Book** p.142/168 Photocopiable 5A *Countable and uncountable combinations* | **eText IWB** Extra activity | **MyEnglishLab: Cambridge First**, Vocabulary 19 *Food*; Use of English 4 *Plurals and articles: The right choice*

Use of English focus

▶ p.48

Open cloze (Part 2)

Aim

- to complete an exam-style open cloze task (Reading and Use of English, Part 2)

1 Put students in pairs to discuss whether they agree with the statements. Ask for a show of hands of who agrees with each statement.

2 Ask students to turn to the **Exam Focus** on page 201 and read through it with the class (on eText if using it), checking they understand everything. Focus on strategy 1 and ask students to read the text quickly for gist. Ask students to choose the correct words in the statements, then elicit the answers.

3 Read the question aloud, then re-read strategy 2 and the **Exam Tip**. Focus students' attention on the example (0) and elicit what kind of word this is (a quantifier). Then look at the first gap (1) and elicit what kind of word fits (a quantifier). Ask students to work through the exercise in pairs, discussing and noting what kind of word fits in each gap, then elicit responses. Elicit which gaps require an expression of quantity.

4 Re-read strategy 3 and the question, emphasising that there is only one word in each gap. Students work through the activity. When they have finished, re-read strategy 4 and give students time to read the whole text and check their answers. Students can then compare their answers in pairs before you check as a class.

5 Put students into pairs to discuss the questions. Elicit examples of foods or drinks that students disliked in the past but enjoy now.

6 Give students a few minutes to underline all the prepositions in the text and the structures listed in 1–3. If using eText, ask a volunteer to come to the board to underline them.

Answers

1 Students' own answers

2 1 doesn't like 2 isn't

3 Gaps 1, 5, 6, 8 can be filled by an expression of quantity.

4 1 many 2 get/become/grow 3 why 4 which 5 any 6 few 7 been 8 every

5 Students' own answers

6 1 go through
2 pour over, use in
3 for the sake of

Teaching tip

Making the most of the interactive whiteboard

- Give all students an opportunity to practise writing on the board.
- Demonstrate how to touch and write firmly on the board.
- If students' hands are sweaty, they may need to wipe them first.
- Make sure extra body parts are not touching the board.

ADDITIONAL PRACTICE | **Maximiser** p.35, Use of English 1–2 | **Teacher's Book** p.142/169 Photocopiable 5B *What's the connection?* | **MyEnglishLab: Cambridge First**, Use of English 9 *Prepositions: What exactly did she say?*

Listening focus ▶ p.49

Sentence completion (Part 2)

Aim

- to complete an exam-style listening task (Listening, Part 2)

1 Put students into pairs to discuss the questions, then elicit a few responses to each one.

2 Ask students to turn to the **Exam Focus** on page 204 and read through it with the class (on eText if using it), checking they understand everything. Then read the rubric aloud. Look at the first example together and elicit what kind of word it is (a noun) and how we know (it is preceded by the preposition *of*). Ask students to note down what kind of word they think would fit in each gap, then go through them as a class.

3 Give students a few minutes to underline the key words (as per strategy 1). Circulate and provide help with vocabulary as needed. Encourage students to guess unknown vocabulary from context if possible.

4 Read the **Exam Tip** aloud, and re-read strategies 2 and 3. Play the recording once while students complete the sentences. Read strategy 4, then play the recording again for students to fill any blanks.

5 Refer to strategy 5 and give students time to check their sentences and compare their answers with a partner. Then go through the answers as a class. If you are using eText, you could open up the audio script and ask students to find and highlight the parts that answered each question.

6 Students discuss the questions in small groups.

Answers

1 Students' own answers

2 1 noun 2 adjective 3 noun 4 verb 5 verb 6 noun 7 noun 8 verb 9 noun 10 noun

3 1 percent, chimpanzee, diet, fruit 2 chimpanzee food, tastes, humans 3 can't survive, fruit, have, small 4 cooking, spent, time 5 benefit, cooking 6 cooking, resulted, increase 7 sharing 8 waiting, food, cooked 9 early humans, used, cooking 10 ice age, cooked food, survive

4 1 fruit 2 bitter 3 stomach 4 finding 5 preserve 6 brain 7 (family) meal 8 stolen 9 (a) fire 10 energy

5–6 Students' own answers

Additional activity: Useful websites

At **www.examenglish.com** there are practice tests for listening. These could be played through an interactive whiteboard. Alternatively, it could be completed on individual computers (or at home) by students.

The Food Programme by BBC radio (**http://www.bbc.co.uk/podcasts/series/foodprog**) offers podcasts on food-related topics for additional listening practice.

ADDITIONAL PRACTICE | **Maximiser** p.35, Listening 1–2 | **eText Game**: Sheep out (cooking) | **MyEnglishLab: Cambridge First:** Listening 15 *Listening for detail: What exactly did she say?*

Reading focus ▶ p.50

Speaking

Aim

- to provide spoken practice and to activate prior knowledge on the topic of eating out

1 Students discuss the questions in pairs. Elicit a few answers from the class for each question.

Answers

1 Students' own answers

Multiple choice (Part 5)

Aim

- to complete an exam-style multiple-choice task (Reading and Use of English, Part 1)

2 Refer students to the **Exam Focus** on page 202 and turn to it on eText if you are using it. Read through it with students, making sure they understand everything. Refer to strategies 1 and 2 and tell students that the picture is of a New York food critic called David Fishman. Elicit the meaning of *critic* (someone whose job is to make judgments about the good and bad qualities of art, music, films and, in this case, food). Give students about five minutes to read the article to get a general idea of what it is about, then elicit why they think David is unusual.

3 Refer to strategy 4 and demonstrate by eliciting which part of the text question 1 refers to (paragraph 1). Ask students to work in pairs and identify which part of the text each question relates to. Then demonstrate underlining the key words in the options by eliciting the key words for the options in question 1. Students continue working in their pairs to underline the key words in the remaining options.

4 Re-read strategy 5 with the class and demonstrate by eliciting the correct answer to question 1 from the class. Read the exam tip aloud, then give students about ten minutes to answer the questions. After students have answered individually, give them time to compare in pairs, then check as a class.

Answers

2 David is very young to be a restaurant critic and is an adventurous eater.

3 (parts of the text for each question)

1 para 1 **2** para 2 **3** para 3 **4** para 4 **5** line 53 **6** line 67

(key words in the options)

1 A prefers, Italian; B attracted, appearance; C wanted, write, review; D prefers, restaurant
2 A wasn't keen, serve, child; B tables reserved, celebrities; C completely booked; D couldn't afford
3 A worried; B interested; C wanted, opinions; D talk to him, lonely
4 A fuss; B unusual food, free; C explained, food, made; D didn't treat him, child
5 A part of animal; B why; C how; D kind of animal
6 A nature; B youth; C child-like; D lack, qualifications

4 **1** B **2** C **3** B **4** D **5** D **6** B

ADDITIONAL PRACTICE | **Maximiser** p.36–37, Reading 1–3 | **eText IWB** Extra activity

Speaking

Aim

- to provide spoken practice

5 Put students into new pairs to discuss the questions, then elicit a few answers from the class.

Answers

5 Students' own answers

Vocabulary

phrasal verbs with *turn*

Aim

- to review the meaning of phrasal verbs with *turn* and to use them in spoken practice

6 Students match the definitions with the phrasal verbs in the text. Give students time to compare their answers in pairs before you check as a class.

7 Put students into pairs to write a paragraph that includes four of the phrasal verbs. Circulate, providing assistance as required. Form larger groups of six for students to share their paragraphs. If you think students will find this activity challenging, you could first write a paragraph on the board with the whole class as a shared writing activity, as an example.

Answers

6 **1** turn down **2** turn up **3** turn on **4** turn out **5** turn off **6** turn away

7 Students' own answers

Additional activity: Useful websites

The BBC Learning English website has a section called Funky Phrasals which contains explanations and activities for collections of phrasal verbs by topic. This is a great resource for students who would like to continue to extend their knowledge of these useful verbs.

http://www.bbc.co.uk/worldservice/learningenglish/radio/specials/148_phrasalverbs/index.shtml

ADDITIONAL PRACTICE | **Maximiser** p.37, Vocabulary 1–2 | **MyEnglishLab: Cambridge First**, Reading 3 *Scanning for detail: Where does he say this?*

Grammar focus ▶ p.52

Passive forms

Aim

- to review passive forms

Warmer: Discussion

Ask students if they have ever been to Thailand or tried Thai food. If not, ask what unusual foods they have tried, or would like to try. Elicit a variety of answers.

1 Ask students to read the extract from the article and elicit what is unusual about the celebration.

2 Focus students on the first underlined form in the article (*will be organised*) and the active form in the example. Point out that in the article, no subject is given, so *people* has been used. Do the next example together on the board, changing it to the active form *Local people will provide vegetables.* If students find this difficult, encourage them to first work out who, or what, the subject of each sentence is. Ask for volunteers to write each of the active sentences on the board to check.

Read the **Language Tip** aloud, then ask students to turn to the **Grammar Reference** on page 172 and go through it together (on eText if using), checking that students understand everything.

3 Complete the first sentence with the class on the board, then ask students to complete the rest. Put students into pairs to check, then elicit answers.

4 Ask students to discuss the questions in pairs.

Answers

1 The celebration is held in honour of monkeys.

2 will be provided → Local people will provide a huge amount of fruit and vegetables.

have been invited → People have invited chefs to prepare a wonderful meal.

can be seen → You can see monkeys everywhere in this jungle town.

is being held → People are holding the feast as they do every year.

are believed to bring → People believe monkeys bring wealth.

3 **1** were given away **2** have been eaten **3** being given **4** be made **5** are going to be served **6** to be asked

4 Students' own answers

Additional activity: Writing

Ask students to write a paragraph introducing one of the foods they mentioned in Activity 4, explaining when it is eaten, how it is served, etc. Students could either record themselves talking about the food for a podcast (see page 10 for recording tips), read their paragraphs aloud in small groups, or post them on a forum (see page 12 for tips on setting up a blog or forum for your class).

Passive reporting verbs

Aim

- to review and use passive structures to report what people say, believe or think

5 Give students time to read the sentences, then elicit the answers to the questions. Read the **Language Tip** aloud and, as a class, match the structures in the **Language Tip** to sentences B and C.

6 Complete the first sentence as a model on the board, then give students time to copy out and complete the rest of the sentences. Ask students to compare their answers in pairs, then check as a class.

7 For this activity, it may help if you bring in a few newspapers or give students some time to look at the headlines online to remind them of current affairs. If these are not available, spend a few minutes brainstorming some stories in the news and listing them on the board before students complete the activity.

Answers

5 B and C avoid saying *who* believes C uses an impersonal third person pronoun.

6 **1** are expected to carry **2** are known to be **3** is claimed that **4** are believed to have been **5** has been estimated **6** are thought to get

7 Students' own answers

Alternative activity

If students do not have much interest in or knowledge of current events, instead of Activity 7, ask students to discuss 'old wives tales' about food and whether they believe them. Share some examples such as the ones below and then ask students if they can think of any similar beliefs in their own culture. Some examples:

It is said that you should wait an hour after eating before swimming or you'll sink.

People say that eating carrots helps you see in the dark.

It is said by some that eating your vegetables will make your hair curl.

It is believed that an apple a day keeps the doctor away.

ADDITIONAL PRACTICE | **Maximiser** p.38, Grammar 1–3 | **eText IWB** Extra activity | **MyEnglishLab: Cambridge First** Use of English 12 *Passive: Correct the mistakes*

Speaking focus ▶ p.53

Long turn (Part 2)

comparing and giving a reaction

Aim

- to review vocabulary and comparative structures and to use them in an exam-style speaking task (Speaking, Part 2)

Ask students to turn to the **Exam Focus** on page 206 and display on eText if using. Go through it on the board, checking that students understand everything.

1 Ask students to look at the photos and the task and tick the statements they agree with. Put students into pairs to compare their ideas, then elicit ideas from the class.

2 Ask students to underline the linking expressions in the statements in Activity 1. Ask students to turn to the **Grammar Reference** on page 165 (and turn to it on eText if using) and go through the notes and examples with the class.

3 Students work in pairs to match the sentences to the photos (A is on the left; B is on the right). Elicit answers from the class.

Answers

1 Students' own answers

Suggested answers:

Formal restaurants: more special, better for a celebration, expensive, food more adventurous and interesting

Fast food restaurants: more casual, simpler/more basic food

2 **1** Although **2** whereas **3** While **4** Both

3 **1** A **2** A **3** B **4** B **5** A **6** A

Additional activity: Vocabulary

Elicit some possible opposites for each sentence in Activity 3, e.g.

1 You have to dress up. There's a dress code.
2 It's nice and quiet. There's a peaceful ambience.
3 It's good value for money.
4 They're good for informal get-togethers.
5 The atmosphere is quite formal.
6 The food's a bit fancy.

Listening

Aim

- to listen to a model of a student completing an exam-style speaking task (Speaking, Part 2)

4 Ask students to read the questions, then play the recording. Ask students to compare answers in pairs. Play the recording again before eliciting responses.

Answers

4 1 She mentions differences of price, food, service, reasons why you might go there.
2 She imagines how the restaurants make the customers feel.

Speaking

Aim

- to complete an exam-style speaking task

5 Put students into pairs and tell them they are going to complete an exam-style speaking task. Give them three minutes to look at the task on page 152, then read the **Exam Tip** aloud. Prompt students to start, allowing them about three minutes. Ask whether they used any of the linking expressions from Activity 2 and if they answered both questions. Then ask students to repeat the task, this time with a timer on for one minute. Ask students to swap roles and turn to page 154.

ADDITIONAL PRACTICE | **Maximiser** p.38–39, Speaking 1–3

Writing focus ▶ p.54

Reading

Describing a personal experience

Aim

- to familiarise students with the language and structure of a review as a model for a Writing, Part 2 task

Warmer: Discussion

Ask *How often do you eat in restaurants? How do you choose where to eat? Do you read online reviews? Do you listen to recommendations from friends?* Alternatively, if students don't eat out much, ask them similar questions about how they decide what purchases to make, e.g. *If you want to buy something such as a new computer, how do you choose? Do you ever read online reviews?*
Allow students a few minutes to discuss the questions, then elicit some responses from the class.

1 Focus attention on the photo of the Hard Rock Café in London. Ask if anyone has been there and elicit anything they know about it. Explain that the Hard Rock Café is a music-themed restaurant chain with over 153 cafés in 51 countries, founded in 1971. The walls are decorated with music memorabilia. Ask students to read the review and tick the things that are mentioned, then elicit the answers.

2 Students discuss the questions in pairs.

3 Copy the table onto the board (or use eText). Ask volunteers to come up in turn and write one or two examples in the table. Check that students understand all the words and phrases and elicit others that could be added to the table.

4 Find the first example together as a class and underline it on eText if you are using it (*the atmosphere didn't disappoint*). Ask students to find other examples of the structures 1–4 and to discuss in pairs why they are used. Elicit responses from the class.

5 Give students a few minutes to answer the questions, then elicit answers as a class. Write the following paragraph plan on the board as a guide for students when they write their own reviews:
Para 1 – basic information
Para 2 – details
Para 3 – who you recommend the restaurant for.

Read the **Language Tip** aloud. Give another example, e.g. *I'd strongly recommend arriving early* and elicit how this could be reworded with a clause: *I'd strongly recommend that you arrive early.* Then give an example using a clause, e.g. *I'd recommend that you try their soup* and elicit the *-ing* form: *I'd recommend trying their soup.*

Answers

1 staff, writer's expectations, location, atmosphere, food, service

2 Students' own answers

3 food: poor quality, overpriced, outstanding, stodgy, perfectly cooked, bland, not much to tempt me on the menu, far from bland; staff: welcoming, friendly, helpful; atmosphere: full of tourists, certainly didn't disappoint, busy, packed, great place

4 1 *the atmosphere certainly didn't disappoint, far from bland:* using negatives with a positive meaning for emphasis 2 *extremely, certainly, pleasantly, perfectly, just, literally*: a wide range of adverbs give emphasis, make the review more interesting and add impact 3 *was served*: passive is used here because it's unnecessary to mention the waiter 4 *I'd always avoided, I'd heard*: past perfect is used because the writer is talking about her expectations before visiting the restaurant

5 A 2 B 3 C 1

Review (Part 2)

Aim

- to complete an exam-style writing task (Writing, Part 2)

Refer students to the **Writing Reference** on page 186. Read through the tips attached to the model answer with the class and point out the Useful language panel. If you are using eText, you could leave this displayed while students complete the writing task.

6 Give students a few minutes to read the task. Encourage them to make notes under the paragraph headings in Activity 5 before beginning to write. Read the **Exam Tip** aloud and ask students to check they have included at least two positive and negative comment ideas in their notes. The writing task can be completed in class or set as homework. Collect the reviews and provide individualised feedback.

Answer

6 Sample answer

I have just discovered a great Italian restaurant called Fratelli's in Manchester. It's a small restaurant tucked away in a side street near the city centre. From the outside, it doesn't look very special, but you won't regret stepping inside.

The atmosphere is quiet and relaxed. Although the restaurant is always full, the staff never seem rushed and they always have time to talk about the food and make recommendations. The food is all freshly-cooked and full of flavour. There are delicious pizzas and pasta dishes and some wonderful meat and fish dishes. My personal favourite is the pasta, which is freshly made every day in the kitchens. The prices are a nice surprise too, as it isn't too expensive.

This is a great restaurant for anyone who wants a quiet meal with family or friends and wants to enjoy top-quality food at very reasonable prices.

Alternative activity: Writing

If students find writing challenging, either ask them to complete the task in pairs or create a model review on the board with the whole class. You may differentiate by allowing those who would like to write independently to do so, while working with a small group by the board to write a review together.

Additional activity: Writing

Before class: Photocopy page 193 of the Coursebook, with one photocopy for each pair of students. Cut the sheet into five parts: the task, the two individual sample answers and the two sets of comments.

In class: Put students into pairs and give them the task. Ask them to make a list of information that should be included in the review. Elicit ideas from the class. Hand out the two sample answers. Ask students to work in their pairs and make comments on the reviews, pointing out good and bad features of each. Circulate and help as necessary. Hand out the two sets of comments and ask students to match them to the model answers and compare them with their own comments. Students could finish by writing their own film review in pairs.

ADDITIONAL PRACTICE | **Maximiser** p.39, Writing 1–3 | **MyEnglishLab: Cambridge First**, Writing 3 *Understanding the question in Part 2: Get the order right*

Progress test 1 ▶ p.55

Aim

- to revise structures and vocabulary covered in Units 1–5

Set the tests as a homework activity and then go through the interactive activities on eText to check.

Answers

1 1 up 2 down 3 away 4 off 5 out 6 on 7 up 8 over 9 off 10 after

2 1 C 2 A 3 A 4 A 5 B 6 C

3 1 little 2 many 3 no 4 hardly 5 being 6 has 7 be 8 are

4 1 ~~live~~ have lived 2 ~~more fastly~~ faster 3 ~~isn't having~~ doesn't have 4 ~~hardly~~ hard 5 ~~a~~ very few 6 ~~more~~ most 7 ~~run~~ been running 8 ~~gets~~ is getting 9 ~~like~~ as 10 ~~lot~~ a lot 11 ~~frightened~~ terrified 12 ~~travel~~ travelling 13 ~~already left~~ had already left 14 ~~the~~ golf 15 ~~taking~~ to take

5 1 across 2 taste 3 released 4 unpredictable 5 difference 6 make 7 by 8 short 9 caught 10 strong 11 icy 12 impatient 13 taking 14 like 15 embarrassing

6 1 A 2 D 3 A 4 A 5 A 6 C 7 B 8 C

7 9 their 10 enough 11 to 12 so 13 the 14 which 15 off 16 If

8 17 spicy 18 sight 19 colourful 20 adventurous 21 surprisingly 22 fascinating 23 daily/everyday 24 fortunate

9 25 can't sing as well 26 have been taken over by 27 are hardly any cheap/inexpensive 28 haven't seen him for 29 don't remember locking 30 always turning up

ADDITIONAL PRACTICE | **OnlineTestmaster** Unit 5 Test; Progress Test 1 **MyEnglishLab: Cambridge First**, Vocabulary 1 *Phrases with 'make'*; Vocabulary 2 *Phrases with 'do'*

On camera

Speaking focus ▶ p.58

Speaking

Aim

- to introduce the topic of performance and to provide spoken practice

1 Put students into pairs to discuss the questions. Elicit a few responses for each question. Check or teach the word *busker* (someone who plays music in a public place in order to earn money). Ask students if they have ever seen a circus or circus performers, and elicit the kinds of things a circus might include, such as *clowns, acrobats, trapeze artists, horseback riders, animal tamers, flame-throwers, jugglers,* etc.

2 Give students time to choose the word which does NOT fit in phrases 1–3. Students compare their answers in pairs, then check as a class.

3 Read the question aloud and display on eText or write on the board the phrases from Activity 2 which can be used for the discussion. Students discuss their ideas with their partner using the phrases from Activity 2.

Answers

1 Students' own answers
2 **1** highest **2** One different **3** large
3 Students' own answers

Discussion (Part 4)

Aim

- to complete an exam-style discussion task (Speaking, Part 4)

Ask students to turn to the **Exam Focus** on page 207 and display on eText if using. Go through it with students, checking they understand everything.

4 Tell students these are examples of the kind of question they might have to answer in Part 4 of the Speaking exam. Ask students to read the questions and underline key words before listening. Make sure students understand that *The X Factor* is a British TV talent show. Play the recording once, then ask students whether they agreed with Roberto and Beata.

5 Ask students to read the questions, then play the recording again while students note down the phrases they heard. Elicit responses and if you are using eText, highlight them in the audio script on the board.

6 Elicit responses from the class, making sure students give reasons to justify their answers.

7 Read the **Exam Tip** aloud and elicit some phrases that can be used to include someone else in the discussion, e.g. *Would you agree with that? What do you think? How about you?* Students discuss the questions from Activity 4 in pairs.

Answers

4 Students' own answers

5 1 Roberto: Would you agree with that, Beata?
2 Beata: Basically, you're saying you don't really need any talent to succeed.
3 Roberto: Yes, I suppose you are right.

6–7 Students' own answers

ADDITIONAL PRACTICE | **Maximiser** p.40, Speaking 1–3

Vocabulary

the arts

Aim

- to develop vocabulary related to the arts

Warmer

Elicit different art forms included within 'the arts', e.g. *painting, sculpture, theatre, film-making*. Students brainstorm on the board any words or phrases they associate with each of these art forms.

8 Ask students to complete the sentences with one of the words in the box, then compare in pairs before you check as a class.

9 Ask students if they recognise any of the paintings. Students discuss in pairs which one they like the most, then match the words with the pictures. If you have an interactive whiteboard with internet access, you may like to show additional examples of paintings by doing an image search for each style.

10 If students have access to the internet, ask them to search for a photograph or picture before the activity. Otherwise, students can work from memory. Give students a few minutes to make notes before they discuss their favourite painting or photograph with a partner.

Answers

8 1 set 2 critics 3 production 4 script

9 1 portrait 2 graffiti 3 still life 4 landscape 5 abstract

10 Students' own answers

Additional activity

Bring in a set of photos or art works, for example from a magazine or from the internet. Distribute them and ask students to discuss them, comparing and contrasting them and discussing their opinion of each.

Additional activity: Art gallery critics

IWB: Search the internet for a large artwork and display it on the IWB so that it takes up the full screen. Explain to students that this is an art gallery and that you are going to walk by the piece of art and make a comment. Invite a student to walk with you. Walk up to the board, acting as if you are in an art gallery and making comments about the artwork. Then walk past it.

Then pin a range of artworks around the class (or ask students to each draw/bring one to class) and ask students to walk around the class in pairs, discussing the artworks as if they were visiting a gallery. Encourage them to use the language from Activity 10. Alternatively, take a trip to a local art gallery with the class and do the activity in a real-life setting.

ADDITIONAL PRACTICE | **Maximiser** p.41, Vocabulary 1–2 | **MyEnglishLab: Cambridge First,** Speaking 17 *Part 4 Expressing opinions: What's missing?*; Speaking 18 *Part 4 Sharing ideas and opinions: Put these in order*

Listening focus ▶ p.60

Multiple choice: short extracts (Part 1)

Aim

- to complete an exam-style listening task (Listening, Part 1)

Warmer: Noughts and crosses game

If you are using eText, open the noughts and crosses game for Unit 6. If you are using a traditional whiteboard, draw a noughts and crosses grid and write the key words in each of the nine squares. Suggested words: *critics, production, set* (noun), *abstract, busker, script, display, graffiti, landscape*. Divide the students into two teams: noughts and crosses. One team sends a student to the board to select a square. The team has 30 seconds to use the word appropriately in a sentence. If they do this correctly, they put their sign in that square by erasing the verb and drawing their sign. Teams continue to alternate turns until one team wins by having three noughts or three crosses in a row horizontally, vertically or diagonally.

Ask students to turn to the **Exam Focus** on page 204 and display on eText if using. Go through the notes with the class, checking they understand everything.

1 Read the rubric aloud. Give students time to underline key words and if you are using eText, demonstrate this on the board, underlining *dislike*. Then play the first part of the recording.

2 Give students time to check their answer with a partner and to answer the questions. Play the recording again and then elicit the answers as a class.

3 Give students time to underline key words before they listen. Read the **Exam Tip** aloud, then play the recording and ask students to choose the correct answers. Refer students to strategies 3 and 4 in the **Exam Focus** on page 204. Play the recording a second time for students to check and complete their answers. Ask students to compare in pairs, then play the recording again to check the answers, pausing after each question.

4 Ask students to work with a new partner for the discussion, then elicit a few responses.

Answers

1 *dislike, play;* A

2 1 no 2 yes, *music* is mentioned 3 no
4 lighting: *semi-darkness, see clearly*
costumes: *jeans and hoodies*
music: *specially composed, welcome, helps to create*
5 *But …, I just wish I'd been able to …*

3 (key words in brackets)
2 B (why, meet, 6p.m.)
3 C (where, see, actor) 4 C (why, different)
5 C (why, retire) 6 A (exhibition, special)
7 A (actress, doing) 8 C (what, talking about)

4 Students' own answers

ADDITIONAL PRACTICE | **Maximiser** p.41, Listening 1 | **Teacher's Book** p.143/170 Photocopiable 6A *Listen carefully* | **MyEnglishLab: Cambridge First**, Listening 5 *Understanding how conversations are organised: What's the right order?*; Listening 8 *Understanding speaker purpose: Why is the speaker calling?*

Grammar focus ▶ p.61

Future forms

Aim

- to revise the use and pronunciation of the future forms *will, going to* and present continuous

Warmer

Ask students if they like being in the spotlight (being the centre of attention). Ask if they have ever been in a performance/have ever dreamed of being on stage or in show business.

Tell students that the dialogue in Activity 1(1) is about being on stage. Ask for two volunteers to read parts A and B in the dialogue.

1 Give students a few minutes to identify the future forms. Students can then compare answers in pairs before you check as a class.

2 Ask students to match the numbered future forms in the dialogue with their uses A–G, then elicit answers.

3 Elicit *may* and *might*. Tell students that, in English, *could/may/might* can be used interchangeably to indicate future possibility. The degree of probability of an event occurring is conveyed by context and the speaker's tone. Refer students to the **Grammar Reference** 21.8 on page 177 and go through it as a class, on eText if you are using it. Go through the notes and examples, checking that students understand everything.

4 Give students time to complete the gap fill. Students compare answers in pairs. Play the recording once, then play it a second time, pausing if necessary to give students time to check their answers. If students found the activity difficult, go through the answers carefully, matching the use in each sentence to the uses in the **Grammar Reference**.

5 Tell students that, in English, sentence stress helps convey meaning. Play the beginning of the recording to hear the example. Elicit how the stress is indicated (by words being pronounced slightly louder, slower and more emphatically than the words around them). Play the recording again while students underline the stressed words. If you are using eText, display the audio script and underline the stressed words on the board.

6 Before you begin, play the recording line by line and ask students to repeat aloud after the recording, copying the intonation. Ensure students know how to pronounce the contractions, particularly the negative forms. Then give students about ten minutes to practise the dialogues in pairs, circulating to provide feedback on pronunciation. Read the **Language Tip** aloud. Elicit a further example of using the present simple with each of the time expressions.

Answers

1 Examples include: present continuous: *when are you starting …*; present simple: *performances start in three weeks*; will: *it'll be …*; going to: *he's going to tell us …*; modal verbs: *it could be …*

2 1 E 2 G 3 D 4 B 5 F 6 C 7 A

3 may, might

4 1 are you doing 2 'm going 3 's moving 4 'll enjoy 5 'm going to buy 6 'll get 7 does it start 8 'm going to leave

5 1

What are you doing this weekend?

I'm going to the dance festival in the park. It's on all weekend.

Oh, I'd really like to go but my brother's moving house and I have to help him.

That's a shame!

Never mind. I'm sure you'll enjoy it.

Yes. It should be fun, especially as I think the weather'll be good.

2

Hi Ben! Are you going to the film festival at the weekend?

Yes, on Saturday. I'm going to buy the tickets online today.

How much are they?

Only £15. I'll get you one if you like.

That would be great. What time does it start?

At 7.30. But I'm going to leave home early, at six o'clock because of the traffic. I'll pick you up on my way, if you like.

6 Students' own answers

ADDITIONAL PRACTICE | **Maximiser** p.42, Grammar 1–2 | **MyEnglishLab: Cambridge First** Use of English 13 *Future tenses: Choose the right tense*

Speaking

Aim

- to practise selecting future forms appropriately and to use them with the correct stress in spoken contexts

7 Give students a few minutes to think about their own answers, then put them into pairs to share their ideas. Circulate, listening to the future forms and noting any errors for correction. Elicit a few answers, then write any errors you heard on the board (without identifying students) and elicit corrections.

Answers

7 Students' own answers

Additional activity: Predicting stories/films

Encouraging students to predict what is going to happen next in a story or film will give useful practice of these structures, in addition to practising the skill of prediction to foster comprehension. You can use any story or video, pausing it at a climactic moment, although stories with many possible outcomes are best.

Reading focus ▶ p.62

Speaking

Aim

- to provide spoken practice and to activate prior knowledge on the topic of the future of entertainment

1 Put students into pairs to look at the pictures and discuss the questions. Make sure students understand *blockbuster* (informal, a book or film that is very good or successful) and *independent film* (one not made or produced by a large film production company).

Answers

1 Students' own answers

Gapped text (Part 6)

Aim

- to complete an exam-style gapped text task (Reading and Use of English, Part 2)

Elicit what students remember about Reading and Use of English, Part 2, asking them: *What is being tested? What do you have to do?* If students aren't sure, ask them to turn to the **Exam Focus** on page 202, displaying it on eText if you are using it and go through the notes together. Leave the **Exam Focus** on eText while students complete the task.

2 Refer students to strategy 1 and ask them to read the title and subheading carefully. Ask why they think this is important (the title and introduction generally summarise what the text is about and focusing on these first helps understand the text as a whole). Then ask students what they think the article is about. Elicit the meaning of *niche* (adj) (relating to selling goods to a particular small group of people who have similar needs/ interests, etc.). Then ask students to read the article quickly to answer the question. Elicit a few responses.

3 Focus students on the text around the first gap, then put students into pairs to answer the questions. Elicit responses from the class. Tell students that these questions are a useful strategy to employ in this part of the exam, and refer to strategies 3 and 4 in the **Exam Focus**. Read the **Exam Tip** aloud.

4 Ask students to choose the option that best fits the gap (strategy 5), then to repeat strategies 3–5 with the rest of the gaps. Then refer them to strategy 7 and ask them to see if their leftover sentence could fit in any of the gaps. Students compare answers in pairs, then check as a class.

Answers

2 *Blockbusters* appeal to a lot of people (*the mass market*) and *niche* products appeal to small groups of people with specific interests.

3 1 *that* refers back to *the internet would vastly increase the supply of small independent films and other niche media products.*
2 It contrasts with it.
3 Something which says that it's not only niche products which are popular.
4 *but, however* or *yet*

4 1 E 2 G 3 A 4 F 5 C 6 B

Speaking

Aim

- to provide spoken practice and to use vocabulary related to entertainment in context

5 Students discuss the questions in pairs. Elicit a few responses for each question.

Answers

5 Students' own answers

Vocabulary

word formation: adjectives from nouns; nouns from verbs

Aim

- to identify patterns in word transformation in adjectives from nouns and nouns from verbs and to provide spoken practice using these in context

6 Read the question aloud, then elicit the adjective form of *access* as an example (*accessible*). Ask students to find it in the article (two lines above gap 3). Ask students to form the remaining words then check with the text. Elicit the answers and the pronunciation of both forms of each word.

7 Students tick the statements they agree with, then discuss their opinions in small groups. Circulate, encouraging students to develop their answers with reasons and examples. Ask each group to report back to the class on their discussion.

Answers

6 1 accessible, anxious, romantic, successful
2 choice, entertainment, growth, living, product/ production, separation, supply

7 Students' own answers

ADDITIONAL PRACTICE | **Maximiser** p.42–44, Reading 1–5 | **eText IWB** Extra activity | **MyEnglishLab: Cambridge First**, Reading 12 *Text structure – examples: What's it an example of?*

Grammar focus ▶ p.64

Future perfect and continuous

Aim

- to compare the uses of the future perfect and continuous and to use them accurately in spoken and written practice

1 Focus on the pictures and elicit or teach the word *avatar* (a picture of a person or animal that represents you on a computer screen, for example in some chat rooms or when you are playing games over the internet). Read the two predictions aloud. Ask students to discuss with a partner whether they agree with them.

2 Students complete the activity, then compare their answers in pairs before you check as a class.

3 Either write the notes on the board or focus on them in eText, and elicit the best way to complete them. Read the **Language Tip** aloud and elicit additional examples such as: *I think I'll be coming to class on Friday. He'll be bringing Sasha along with him as usual.* Refer students to the **Grammar Reference** 21.8 on page 177 for more information and turn to it on eText if using. Go through the notes and examples, checking students understand everything.

4 Students choose the correct alternative, comparing in pairs before you check as a class.

5 Ask students to tick which sentences they agree with, then put them in new pairs to compare.

6 Write on the board: *In 50 years' time …* and elicit a few predictions. Write students' ideas on the board. Then put students into new pairs and ask them to think of at least five more predictions, using the ideas in the box. Put pairs together into groups of four to share their predictions. Ask each group to report back to the class.

Answers

1 Students' own answers

2 1 By (2020) … ; In (twenty-five years) …
2 we'll be watching, will be controlling (future continuous)
3 might even have found, will have learnt (future perfect)

3 *be*; *have*, past

4 1 have closed 2 be using 3 be choosing
4 be interacting 5 have invented 6 be projecting

5–6 Students' own answers

Additional activity: Useful websites

There are many websites that have interesting articles about the future. Students can read them, then discuss in pairs or small groups how likely they think the predictions are. They could write their own news article with predictions about the future. For example:

http://www.economist.com/node/17730434 The future of English (advanced text).

http://www.news.com.au/travel/news/the-future-of-travel-floating-on-a-cloud/story-e6frfq80-1226170751801 The future of travel: Floating on a cloud?

http://www.dailymail.co.uk/sciencetech/article-507617/Robot-servants-housework-British-homes-years.html The future of housework: Robot servants that do the housework.

ADDITIONAL PRACTICE | **Maximiser** p.44, Grammar 1 | **Teacher's Book** p.144/172 Photocopiable 6B *First to 30* | **eText IWB** Extra activity

Use of English focus ▶ p.65

Vocabulary

expressions with *get*

Aim

- to revise different meanings of the word *get* and to use them in spoken practice

Warmer: get

Put students in pairs and ask them to write three sentences using different meanings of the word *get*. Ask students to put them aside for later in the lesson.

1 Students work individually to replace the word *get* with the verbs in the box. Students compare their answers in pairs, then check as a class. Students ask and answer the questions.

Additional activity

Ask students to look at their sentences from the warmer and see if they can replace *get* with one of the verbs in the box, or a different verb. Put pairs together into groups of four to compare their sentences.

Answers

1 1 understand 2 persuade 3 have 4 become
5 move/travel 6 receive (Students' own answers)

Multiple-choice cloze (Part 1)

Aim

- to complete an exam-style multiple-choice cloze task (Reading and Use of Enghlish, Part 1)

Refer students to the **Exam Focus** on page 200 and turn to it on eText if you are using it. Read through it with students, making sure they understand everything.

2 Read the rubric and questions aloud, then give students three minutes to quickly read the text to answer the questions. Remind students that they should not worry about the gaps at this stage. Elicit the answers to the questions, then focus students on the **Exam Tip**.

3 Remind students of the strategies in the **Exam Focus** and display them on eText if using. Ask students to cover the possible answers and read the text again in pairs, discussing what the missing word might be in each gap. Students then work individually to choose the correct answers. Read strategy 4 with the class and give students time to check their answers in pairs. Check answers as a class.

4 Students discuss the questions in small groups.

Answers

2 It predicted touchscreen technology but other things it predicted have not come true: hoverboards, domestic robots, flying cars, pills to replace food. It did not predict the microchip.

3 **1** A **2** A **3** B **4** D **5** B **6** C **7** C **8** B

4 Students' own answers

ADDITIONAL PRACTICE | **Maximiser** p.44–45, Use of English 1–3 | **MyEnglishLab: Cambridge First**, Use of English 5 *Collocations: Put the words in order*; Vocabulary 4 *Phrases with 'get'*

Writing focus ▶ p.66

Report (Part 2)

Aim

- to identify key features of a report and to complete an exam-style writing task (Writing, Part 2)

Remind students that a report may be one of the options in the Writing Task, Part 2 (see **Exam Focus** on page 203 of the Coursebook for more details on the writing paper).

Ask students to turn to the **Writing Reference** on page 184 and open it on eText if using. Ask students to read the task in the **Writing Reference**. Put students into pairs and give them a few minutes to think of three benefits of buying computers and three of improving the library. Elicit ideas and write them on the board. Then give students a few minutes to think of possible disadvantages of each option. Elicit ideas and write these on the board.

Ask students to read the model answer to see which of their ideas were used and whether the student had any additional ideas. Go through the *Dos* and *Don'ts* with the class. Ask students to re-read the report and highlight any phrases they think would be useful in writing reports. Finally, go through the Useful Language. Then turn back to page 66.

1 Give students a few minutes to read the report and answer the questions. Elicit responses.

2 Give students time to match the headings to the paragraphs and then elicit responses.

3 Go through each example of underlined text, eliciting the type of example (passive form/linking word/clause of purpose) and why they are commonly used in reports.

4 Ask students to read the exam task and underline key words. If you are using eText, ask for a volunteer to underline key words on the IWB.

5 Write the headings *Advantages* and *Disadvantages* on the board and elicit which side each point goes under. Record the points (or ask a student to record them) on the board.

6 Read the **Exam Tip** aloud. Remind students about the Useful Language on page 184. Then either give students time in class to write this (30 minutes – having allowed ten minutes of the exam allocation to plan) or set as a homework task. When students have finished writing, ask them to check their writing against the list of *Dos* and *Don'ts* in the **Writing Reference** on page 184 and edit as appropriate before you collect the reports in for individualised feedback.

Answers

1 1 to look at the advantages and disadvantages of a college cinema, and make a recommendation on the possibility of having one

2 to go ahead with the idea

3 semi-formal (passive forms, words and expressions such as *all things considered, the benefits outweigh the disadvantages, therefore*, etc.)

2 1 Introduction 2 Advantages 3 Potential problems 4 Recommendations

3 passive forms/reporting verbs: *were consulted, was generally believed, It was suggested, could be shown, also be used, were raised*. These are used to make the tone impersonal and to avoid focusing on individual people.

linking words: *However* (to express contrast), *therefore* (to express a conclusion).

clauses of purpose: *In order to* (to show purpose), *Since* (to show reason).

4 your college, visit, self-study centre, local university, successful, recommend

5 advantages: 2, 4, 6

disadvantages: 1, 3, 5, 7, 8

6 Sample answer

Introduction

The aim of this report is to outline the advantages and potential problems of investing money in a self-study centre for our college. In order to do this, I have visited the self-study centre at Central English University.

Advantages

There are several advantages of the facility at Central English University. Firstly, it helps to attract potential students to the university. Secondly, many students have also found the space and worksheets that are provided very useful.

Disadvantages

The main disadvantage is the significant cost. Despite many people from the community using the centre facilities, which helps to fund it, it cost a significant amount to set up and there is also the cost of having a full-time assistant on duty, even if the centre is empty. In addition, writing materials for the centre is time-consuming for the teachers.

Recommendations

Although there would be some students who would benefit from a self-study centre, the significant costs of time and money would outweigh the advantages. I would therefore recommend looking at other options.

Additional activity: Writing

For additional practice, refer students to the **Writing Reference** on page 191. Read the task with the class. Ask students to cover the examiner's comments and read the student's report. Elicit a few ideas on how good the report is and how well it completes the task. Refer students back to the *Dos* and *Don'ts* in the **Writing Reference** on page 184. Ask students to read the report again and write comments on it, as if they were examiners. Tell them they should think about the content and also the style. When students have finished, they can look at the examiner's comments on page 191 and compare them with their own. Students can then work in pairs to improve the report.

ADDITIONAL PRACTICE | **Maximiser** p.45, Writing 1–4 | **MyEnglishLab: Cambridge First**, Writing 9 *Text structure: The right references*

Review ▶ p.67

Aim

- to revise structures and vocabulary covered in Unit 6

1–4 Ask students to complete the activities, circulating to provide assistance. Ask students to check in pairs before checking as a class on eText. Alternatively, set as a homework activity and then go through the interactive activities on eText to check.

Answers

1 1 entertainment 2 growth 3 successful 4 accessible 5 anxious 6 choice

2 1 B 2 A 3 B 4 B 5 C 6 A 7 C 8 A

3 1 through 2 round 3 over 4 down 5 away 6 into

4 1 be learning 2 have started 3 show/be showing 4 use/be using 5 watch/be watching 6 have lost

ADDITIONAL PRACTICE | **Maximiser** p.46–47, Use of English | **Online Testmaster** Unit 6 Test | **MyEnglishLab: Cambridge First**, Practice Test: Reading and Use of English

MyEnglishLab tip

Practice Tests

MyEnglishLab Practice tests are an opportunity for students to practise a full exam paper for each of the four papers: Reading and Use of English, Writing, Listening and Speaking. They are able to re-attempt the question multiple times for extra practice.

A home from home

Reading focus ▶ p.68

Speaking

Aim

- to provide spoken practice and to introduce the topic of emigration

1 Read the rubric aloud. Ensure students understand the word *emigrate* (to leave your own country in order to live in another country). Also elicit *emigrant* (someone who leaves their own country to live in another), *immigrate* (to come into a country in order to live there permanently) and *immigrant* (someone who enters another country to live there permanently). Put students into pairs to discuss the questions. Ask pairs to report back to the class on their ideas.

Answers

1 Students' own answers

Multiple choice (Part 5)

Reading for detail

Aim

- to practise reading for detail and to complete an exam-style multiple-choice task (Reading and Use of English, Part 5)

Refer students to the **Exam Focus** on page 202 for more information about Reading and Use of English, Part 5. Turn to it on eText if you are using it and go through it with the students, checking they understand everything.

2 Ask students to skim the text to get a general idea of what it's about (strategy 2), then ask students how Eilis feels about the move.

3 Ask students to highlight key words in the questions (strategy 3), then highlight the part of the text it relates to (strategy 4). Students should then read the text again, then look at the four options for each question and choose the correct one.

4 Read the **Exam Tip** aloud and refer students back to strategies 6–7. Put students in pairs to compare and discuss their options, then check answers as a class. As you go through the answers, elicit the part of the text that answered each question.

5 Students discuss the question in small groups. Ask each group to report back to the class.

Answers

2 negative, but trying to be positive

3 (key words and answers in text in brackets)
1 A (worried; fear, in case she lost her nerve)
2 D (avoid talking about emotions; do anything to distract themselves from the thought)
3 B (not feel at home; the rest of her life would be a struggle with the unfamiliar)

4–5 Students' own answers

ADDITIONAL PRACTICE | **Maximiser** p.48–49, Reading 1–2 | **Maximiser** p.48, Vocabulary 1 | **eText IWB** Extra activity | **MyEnglishLab: Cambridge First**, Reading 4 *Scanning for detail: The facts about Liverpool*

Vocabulary

deducing meaning

Aim

- to practise guessing the meaning of unknown words from context

6 Students work through the options in pairs. Then elicit some answers, focusing on how students made their choices.

7 Students try to work out the meanings of these words in pairs from the context. Elicit answers from the class and discuss what helped students guess the meanings.

8 Students discuss the questions in small groups. Ask each group to report back to the class.

Answers

6 1 C 2 A

7 1 presumed: thought something was true, although she was not certain 2 singled out: chose one person or thing from among a group because they were better, worse, more important, etc. than the others 3 lost her nerve: became very nervous so that she could not do what she intended to do 4 taken aback: was very shocked or surprised by something 5 unbidden: without being asked for, expected, or invited
6 dread: (the fear of) what she was most anxious about

8 Students' own answers

ADDITIONAL PRACTICE | **Maximiser** p.50, Vocabulary 1

Grammar focus ▶ p.70

Modal verbs

possibility and certainty

Aim

- to review modal verb forms and uses to express possibility and certainty

Warmer

Ask students to discuss in pairs what they remember about the extract from the novel on page 68.

1 Ask students to read the statements and decide whether they agree or disagree with each one, referring back to the text on page 68 as necessary. Put students into pairs to discuss their answers, then compare as a class. Check that students know that *Father* is a title used for priests, especially in the Roman Catholic Church.

2 Students underline the modal verbs in the statements. If you are using eText, invite a student to underline them on the board or alternatively write the verbs from the statements on the board. Then ask students to complete the gaps, working in pairs. Elicit the answers.

3 Students answer the questions, then compare their ideas in pairs before you check as a class. Refer students to the **Grammar Reference** on page 170 and display it on eText if using. Go through the notes and examples with students, checking they understand everything. Read the **Language Tip** and drill the weak form on its own and in the sentence.

4 Ask students to choose the best alternative in the sentences, then compare in pairs before you check as a class. Give students a chance to repeat the modals aloud, concentrating on the weak forms.

5 Model the exercise by selecting a student to read the statement 1A and asking another student to respond using the cues in brackets (*He must have given up work*). If students find this challenging, give them a chance to prepare the answers first. Alternatively, ask students to complete the activity orally then write down the answers with the correct modal forms afterwards. Check as a class.

6 Elicit what kind of animal is in the picture (a camel) and then ask students to discuss in pairs what might be happening. If you think students will need prompts, elicit some starters and write them on the board using the modals, such as *The camel could be … The camel might have … The person might be … .*

Answers

1 1 No, he can't be, because her father is dead. 2 Yes 3 No, he must be living there because he's writing to Eilis. 4 Yes 5 Yes

2 1 could 2 might 3 can't 4 couldn't 5 may
A must B can't, couldn't C may, might, could

3 1 present: 1, 2, 3; past: 4, 5
2 a) infinitive without *to* b) *have* + past participle

4 1 must 2 can't 3 must have decided
4 can't be playing 5 can't have been
6 may have seen

5 1 He must have given up work.
2 It can't be Alfie, because he never takes any exercise.
3 She may be expecting a message.
4 She might have run out of money.
5 They may have gone on holiday.
6 She may be wearing contact lenses.
7 They must have spent a fortune on it.
8 It may be hiding in the shed.

6 Sample answers
the camel might have swallowed something; the person could be trying to get it out;
the camel might be ill; it must be very uncomfortable for the person!

ADDITIONAL PRACTICE | **Maximiser** p.50, Grammar 1–2 | **eText IWB** Extra activity | **MyEnglishLab: Cambridge First** Use of English 19 *Modal Verbs: What does it mean?*

Speaking focus ▶ p.71

Long turn (Part 2)

Aim

- to practise using a range of different phrases to speculate

1 Focus students on the photographs (on eText if you are using it). Read through the expressions and check that students understand them all. Put students in pairs and ask them to compare the photographs using the language in Activity 1.

Answers

1 Students' own answers

ADDITIONAL PRACTICE | **Teacher's Book** p.145/173 Photocopiable 7A *It looks like …*

Listening

Aim

- to use a range of different phrases to speculate and to complete an exam-style speaking task (Speaking, Part 2)

Refer students to the **Exam Focus** on page 206 and turn to it on eText if you are using it. Read through it with students, making sure they understand everything.

2 Ask students to read the task. Play the recording once and then elicit which place the student chose.

3 Ask students to complete the sentences, then play the recording again while students check their answers, pausing and replaying as necessary.

4 Display the audio script on eText if you are using it. Play the recording and ask students to underline the stressed words. Then play the recording again, pausing after each sentence to give students a chance to repeat the intonation.

Read the **Exam Tip** aloud and elicit the main similarity and difference that students would talk about if they were doing the task in Activity 2, e.g. *Both photos show unusual places to stay, but the locations are very different.* Then ask students in pairs to take turns to practise doing the task from Activity 2, using some of the language from Activity 1 and Activity 3. Circulate and monitor, making sure that they summarise the main similarities and differences.

5 If you are using eText, display the expressions from Activity 1 on the board while students complete the tasks on pages 153 and 155. For additional practice, ask students to repeat both tasks with a new partner, swapping the roles they took originally.

Answers

2 the treehouse

3 **1** certain **2** could **3** seems **4** looks **5** appears **6** definitely **7** must **8** imagine

4 Well, I'm not absolutely certain what the place on the right is.
 2 It could be an underwater hotel.
 3 The other one seems to have been built in the trees.
 4 The underwater hotel looks quite luxurious.
 5 The treehouse appears to be more basic.
 6 It would definitely be less expensive to stay at.
 7 It must be an interesting experience to stay at both of them.
 8 I'd imagine the treehouse might not be such fun in bad weather.

5 Students' own answers

ADDITIONAL PRACTICE | **Maximiser** p.50–51, Speaking 1–3 | **MyEnglishLab: Cambridge First**, Speaking 9a *Part 2 Speculating: Matching halves*, Speaking 9b *Part 2 speculating: Practice*

MyEnglishLab tip

Customisable attempt number

The number of attempts students have on each MyEnglishLab exercise is customisable so that you can either set attempts to one or allow unlimited attempts. The default setting is three attempts.

Listening focus ▶ p.205

Vocabulary

describing places

Aim

- to revise and expand vocabulary for describing places

1 Focus attention on the photo of the monastery in Tibet and put students in pairs to discuss which adjectives could be used to describe it. Check answers, then elicit any other adjectives that students think could be used to describe the monastery.

2 Ask students to underline the stressed syllable in each adjective then play the recording, pausing to drill each word. Put students into pairs and ask them to practise saying the words in sentences as they describe the monastery, focusing on the pronunciation of the adjectives, e.g. *It looks very remote and peaceful.*

3 Focus attention on the dictionary entry. Elicit anything that students know about Shangri-La (a place that was first mentioned in *Lost Horizon*, a novel by the English writer, James Hilton **http://en.wikipedia.org/wiki/James_Hilton_(novelist)**, first published in 1933; pictured). Students discuss the second question in pairs.

Answers

1 Students' own answers

2 breathtaking, inspirational, luxurious, magnificent, mysterious, peaceful, remote, spiritual

3 Students' own answers

Teaching tip

Dictionary use

For more information, go to:
http://www.pearsonelt.com/professionaldevelopment
Click on Articles and look for Philip Schofield 'Monolingual versus bilingual dictionary use'

professionaldevelopment/downloads/articles/dictionaries/Monolingual-versus-bilingual-dictionary-use.pdf

Multiple choice (Part 4)

Aim

- to complete an exam-style listening task (Listening, Part 4)

Refer students to the **Exam Focus** on page 205 and turn to it on eText if you are using it. Read through it with students, making sure that they understand everything.

4 Ask students to read the rubric. Give students a few minutes to read the questions and underline key words. Then play the recording for students to listen and choose the correct answers.

5 Play the recording again, pausing after the words *peaceful and harmonious* and then elicit the answers to the questions, replaying the first section again if necessary. Then elicit the rest of the answers to Activity 4, pausing and replaying the recording if necessary. Then play the rest of the recording, pausing for students to check their answers.

6 Students discuss the questions in small groups.

Answers

4 (key words in brackets)

1 A (popular; escape, reality; believed, real; interested, Tibet)
2 A (travellers, get; guides; plane, crashed; found; map)
3 B (special; wise; live long time; speak every language)
4 C (author; Buddhist; one trip, Tibet; ideas, books, magazines)
5 A (similarities, show; interested, Tibetan, culture; believed, could exist; unable, original ideas)
6 C (Zhongdian; originally called Shangri-la; monasteries; new, income)
7 C (modern-day Shangri-la; shocked; confused; disappointed)

5 1 Tibet, place
2 only too keen to forget their troubles; fantasy
3 very little known about Tibet (doesn't say it was popular); fantasy (it wasn't a real place)

6 Students' own answers

ADDITIONAL PRACTICE | **Maximiser** p.51, Listening 1–2 | **MyEnglishLab: Cambridge First**, Listening 13 *Dealing with distraction: Who says what?*; Listening 16 *Sentence stress in listening: What do they mean?*

Vocabulary

travel and expressions with *world*

Aim

- to revise and expand knowledge of collocations related to travel and expressions with *world*

7 Do number 1 as an example with the class by eliciting the collocations and crossing out the word that doesn't collocate (*seasonal*). Ask students to complete the remaining questions. Allow students time to compare their answers in pairs, then elicit the answers.

8 Students complete the expressions with the correct prepositions, then check their answers in pairs. If you think students will find this difficult, write the prepositions on the board for students to match with the gaps in the expressions: *in* (x2), *to, of, off, over, out, at*. Check answers with the class.

9 If you have a multilingual class, put students into small groups to compare. If you have a monolingual class, elicit a few responses.

10 Give students a few minutes to think about the question, then put them into small groups to talk about their special places.

Answers

7 1 seasonal 2 direct 3 round 4 package 5 long-distance 6 direct

8 1 off 2 over/around 3 out 4 of 5 in 6 at 7 to 8 in

9–10 Students' own answers

Additional activity: PechaKucha

Ask students to present a PechaKucha mini-presentation on their special place.

PechaKucha 20x20 is a simple presentation format in which you show 20 images, each for 20 seconds. The images forward automatically and you talk along to the images. You can find more details at **http://www.pechakucha.org/what**.

PechaKucha in the EFL classroom (or mini PechaKucha of five or ten images for 20 seconds each) provides an opportunity for students to gain fluency in front of an audience and helps presentations to be snappy and interesting, as there is no time to waffle when the slides are forwarding automatically. Talks can be prepared in presentation software such as Microsoft Powerpoint or Google Presentations.

ADDITIONAL PRACTICE | **Maximiser** p.52, Vocabulary 1 | **MyEnglishLab: Cambridge First**, Vocabulary 14 *Topic: Environment*; Vocabulary 17 *Topic: Transport*

Grammar focus ▶ p.74

Relative clauses

Aim

- to revise the formation and use of relative clauses including identifying defining and non-defining relative clauses and to practise selecting appropriate relative pronouns

1 Focus attention on the picture and ask students to read the text. Ask *Where do you think the place is?*

2 Elicit an example of a defining relative clause and a non-defining relative clause in the text. Then ask students to find the remaining defining and non-defining relative clauses. Allow them time to compare their answers in pairs before you elicit responses as a class.

3 Elicit responses to the questions, then read the **Language Tip** aloud. Refer students to the **Grammar Reference** on page 172 and turn to it on eText if using. Go through the notes and examples with students checking they understand everything.

4 Join the first two sentences on the board as an example, then give students time to complete the remainder, circulating to help as necessary.

5 Either set this as a homework task or ask students to complete it in class. Encourage them to use some of the vocabulary on pages 72–73 along with the relative clauses.

Answers

1 Iceland

2 **A** 9 (tourists who come to the island …), 11 (… summer, when there are over …), 15 (One of the places which …) **B** 1 (The island, which is …), 4 (… southwest of the country, where the capital …), 5 (the island, whose main attraction is …), 13 (winter temperatures, which average …), 18 (a lava field, in which you can …)

3 **A** 15 (One of the places that tourists most want to visit …) **B** 15 (One of the places tourists most want to visit …) **C** 15 (One of the places where tourists most want to visit …)

4
1 The nearest town, which is 5km from here, doesn't have a train station.
2 The local people, who used to work in the fishing industry, now work in tourism.
3 Where's the bus that/which goes to the beach?
4 The woman who owns the hotel isn't here at the moment./The woman whose hotel it is, isn't here at the moment.
5 In summer when the water is warm you can go swimming./You can go swimming in summer, when the water is warm.
6 The man who/that (whom) I met yesterday is a tour guide.
7 The road, which is very steep, takes you to the top of the mountain./The road that takes you to the top of the mountain is very steep.
8 The place where we stayed/that we stayed in last summer is very beautiful.

5 Students' own answers

ADDITIONAL PRACTICE | **Maximiser** p.52, Grammar 1–3 | **eText IWB** Extra activity | **MyEnglishLab: Cambridge First**, Use of English 17 *Make one sentence out of two*

Use of English focus ▶ p.75

so, such, too, very, enough

Aim

- to compare the meanings and uses of *so, such, too, very* and *enough* and to practise using each one accurately

1 Put students into pairs to select the correct alternatives. Elicit answers as a class.

2 Ask students to complete the rules and then check with their partner. Elicit answers as a class, then ask students to turn to the **Grammar Reference** on page 175 for more information. Turn to it on eText if using and talk students through the notes and examples.

Answers

1 1 such, so 2 very, too 3 very, so 4 too, enough 5 so, enough 6 Very, so

2 1 so, too, very 2 enough (also *too* but only when it means *as well*) 3 enough 4 so, too, very 5 too 6 very, so

Additional activity: Status updates

Ask students if they ever post to social networking sites such as *Facebook* or *Twitter* when they are on holiday. Write the following statements on the board and tell students that they are status updates.

10.37 a.m. Well, I'm finally here and it's not what I expected at all, it's so …

11.24 a.m. Accommodation here is very …

12.13 p.m. Having lunch, food is so … here

7 p.m. What a day, this whole place is such a …

Put students into pairs. Tell half of the pairs to complete the status updates with a positive experience and the other half to complete them with a negative. If you have a small class, ask pairs to swap their status updates and read everyone else's. Alternatively, if you have a large class, put pairs together into groups of eight with both positive and negative in a group to share their answers.

Speaking

Aim

- to practise using *so, such, too, very* and *enough* in a spoken context

3 Give students five minutes to complete the sentences, then ask them to compare with a partner. Ask one student from each pair to report back on how similar or different their sentences were.

Answers

3 Students' own answers

Additional activity

Ask students to reframe the sentences as questions, then write them on the board, e.g. *Have you got enough time to …? Is it a long time since you've …? When was the last time you felt so excited about something? Do you think you're old enough to …? Do you think you have enough …? What do you find too expensive?* Put students into pairs to complete the questions, then ask them to walk around the class and ask at least five different people one of the questions. Ask students to report back on what they learnt about their classmates.

Key word transformations (Part 4)

Aim

- to complete an exam-style sentence transformation task (Reading and Use of English, Part 4)

Refer students to the **Exam Focus** on page 201 and turn to it on eText if you are using it. Read through it with students, making sure they understand everything.

4 Ask a student to read the rubric aloud, then read the **Exam Tip** aloud. Focus attention on the example, then students complete the task. Ask students to check that they have used 2–5 words in each gap and that their sentence has exactly the same meaning as the original sentence. Students can compare their answers in pairs before you check as a class.

Answers

4 1 so foggy that we could
2 didn't have enough money
3 such a lot of traffic
4 could have seen
5 can't be telling
6 may have been taken

ADDITIONAL PRACTICE | **Maximiser** p.52, Use of English 1 | **MyEnglishLab: Cambridge First**, Writing 12 *Linking: Find the right connection*

Writing focus ▶ p.76

Essay (Part 1)

including a range of structures

Aim

- to practise including a range of structures in writing and to complete an exam-style writing task (Writing, Part 1)

1 Put students in pairs to discuss statements 1–5 about travel. Remind students to give reasons as well as their opinions. Call out statements and elicit answers from the class: *Travel broadens the mind* **because** …; *It is better to spend money on possessions* **because …; *You don't need to travel*** *because* … . Encourage students to supply as many different answers as they can as quickly as possible.

2 Ask a student to read the essay task aloud, or if you are using eText IWB, show the page on the board. Ask students to think about the points they discussed in Activity 1 and to make notes on points for and against the value of travelling abroad.

3 Read the model essay aloud and ask students to underline the main points and supporting information in each paragraph. If you are using eText IWB, a student can do this on the board. Check answers as a class. Ask students to look back at the notes they made in Activity 2. Did the model essay include any of the same ideas?

4 Ask students to do the activity, then they compare their answers in pairs.

5 Read the **Exam Tip** aloud, then refer students to the **Writing Reference** on page 181 or, if you are using eText IWB, show it on the board. Go through the Useful language and the *Dos* and *Don'ts*. Then ask students to turn to page 159. Brainstorm ideas for points that could be included in the essay and put students in pairs to discuss how they would organise it. Remind them to include a range of structures in their work. Students then complete the essay.

6 Put students in pairs to look through each other's essays. Ask them to go through questions 1–4 and give feedback.

Answers

1 Students' own answers

2 Students' own answers

3 Paragraph 1: introduction (rephrasing the task); paragraph 2: it costs money (you have to pay to get there); paragraph 3: it doesn't necessarily help you to be independent (some people mix with their own nationality); paragraph 4: it can be useful for CVs (shows you have some life experience); paragraph 5: conclusion/ opinion

4 1 Even if, which 2 so that 3 unless, This 4 If

5 Sample answer

Is it better to have a holiday abroad or stay in your own country?

For many people, having a holiday abroad seems much more attractive than a holiday at home. There are new sights to see and the opportunity to experience another culture. However, there are many advantages to a holiday at home.

The first thing is the expense. There is the cost of flights as well as the cost of accommodation and entertainment. When you are in another country, you can end up spending more than you planned. It is easier to calculate the cost of a holiday at home, and it is often cheaper.

The next thing is the environment. Most holidays abroad involve air travel, which harms the environment. In addition to this, tourism may have an impact on the wildlife of the local area. If you have a holiday at home, you can reduce your impact on the environment by taking train journeys, for example.

Finally, it can be more relaxing. You don't have to worry about delays or long waits at the airport and there are no communication problems. Sometimes when you come back from a holiday abroad, you feel you need another holiday.

In my opinion, a holiday at home is a good idea. You may discover surprising things about your own country.

6 Students' own answers

ADDITIONAL PRACTICE | **Maximiser** p.53, Writing 1–7 | **Teacher's Book** p.145/175, Photocopiable 7B *Putting it all together* | **MyEnglishLab: Cambridge First**, Writing 12 *Linking: Find the right connection*

Review ▶ p.77

Aim

- to revise structures and vocabulary covered in Unit 7

1–3 Ask students to complete the activities, circulating to provide assistance. Ask students to check in pairs before checking as a class on eText. Alternatively, set as a homework activity and then go through the interactive activities on eText to check.

Answers

1 1 must have been 2 may have had 3 could have been 4 might have mistaken 5 must have been 6 can't be/can't have been

2 1 which 2 who 3 that/who 4 where 5 which 6 which 7 which 8 where

3 1 C 2 B 3 C 4 D 5 C 6 B

ADDITIONAL PRACTICE | **Online Testmaster**, Unit 7 Test | **MyEnglishLab: Cambridge First** Practice Test: Writing

Moving on

Listening and vocabulary focus ▶ p.78

Multiple matching (Part 3)

Aim

- to complete an exam-style listening task (Listening, Part 3)

Warmer

Tell students this unit is about the future. Focus attention on the pictures. Magnify them on eText if using and elicit ideas of what they show.

1 Put students into pairs to discuss what each job might involve, then elicit a few responses for each one.

2 Ask students to read the options and highlight the key words in each. Read the **Exam Tip** aloud, then ask students to work in pairs and think of synonyms and paraphrases for the key words. Elicit ideas from the class. Play the recording once and get students to mark the option which they think matches most closely. Play the recording again to check answers.

3 Display the audio script on eText if using, or ask students to turn to the audio script on page 160. Refer back to the **Exam Tip** and elicit the part of the text that gives the correct answer for Speaker 1 (see answers).

4 Play the recording once more and ask students to underline the key phrases that give the answers. Finish by checking the answers as a class.

Additional activity

Students look at the audio script again and find examples of words from the rubrics that are in the audio script as distractors (as mentioned in the **Exam Tip**). Students could find the words and discuss as a class why they don't necessarily mean that a particular option is correct.

Answers

1 Students' own answers

2 1 E **2** D **3** A **4** C **5** H
(Key words in the options and audio script in 3 and 4.)

3 Speaker 1: E (available on demand) easier for people to contact us when they need us

4 Speaker 2: D (costs less) becoming more affordable
Speaker 3: A (new employees) recruit, train
Speaker 4: C (wide range of people) people from all sorts of companies
Speaker 5: H (fast and efficient) under two hours, no pollution, water is recycled

ADDITIONAL PRACTICE | **Maximiser** p.54, Listening 1–2 |
MyEnglishLab: Cambridge First, Listening 20 *Listening to identify the topic: What are they talking about?*

Speaking

Aim

- to give spoken practice on the topic of work

5 Put students into pairs to discuss the questions, then elicit a few responses for each.

Answers

5 Students' own answers

Additional activity: Useful websites

There are several websites where students can learn more about vertical farming. For example:

http://www.verticalfarm.com/ On the home page there is a great two minute overview video of what vertical farming is, with cartoons and visuals.

http://www.bbc.co.uk/news/uk-england-manchester-14201793 This is an article about a vertical farm in Manchester.

Vocabulary

collocations and phrasal verbs with *work*

Aim

- to review and extend knowledge of collocations and phrasal verbs with *work* and to use them in spoken practice

Warmer

Write the following words on the board: *work, job, employment, career, profession, occupation.* Elicit examples of how each could be used, eg. *go to work, be at work, get a job,* etc. Students could use the Longman Dictionary of Contemporary English online to find further examples and collocations. Point out that *work* and *employment* are uncountable but the others are all countable.

6 Put students into pairs to work through the activity, then elicit the answers.

7 Ask students to do the matching activity. Allow students to check their answers in pairs before you check with the class. Read the **Language Tip** with students. Put students in pairs and ask them to write three sentences using the phrasal verbs in Activity 7. Elicit some sentences and write them on the board, checking the phrasal verbs have been used accurately.

8 Give students about ten minutes to discuss the questions, encouraging them to extend their answers as much as possible. Students could change partners for extra practice or make up four new questions using the phrasal verbs to ask their partner.

Answers

6 **1** job **2** job **3** occupation **4** profession **5** employment **6** career

7 **1** D **2** C **3** B **4** A **5** F **6** E

8 Students' own answers

ADDITIONAL PRACTICE | **Maximiser** p.54, Vocabulary 1 | **MyEnglishLab: Cambridge First**, Vocabulary 13 *Topic: Learning and training*; Vocabulary 18 *Topic: Work;* Reading 17 *Text structure – vocabulary groups: Put the words into groups*

Speaking focus ▶ p.80

Collaborative task and discussion (Parts 3 and 4)

agreeing and disagreeing

Aim

- to practise using intonation appropriately when agreeing and disagreeing and to complete an exam-style collaborative task

Warmer: Discussion

Ask students to think of as many jobs/professions as they can. Point out that some job titles are gender-specific, e.g. *fireman*, but others are gender-neutral, e.g. *firefighter*. Explain that in general, the gender-neutral terms are preferred nowadays, because all jobs are done by men and women. Then ask students to discuss with their partner which of the jobs in the exam task appeal to them the most/least, and why.

1 Refer students to the **Exam Focus** on page 207 and turn to it on eText if you are using it. Read through the Part 3 *What do you have to do?* section with students, making sure they understand everything. Then ask students to underline key words in the speaking task.

2 Ask four volunteers to read the statements aloud. Then ask students to indicate which statements they agree with by writing a tick, cross or question mark. Emphasise that there are no wrong answers.

3 Remind students that intonation is important in conveying meaning in English and this is particularly important when disagreeing politely. Play the first phrase as an example and compare it on eText with the arrows marking the intonation. Play the rest of the recording, pausing after each phrase for students to mark the intonation. Then replay the recording for students to listen and repeat, copying the intonation.

4 Put students into pairs to read the statements and agree or disagree. Circulate and listen to students' intonation. If necessary, play the recording again for students to repeat the intonation on the recording.

5 Refer back to the **Exam Focus** on page 207 and read through the Part 3 strategy section. Point out that strategy 2 suggests spending two minutes talking about each prompt in detail, then one minute summarising and agreeing. Read the **Exam Tip** aloud, then set a timer for two minutes while students discuss the prompts in pairs. Ask students if they managed to talk about all the prompts. If not, ask them to repeat this part of the activity before moving on.

6 Revise some useful phrases for summarising on the board, such as *So, all in all …*, *Overall, it seems we agree that …*, before setting the timer for one minute for students to reach a decision.

7 Tell students that these are examples of follow-up questions for a Part 4 discussion. Turn back to the **Exam Focus** on page 207 and go through the Part 4 section with the class. After reading strategy 2, elicit expressions to express opinions, such as *I'm convinced/not convinced that …*; *I see what you mean, but …*; *In my view, …*. Write these on the board for students to refer to. Then give students time to discuss the questions.

Answers

1 Suggested answers: careers advice for students, jobs, students, choose in the future, discuss, how rewarding

2–7 Students' own answers

ADDITIONAL PRACTICE | **Maximiser** p.55, Speaking 1–3 | **MyEnglishLab: Cambridge First**, Speaking 16 Part 4 *Discussing opinions: Put the discussion in order*

Grammar focus ▶ p.81

Listening

Aim

- to gain listening practice and to provide conversations to report in the next activity

1 Tell students they are going to listen to three work-related situations. Ask students to read the questions and underline the key words in pairs. Check students have underlined the correct words. Ask students to read the options A–C for each situation and elicit some predictions of synonyms or paraphrases that they might hear in the recording. Play the recording. Students listen and choose the correct answers, then compare their answers in pairs before hearing the recording again. Elicit answers from the class. Display the audio script on eText if using and ask students to identify the key phrases.

Answers

1 (key words and phrases from the audio script in brackets) **1** C (manager, employee, what, doing; Remember …, Don't …, summarise) **2** A (radio job interview, recommend; find out, prospective employer) **3** B (colleagues, what, woman, doing; Why wasn't I given the messages?)

Reporting verbs

Aim

- to compare and contrast reporting verbs meaning and patterns

2 Put students into pairs to complete the activity, then elicit answers. Read the **Language Tip** aloud and elicit some other examples with *recommend* and *suggest*.

3 Ask students to match the reporting verbs with the structures. Elicit answers. Turn to the **Grammar Reference** on page 173 on eText and go through it with the class, checking that students understand everything. Put students in pairs and ask them to write five more examples using the verbs. Ask pairs to read out some of their examples.

Answers

2 **1** advised/asked/reminded/told/warned
2 explained/recommended/suggested
3 advised/recommended/suggested **4** accused
5 denied **6** offered

3 **A** advise, ask, remind **B** offer
C advise, suggest, deny, recommend **D** accuse, remind
E advise, ask, deny, explain, recommend, suggest, warn

ADDITIONAL PRACTICE | **Maximiser** p.56, Grammar 1–2 | **eText IWB** Extra activity

Speaking

Aim

- to provide spoken practice of using reporting verbs

4 Read the rubric aloud, then revise expressions for giving advice, e.g. *You should/You must/It's a good idea to ....* Put students into small groups to prepare their advice. Give them ten minutes to write, then ask groups to swap their advice. Students read the advice given to them, then report it using the reporting verbs in Activity 2.

Answers

4 Students' own answers

Alternative activity

If you don't think the topic of job/college interviews will appeal to your students, ask them to prepare advice on a different topic, e.g. advice for travelling, for choosing a new mobile phone or a gift for a friend, for someone entering their profession.

Reading focus ▶ p.82

Speaking

Aim

- to introduce the topic of living abroad and to provide spoken practice

1 Focus attention on the picture and tell students they are going to read an article about people whose work involves living abroad. Put students into pairs to discuss the questions. Elicit answers and make a list of the kinds of jobs that might require a person to live abroad.

Answers

1 Students' own answers

Multiple matching (Part 7)

Aim

- to complete an exam-style reading task (Reading and Use of English, Part 7)

Refer students to the **Exam Focus** on page 203 and turn to it on eText if you are using it. Read through it with students, making sure they understand everything.

2 Before students read the questions, refer to strategy 1 and ask students to read the title and subheading, then give them a few minutes to do strategy 2 (skim each text to see what it is about). Elicit a few answers from the class, then ask students to read the questions and underline key words (strategy 3).

3 Focus on the highlighted words in B and point out that they match the key words in question 1. Then focus on the key words in 2 and ask students to scan the texts to find and highlight words or phrases with similar meaning (Text A: wasn't really stretching me enough). Students then work independently to find and highlight phrases for the remaining questions. Refer students to strategies 6 and 7, and allow them time to check their answers. You may like to give students a time limit (15 minutes) for this task to encourage them to work quickly as they will need to in the exam. Put students into pairs to compare answers then check as a class, eliciting the phrases that correspond to the key words in each case (see answers).

Answers

2 Suggested key words: **1** passion to see the world **2** more, challenge **3** less expensive **4** a while to adapt **5** found ideal job by accident **6** discovered unexpected things **7** regularly travels long distances **8** sacrificed career opportunities **9** appreciates long holidays **10** primitive environment

3 (phrases from text in brackets) **2** A (wasn't really stretching me) **3** C (enjoy the same lifestyle for far less) **4** D (help me settle in; four months on) **5** B (stumbled across an advert) **6** E (lots of surprises) **7** A (covering 800 miles) **8** D (was building a career) **9** B (take time off to go travelling for a couple of months) **10** E (only the basic requirements)

Speaking

Aim

- to give spoken practice on the topic of jobs

4 Give students time to discuss the questions in pairs.

Answers

4 Students' own answers

Vocabulary

linking words and expressions

Aim

- to review the uses of linking expressions in context

5 Ask students to match the expressions to the purposes, then check as a class.

6 On eText, magnify the area around each underlined word and encourage students to share observations, including the context and punctuation for each one. Put students into pairs to complete the gap fill and finish by checking the answers with the class.

Answers

5 1 as well as, too, also, as well 2 so, that's why, since, as, because 3 so that, to, in order to 4 while, although, still, despite, however, even though

6 1 However 2 although 3 That's why 4 so 5 As well as 6 in order to 7 Despite 8 ,too

ADDITIONAL PRACTICE | **Maximiser** p.56–57, Reading 1–4 | **eText IWB** Extra activity | **eText Game**: Pelmanism (linking words) | **MyEnglishLab: Cambridge First**, Reading 6 *Inferring facts from a text: What do we learn about the writer?*

MyEnglishLab tip

Messaging

In MyEnglishLab you can send online messages to individuals or groups of students. Use the 'Message' feature for reminders or encouragement. It can also be a forum for students to ask you a question which you can reply to at a time that suits you.

Grammar focus ▶ p.84

Listening

Aim

- to provide listening practice and to provide direct speech examples for use in the contrasting activities (3–6)

Warmer: Discussion in pairs

Ask students if they have ever had a job interview, and ask *Was it a face-to-face, phone or video interview? What kinds of questions did the interviewer ask?* Elicit some answers, then put students into pairs to make a list of the kinds of questions they might expect in a job interview for a holiday job in Greece.

1 Ask students to read Lauren's email to her mum. Tell students that there are eight mistakes in the email. Focus on the example answer and point out that the mistakes are related to content. Play the recording for students to listen and underline the mistakes.

2 Put students into pairs to discuss and correct the incorrect details. Then play the recording again for them to check. Check answers with the class, playing the recording again as necessary. Elicit the incorrect details from the class.

Suggested answers

1–2

Hi Mum,

The interview for the job in Greece went well, I think. First the interviewer asked me how I'd heard about it. I told her I'd spotted the advert *on the internet* ~~in a local newspaper~~ and thought it was something I'd *be good at* ~~enjoy doing~~.

Then she said the job would involve looking after *very young children* ~~young teenagers~~ and asked me whether I'd had much experience of doing this. So I told her that I look after Sandra and Davy *every month* ~~now and again~~ and that I was taking them *cycling* ~~camping~~ the next day. She said I might be unlucky, as she'd heard it was going to *rain* ~~snow~~. Then she told me to enjoy the weekend and said she'd *write* ~~phone~~ soon. She told me not to worry if I didn't hear anything for a few *days* ~~weeks~~.

Fingers crossed,

L x

Reported statements

Aim

- to contrast the structures used in direct speech and reported statements

3 Ask students to turn to page 159 and match the underlined examples to the verb forms in the box. They should then find the reported equivalent in the email on page 84. Questions 12–15 are not reported in the email.

4 Students complete the table, referring to the audio script on page 159 to help. Go through the answers as a class. Read the **Language Tip** aloud and find the example in the audio script and the email. Then refer students to the **Grammar Reference** on page 173 and read through it together (on eText if using it).

Answers

3 1 past simple (how did you hear/how I'd heard) 2 past simple (I spotted/I'd spotted) 3 present simple (I think/I thought) 4 would ('d be good at/would enjoy) 5 will (will involve/would involve) 6 present perfect (Have you had/I'd had) 7 present simple (look after/look after) 8 present continuous (I'm taking/was taking) 9 might (might be unlucky/might be unlucky) 10 present perfect (I've heard/she'd heard) 11 going to (it's going to rain/it was going to) 12 present simple (I'm sure/*not included*) 13 will (we'll/*not included*) 14 present simple (you sound/*not included*) 15 present continuous (we're looking for/*not included*) 16 will (We'll write/she'd write) 17 present simple (you don't hear/I didn't hear)

4

Direct speech	Reported statements
past simple	past perfect
present perfect	past perfect
present simple	past simple
will	*would*
present continuous	past continuous
be going to	*was going to*
would, might	*would/might*

Reported questions and imperatives

Aim

- to contrast the structures used in direct speech and reported questions

5 Refer students to the audio script on page 159 to transform A–D. Go through **Grammar Reference** 18.3 on page 174 together. Point out that there are no question marks in the reported questions.

6 Change the first sentence on the board to reported speech as an example. (*Jack asked her if she got paid well.*) Ask students to change the questions into reported speech. Read the **Language Tip** aloud and ask students to compare their answers in pairs and to check that they have changed the pronouns and time expressions appropriately. Elicit answers from the class.

7 Tell students they are going to play a game. Give students a few minutes to write four statements about themselves; three true and one false. Then put them in pairs to share their statements. They might need to take notes on what the other person said. Then put students into groups of four, made up of two pairs. Tell students to take turns sharing what their partner said (using reported speech) and for everyone to guess which is false.

Answers

5 A How did you hear about this job?
B Have you had much experience of doing this?
C Enjoy your weekend!
D Don't worry.

6 1 He asked her whether she got paid well.
2 He asked her to let him know if there were any more job vacancies. 3 He asked her who she was going to be working with the following week. 4 He asked her what she'd done the previous day. 5 He told her not to forget/reminded her to take some photos. 6 He said they would/promised to email her if they came over to Greece.

7 Students' own answers

Additional activity

Students prepare three questions to ask a partner, using three different tenses. They ask their questions in pairs, then report back on what they asked their partner and what they answered, e.g. *I asked Paolo if he had ever played tennis, and he told me that he had never played*, etc.

ADDITIONAL PRACTICE | **Maximiser** p.58, Grammar 1 | **Teacher's Book** p.146/176, Photocopiable 8A *You say, we report* | **eText IWB** Extra activity | **MyEnglishLab: Cambridge First,** Use of English 11 *Reported speech: What did he say?*

Use of English focus

▶ p.85

Vocabulary

concrete and abstract nouns

Aim

- to compare forms of concrete and abstract nouns and to practise forming abstract nouns

Warmer: *Noun alphabet*

In pairs, students write the letters of the alphabet down the left hand side of their page. Tell them they are going to race to think of one noun in English for every letter of the alphabet. The first pair to complete their alphabet wins. If nobody completes it in 5 minutes, the winners are the pair with the most letters complete.

After you have done Activity 1, ask students to return to their lists and decide which are concrete and which are abstract. How many can they find related abstract/ concrete nouns for?

1 Students discuss the nouns in pairs. Elicit answers.

2 Elicit some suffixes often used to make concrete nouns (e.g. *-or, -er*), then ask students to complete the table and check with a partner before you check as a class.

3 Put students into pairs to divide the list into verbs and adjectives. Check as a class, then elicit the abstract nouns and write them on the board.

4 Ask students to complete the activity, then to check their answers in pairs before you check with the class.

Answers

1 Abstract nouns: engineering, journalism, music, visit
Concrete nouns: engineer, journalist, musician, visitor

2 -er -or -ist -ant -ive -ian
advice – advisor employment – employer/ee
tourism – tourist application – applicant
representation – representative childhood – child
politics – politician

3 (abstract nouns in brackets)
Verbs: arrive (arrival), behave (behaviour), confide (confidence), know (knowledge), permit (permission), progress (progress/progression)
Adjectives: angry (anger), difficult (difficulty), friendly (friendliness), sad (sadness), short (shortage), strong (strength)

4 1 permission 2 progress 3 difficulty 4 a visit
5 strength 6 a friendship

Additional activity: Discussion

Put students into pairs and ask them to prepare three discussion questions using abstract nouns from Activities 1–4. Both partners should write the questions. Separate the pairs and form new groups of 3–4 students to discuss the questions. Then ask the original pairs to re-form to compare the responses to their questions, using the reported speech verbs and tenses from page 84, e.g. *When I asked if they were interested in politics, Suyong said she didn't know much about it but Bernard said he does.*

ADDITIONAL PRACTICE | **Teacher's Book** p.146/177 Photocopiable 8B *Right word crossword*

Word formation (Part 3)

Aim

- to complete an exam-style word formation task (Reading and Use of English, Part 3)

Refer students to the **Exam Focus** on page 201 and turn to it on eText if you are using it. Read through it with the class, making sure they understand everything. Read the exam tip aloud and give students a minute to skim the text, then elicit what it is about (the job of a video game designer).

5 As a class, work through strategies 2–4 with the example (0) by looking at the words before and after the gap and deciding what type of word will fit in the gap (a noun). Put students into pairs to look at the remaining gaps and decide what type of word is missing. Check their ideas, then give them ten minutes to complete the task. Ask students to check their answers in pairs, then elicit answers as a class. Ask students to identify which of the gapped words are abstract nouns (*production, flexibility, responsibility, technology*).

6 Ask students to discuss the question with a partner. Elicit a few answers from the class.

Answers

5 1 flexibility 2 responsibility 3 technology
4 personally 5 artists 6 decisions
7 enjoyable 8 various/varying

6 Students' own answers

ADDITIONAL PRACTICE | **Maximiser** p.58, Use of English 1–2

Writing focus

▶ p.86

Reading

Aim

- to identify key features of an application letter (formal language, paragraph structure and fixed phrases)

Warmer: Discussion

Ask: *Would you like to work in an English-speaking country in the future? Why/Why not?* Elicit a variety of responses.

1 Ask students to read Magda's letter to find out what job she has applied for. Elicit the answer.

2 Elicit whether a job application requires formal or informal language (formal). Ask students to underline the correct alternative. Compare as a class.

3 Students match A–E to the paragraphs. Elicit answers. Tell students that this is a useful standard structure for a job application letter.

4 Tell students there are fixed phrases in job application letters. Ask them to locate the phrases, then check.

Answers

1 hotel receptionist

2 1 position 2 At present 3 obtained 4 require 5 on a number of occasions 6 In addition 7 possess 8 look forward 9 in the near future 10 remaining 11 available 12 I am required

3 A 3 B 1 C 4 D 2 E 4

4 1 following your recent advertisement 2 I would like to apply for 3 I obtained the diploma 4 I would be grateful if you could send me further details of 5 I enclose

Letter of application (Part 2)

using semi-formal language

Aim

- to complete an exam-style writing task (Writing, Part 2)

On eText, go through the **Writing Reference** on page 183 with the class, focusing on the Useful Language box. If possible, leave this displayed on eText while students complete the writing activity.

5 Students complete the activity in pairs, or a volunteer could underline the key information on eText.

6 Suggest that in the exam students spend five minutes planning, twelve minutes writing and three minutes checking. Give students five minutes to make notes.

7 Read the **Exam Tip** aloud. Give students 15 minutes to write their letter, or alternatively set as a homework task.

Answers

5 18+ , activity instructors, Experience not important, training will be given, Love of sport, energy, enthusiasm, ability to relate to young people

6 Sample answer

Para 1: to apply for activity instructor position Para 2: enjoy sports (basketball, tennis, volleyball) Para 3: working with young people; babysitting, coaching junior swim team Para 4: ask for further info about the course Para 5: say when you can come for interview

7 Sample answer

Dear Sir/Madam,

I am writing to apply for the position of summer activity instructor as advertised on your website.

One of the main reasons I am applying for this job is that two of my great passions are sports and young people and I have experience which I think would be very useful.

I enjoy all kinds of sports, especially team sports. I am captain of the volleyball team at college and I also play basketball and tennis and swim regularly.

I have a lot of experience with children and teenagers, including regular babysitting and coaching a junior swimming team at my high school for three years. I am hoping to train to become a sports teacher.

The training course offered as part of the job sounds like an interesting opportunity and I would be grateful if you would send me further details.

Please find enclosed my CV. Thank you for considering my application. I look forward to hearing from you.

Yours sincerely

ADDITIONAL PRACTICE | **Maximiser** p.59, Writing 1–3 | **MyEnglishLab: Cambridge First**, Writing 5 *Appropriateness of language: Choosing the right style*; Writing 8 *Formal functions in writing: What goes in where?*

Review ▶ p.87

Aim

- to revise structures and vocabulary covered in Unit 8

1–3 Ask students to complete the activities, circulating to provide assistance. Ask students to check in pairs before checking as a class on eText. Alternatively, set this section as a homework activity and then go through the interactive activities on eText to check.

Answers

1 1 C 2 A 3 A 4 B 5 A 6 B

2 1 Representatives 2 unemployment 3 application 4 shortage 5 sadness 6 Tourists 7 arrival 8 knowledge

3 1 reminded his colleagues to 2 suggested (that) Carol (should) 3 accused Anna of 4 warned us not to 5 apologised for not 6 his notice the following/next 7 recommended looking/(that) I look/(that) I should look 8 denied breaking/that she had broken

ADDITIONAL PRACTICE | **Maximiser** p.60–61, Use of English | **Online Testmaster**, Unit 8 Test | **MyEnglishLab: Cambridge First** Practice Test: Listening

Lucky break?

Reading focus ▶ p.88

Speaking

Aim

- to introduce the topic of sport and role models, and to provide spoken practice

Warmer: Sport brainstorm

Elicit the meaning of the unit title *Lucky break* (a sudden or unexpected chance to do something that allows you to become successful). Tell students that the term *lucky break* is often used in the entertainment and sports industries and that Unit 9 is about sport and luck. Put students in pairs and give them a few minutes to brainstorm a list of words to do with sport. Encourage them to not only list names of individual sports but also words associated with sport, e.g. *coach, record, game, points, competitive, train,* etc. Elicit words from the class and write them on the board.

1 Put students into pairs to discuss the questions. Elicit the qualities of a great sprinter, e.g. *determination, dedication, strong physique, energy, commitment, speed, passion.*

Answers

1 Students' own answers

Gapped text (Part 6)

Aim

- to complete an exam-style gapped text task (Reading and Use of English, Part 6)

Ask students to turn to the **Exam Focus** on page 202 and talk students through it on eText, checking they understand everything.

2 Read the **Exam Tip,** which relates to **Exam Focus** strategies 1 and 2. Ask students to read the article quickly then elicit some comparisons with their ideas in Activity 1. Teach *scoliosis* (a condition of the spine).

3 Do the first gap with the class as an example, demonstrating how to work through strategies 3–5. Read the sentences before and after the gap and elicit predictions of the missing information (part of a description of Usain Bolt). Then elicit the topics of the sentences before and after the gap (*scoliosis, attitude*). Read through sentences A–G with students and elicit connections that students can see (*condition* in C is a replacement word for *scoliosis*). Remind students of strategy 6 (to move on if they are not sure what goes in the gap), then give students about ten minutes to complete the remaining gaps using the strategies you have demonstrated. Put them into pairs to compare answers before you check as a class.

Answers

2 Students' own answers

3 **1** C **2** E **3** G **4** A **5** F **6** B

Speaking

Aim

- to provide spoken practice

4 Check students understand *grounded* (someone who is grounded understands their own character and knows what is really important) and *legend* (someone who is famous and admired for being extremely good at doing something). Students discuss the questions in small groups.

Answers

4 **1** He suffers from scoliosis, his attitude (he seems to have fun before a race), he parties a lot, he's opinionated, funny, grounded

2 Students' own answers

3 Students' own answers
Sample answers: Roger Federer, Serena Williams (tennis), Tiger Woods (golf), Cristiano Ronaldo, David Beckham (football), Bradley Wiggins (cycling), Ian Thorpe (swimming)

ADDITIONAL PRACTICE | **Maximiser** p.62, Vocabulary 1 | **Maximiser** p.62–63, Reading 1–3 | **eText IWB** Extra activity | **MyEnglishLab: Cambridge First,** Reading 17 *Text structure: The right references*

Vocabulary

collocations: success and failure

Aim

- to revise and expand student knowledge of collocations related to success and failure

5 Ask students to complete the sentences. Point out that the collocations are all used in the text on page 89. Let students check their answers in pairs before you check as a class.

6 Students complete the activity, then find and highlight or circle the phrases in the text to check.

7 Give students about five minutes to discuss the questions in pairs. Ask a few students to report back to the class on their discussion.

Answers

5 **1** have **2** overcome, be **3** set **4** fulfil **5** make, have **6** have

6 **1** with **2** on **3** for **4** on **5** in **6** up **7** down **8** in

7 Students' own answers

ADDITIONAL PRACTICE | **Maximiser** p.64, Vocabulary 1–2 | **Teacher's Book** p.147/178 Photocopiable 9A *You're just like me* | **eText Game**: Pelmanism *(success and failure)*

Speaking focus ▶ p.90

Listening

Aim

- to provide a model of students completing an exam-style speaking task and to revise language related to success for use in the next activities

1 Elicit anything students know about the people in the pictures (American actress Natalie Portman receiving an Oscar for her role in *Black Swan,* 2011; Spanish tennis champion Rafael Nadal celebrating one of his many grand slam wins). Put students into pairs to discuss the question, then elicit a few responses.

2 Ask students to read the question and factors. Elicit the difference between *ambition* (a strong desire to achieve something), *dedication* (hard work or effort that someone puts into a particular activity) and *talent* (a natural ability to do something well). Play the recording for students to listen and note down the factors mentioned. Give students time to compare answers in pairs, then play the recording again and elicit responses as a class. Ask students whether they agree with the students on the recording.

Answers

1 Students' own answers

2 mentioned: ambition, good health, personality, dedication, talent

not mentioned: family support, money

Compensation strategies

Aim

- to practise using compensation strategies

3 Tell students that in the exam (and in real life) it is helpful to know some compensation strategies to correct yourself, check your understanding of what someone else has said and give yourself time to think. Ask students to match the strategies with the examples. Check as a class, then play the recording again while students tick the language they hear in the recording. Display the audio script on eText and have students highlight the expressions to tick.

4 Play the recording, pausing for students to repeat each phrase. Students then practise saying the phrases in pairs.

Answers

3 1 C 2 B 3 A

I'm sorry, did you say …? Well, it's difficult to say …
I mean … What I'm trying to say …
… or rather … Right, er …

4 Students' own answers

Additional activity

Give students a photocopy of the audio script on page 129. Ask students to read the dialogue aloud in pairs. If students have recording devices, they could record themselves and then listen to their pronunciation.

Discussion (Part 4)

Aim

- to practise using compensation strategies in an exam-style speaking task (Speaking, Part 4)

Refer students to the **Exam Focus** on page 207 and turn to it on eText if you are using it. Read through it with students, making sure they understand everything.

Turn back to page 90 and focus students on the **Exam Tip**. Elicit some phrases students could use if they find themselves with no ideas, e.g. *What do you think about …? That's certainly a difficult question. What's your view on the subject?* Write these on the board. Remind students that they should also use some of the fillers from Activity 3. If you are using eText, display these on the board as a prompt during the discussion.

5 Put students into pairs to discuss the questions. Remind them to take turns and involve each other in the discussion. If time allows, put them in new pairs to practise again.

Answers

5 Students' own answers

Alternative activity: Doughnut circle

If you have 8–30 students and plenty of space in your classroom, a doughnut circle discussion gives students the opportunity to work with a number of different partners. Getting up and moving around can also re-energise students, especially if classes are long. Divide students into two groups, A and B. Ask all the As to stand up and make a circle. Then ask them to turn so that they are facing outwards. Ask those in group B to each stand in front of an A student, which means that there should now be two circles (a doughnut). Magnify the first question on eText and give the As one minute to answer that question while Bs listen. Then ask them to swap roles for the next question. Next, ask Bs to move one place in a clockwise direction so they have a new partner. This time Bs start by answering question two for one minute, then A and B swap roles. Students then move again, and so on.

ADDITIONAL PRACTICE | **Maximiser** p.64, Speaking 1–3 | **MyEnglishLab: Cambridge First** Speaking 4 *Discussing opinions: Put the discussion in order*

Grammar focus ▶ p.91

Conditional forms

Aim

- to revise conditional forms and to use them in spoken practice

1 Display the question on eText and ask three volunteers to read the sentences aloud. Ask students to discuss in pairs which situation describes each sentence. Elicit responses.

2 Give students a few minutes to complete the activities in pairs, then elicit responses and underline the verb forms on eText if using. Refer students to the **Grammar Reference** on page 166 and go through it with students on eText if using, checking that students understand everything. Turn back to the activities and read the **Language Tip** aloud. Elicit a few more examples of continuous forms for conditionals, e.g. *If you're coming to the party, would you mind bringing a cake? If I was thinking of going on a holiday next summer, where would you recommend?*

3 Do the first question as an example on the board. Ask students how likely they think it is that someone in the class will become a film star (very unlikely). Ask them which conditional is used for possibilities that are unlikely to happen in the future (second conditional). Elicit the question: *If you became a famous film star, who would you want to act with?* Note that if students think this is likely, they will use first conditional. Students complete the remaining questions, then compare answers in pairs before you check as a class. Students then ask and answer the questions with their partner.

4 Elicit a few possible ways to complete the first sentence e.g. *If I didn't live in London, I'd live in Paris.* Ask students to complete the questions, then elicit a few examples for each sentence, checking that the conditionals are correct. For extra practice, students could turn each phrase into a question. (*If you didn't live in the place you do, where would you live? If you could change one thing in the world, what would it be? If you found some money in the street, what would you do with it? If you could meet three people, who would they be?*) Put students into small groups to share their responses.

Answers

1 a) second conditional b) zero conditional c) first conditional

2 1 zero conditional 2 *may, might, could, can, going to,* present perfect and the imperative 3 *might, could* and *should*

3 1 If you become/became a film star, who will/would you want to act with? 2 If you win/won a lot of money, what will/would you spend it on? 3 If you learn/were going to learn/learnt another language, which one will/would you choose? 4 If you had the money to go to any place in the world, where would you go? 5 If you had the chance to do anything this evening, what would you do? 6 If the weather is good this weekend, what will you/are you going to do? 7 If you get/got/were getting/were going to get married next year, what kind of ceremony will/are you going to/would you have? 8 If someone follows/was following/followed you down the street, what will/would you do?

4 Students' own answers

ADDITIONAL PRACTICE | **Maximiser** p.65, Grammar 1–2 | **eText IWB** Extra activity | **MyEnglishLab: Cambridge First**, Use of English 15 *Conditionals: Which are the right two answers?*

Speaking

Aim

- to provide speaking practice of conditional forms

5 Read the example with the class, then give students a few minutes to prepare their ideas. Put students into small groups to compare their ideas. Ask groups to report back to the class on whose idea seems the most interesting or exciting.

Answers

5 Students' own answers

Listening focus ▶ p.92

Multiple choice (Part 4)

Aim

- to complete an exam-style listening task (Listening, Part 4)

Teaching tip

Vocabulary

It is sometimes worth spending a bit of time looking at very common words, to make sure that students learn their usage in English and don't introduce errors in collocations based on interference from their own language. For example, you could look at *luck* with the class. In English, we do not say that someone *'has luck'*, we say they are *lucky* e.g. *I was lucky and got to the airport just in time. You're so lucky to live by the sea. Have* and *luck* only collocate in expressions such as *bad luck, good luck* and *have no/some/a lot of luck*, e.g. *He's had a lot of bad luck recently. Did you have any luck finding your bag?*

1 Put students into pairs to discuss the questions. Elicit a few responses from the class.

2 Refer students to the **Exam Focus** on page 205 and turn to it on eText if you are using it. Read through it with students, making sure they understand everything. Focus students on question 1 in Activity 3 and brainstorm some possible paraphrases for each option (see answers). Play the first part of the recording and elicit any paraphrases students heard.

3 Give students time to read the remaining questions and underline key words. Then play the full recording. Read the **Exam Tip** with the class, then play the recording again for students to check their answers.

4 Put students into pairs to check their answers, then elicit paraphrases that helped students arrive at the answers. If students have found this difficult, ask them to look at the audio script to locate paraphrases of the options. (You can photocopy pages 29 and 130 or display them).

5 Give students a few minutes to discuss the statement in pairs, then elicit a few responses.

Answers

1 Students' own answers

2 A good fortune (luck)
B hard work (effort, dedication, long hours of practice)
C natural skill (ability you're born with)

3 (key phrases in brackets)
1 B (dedication, ambition and long hours of practice)
2 B (standards in sport are getting higher)
3 C (the child is unlikely to continue to make progress at such a fast rate)
4 B (older brother … happy to fight out endless battles)
5 A (could play whenever they liked)
6 C (a combination of lucky events)
7 B (better at taking chances and finding ways to improve)

4–5 Students' own answers

ADDITIONAL PRACTICE | **Maximiser** p.65, Listening 1–2 | **MyEnglishLab: Cambridge First**, Listening 7 *Listening to predict questions: What's the right question to ask?*

Use of English focus

▶ p.93

Vocabulary

word building

Aim

- to practise word transformations

Warmer: Transformations – *perform*

Write the verb *perform* on the board and tell students that this can be used when talking about sport. Elicit other words that share the same root word, e.g. *performer*, *performance* and elicit an example sentence for each of the words in the word family.

1 Complete the first question together as an example, then give students a few minutes to complete the remaining questions. Circulate and, if necessary, help by eliciting what type of word would fit in each gap and then what kind of prefix/suffix is needed.

2 Elicit the pronunciation of each word in context and mark the stress on the board. Point out the vowel sound change in the second syllables of *compete* /iː/ and *competition* /ə/, and *athlete* / iː/ and *athleticism* /e/.

Answers

1 1 competitive 2 competing 3 perfectionists
4 imperfections 5 athletes 6 athletic

2 (main stress underlined)
1 com<u>pet</u>itive 2 com<u>pet</u>ing
3 per<u>fect</u>ionists 4 imper<u>fect</u>ions 5 <u>ath</u>letes
6 ath<u>let</u>ic

Word formation (Part 3)

Aim

- to complete an exam-style word formation task (Reading and Use of English, Part 3)

Refer students to the **Exam Focus** on page 201 and turn to it on eText if you are using it. Read through it with students, making sure they understand everything. Leave the strategies displayed as a prompt during the task.

3 Ask students to read the text quickly and decide which is the best summary. Point out that this is strategy 1 in the **Exam Focus**. Elicit the answer.

4 Read the **Exam Tip** and point out that this is part of strategy 2. Demonstrate this strategy by looking at the example (0) and the words around it with the class. Read aloud the phrase before the gap and then pause at the full stop after the gap. Ask students what sort of word they would expect to come after *no* (a noun). Elicit a noun related to *connect* (*connection*) and ask students to read the sentence to check. Tell students to follow these strategies to complete the rest of the task. Put on a timer for ten minutes. When they finish, refer students back to strategy 4 and tell them to read their text again with a partner, checking that their answers make sense and are spelt correctly. Then check answers as a class.

5 Put students in pairs to discuss the question, then ask them to change partners and repeat the activity. Some students may like to show any lucky items they have.

Alternative activity

If most students don't believe in lucky charms, they could talk about an item that has sentimental value (important because of feelings or memories relating to them) or a personal tradition instead.

Answers

3 B

4 **1** connection **2** Competitive **3** perfection **4** stressful **5** relaxed **6** confident **7** dangerous **8** dependence

5 Students' own answers

ADDITIONAL PRACTICE | **Maximiser** p.66, Use of English 1–2

Vocabulary focus

▶ p.94

Speaking

Aim

- to review and expand vocabulary related to superstitions and to give spoken practice

Warmer: Pictionary

Ask students to keep their books closed. Put students into groups of three. Each group needs a pen and a blank sheet of paper. Each group nominates someone to go first. Write the word *knife* on a piece of paper. Invite the student going first from each group to come to the front and read the word from your paper (without saying it). These students then return to their groups and pick up the pen and paper but do not start drawing until everyone is ready and you say *go*. They draw the word (no letters allowed) and their group members guess what they are drawing. Repeat, with different students taking turns to draw different words, e.g. *ladder, umbrella, cat, wood, mirror*. Alternatively, this game can be played with the whole class, with one student drawing the word on the board while the rest of the class guesses.

1 Begin by focusing attention on the pictures and eliciting the word *superstition* (a belief that some objects or actions are lucky or unlucky, or that they cause events to happen, based on old ideas of magic). Put students in pairs to complete the superstitions, then check as a class, including whether each phrase is considered lucky/unlucky.

2 Give students time to discuss the questions with their partner. If you have a multi-lingual class, ensure that students are paired with someone of a different nationality.

Answers

1 **1** ladder (unlucky) **2** cat (either lucky or unlucky depending on who you ask!) **3** mirror (unlucky; it brings seven years' bad luck) **4** wood (lucky; people say *touch wood* and touch some wood to prevent something bad from happening, e.g. *I don't think I'll fail the exam, touch wood*). **5** knife (unlucky; especially for a wedding present) **6** umbrella (unlucky)

2 Students' own answers

Additional activity: Useful websites

There is a six-minute podcast about superstitions related to birds from the BBC Learning English team at **http://www.bbc.co.uk/worldservice/learningenglish/general/sixminute/2011/08/110810_6min_english_superstitions_page_latest.shtml**.

Robin and Moira, from Culips ESL podcasts, host a 20-minute discussion about urban myths and legends and superstitions in North America (North American accents) at **http://esl.culips.com/2010/08/urban-legends-old-wives%E2%80%99-tales-and-superstitions-from-north-america/**.

Collocations with *luck*

Aim

- to review and expand student knowledge of collocations with *luck*

3 Ask students to select the correct word in each sentence, then to check their answers in pairs before you check as a class.

4 Remind students that using collocations will help them sound more natural in conversations and in the exam. Make sure they know that some verbs can collocate with more than one noun.

5 While students are completing the sentences, circulate providing help as required. Check answers as a class.

Answers

3 **1** piece **2** bit **3** had **4** wished **5** believe **6** ran

4 **1** give up, miss, waste **2** achieve, give up **3** lose, miss, win **4** beat **5** achieve, miss, reach

5 **1** miss **2** reached **3** win **4** wasted **5** achieve **6** losing **7** beaten **8** gives up

Speaking

Aim

- to give spoken practice on the topic of ambition using collocations with *luck*

6 Ask students to think about their ambitions and what they have achieved or given up. Encourage them to use collocations with *luck* when they talk about their experiences. Then put students into pairs to share their ideas. After a few minutes, put students into new pairs to repeat. To finish, ask a few students to report back.

Answers

6 Students' own answers

Additional activity: Discussion questions

Ask students to discuss these questions in pairs:

Are you competitive? Do you give up easily in games?

In English, we often wish performers luck by saying 'break a leg'. Is there a similar tradition in your country?

Have you ever been in a situation where you couldn't believe your luck?

Ask a few students to report back on their discussions.

Grammar focus ▶ p.95

Third conditional

Aim

- to review the structure and use of the third conditional

Additional activity

Before the lesson, look at videos on **http://www.tomdaley.tv/**. Consider showing students (through the IWB) the first 30 seconds of one of the videos to open the lesson. Resources on this site include Tom's video diary, media interviews with Tom and further biographical information.

1 Focus attention on the picture and article. Tell students to read the article and find out how Tom feels about his monkey. Then elicit answers.

2 Ask students to read the statements and tick ones they agree with. For more information on Serena Williams, students can visit **http://en.wikipedia.org/wiki/Serena_Williams**.

3 Give students a few minutes to complete the activity, then elicit answers as a class. Refer students to **Grammar Focus** 5.5 on page 166 for more information.

4 Put students into pairs to complete the activity, then check answers as a class.

5 Circulate while students complete the sentences, ensuring they use the third conditional accurately.

6 Tell students to compare their answers in pairs. Ask a few students to report to the class anything new they learned about their partner.

Answers

1 A

2 Students' own answers

3 1 past 2 can come first or second
3 past perfect 4 *might* and *could*

4 1 a fifth gold medal if he hadn't been injured
2 trained properly, she might/would have been able to finish the race
3 have met if they hadn't done a scuba diving course in Thailand
4 gone out jogging I wouldn't have fallen over and broken my ankle on the ice

5–6 Students' own answers

ADDITIONAL PRACTICE | **Maximiser** p.66, Grammar 1–2 | **Teacher's Book** p.148/179, Photocopiable 9B *Completely conditional* | **MyEnglishLab: Cambridge First**, Use of English 16 *Conditionals: Match the halves together*

Writing focus ▶ p.96

Essay (Part 1)

structuring a paragraph

Aim

- to review the structure and style of an essay and to complete an exam-style writing task (Writing, Part 1)

Warmer: Discussion

Write on the board: *Shopping has little value as a leisure activity*. Give students a few minutes to discuss the statement in pairs, then elicit a few responses.

Ask students to turn to the **Writing Reference** on pages 186 and 187, displaying it on eText if you are using it. Read the task aloud, then tell students that these sample answers are Band 3 and Band 4. Ask students to read both answers, and as they do so to underline any words, phrases or examples that they see as strengths or weaknesses in each one. Then, read through the comments with the class.

1 Read the writing task together. Then tell students to read the student's introduction and decide whether A and B are true or false.

2 Tell students that the student's second paragraph needs to be re-ordered. Ask them to read the paragraph and re-order the sentences.

3 Give students time to read the rest of the essay and elicit other possible examples to support the arguments.

4 Ask students to look again at the essay in Activity 3 and decide which sentences best introduce the second and third paragraphs, then read the **Exam Tip** aloud.

5 Read the task aloud and ask students to discuss the statement in pairs. The task can be set as a homework activity or completed in class. Before students begin writing, refer them to the **Writing Reference** on pages 180 and 181 and focus attention on the Useful Language for essays. Display this on eText IWB as a reference. Encourage students to work to the time limit of 40 minutes (for writing and checking) which is the time they should allocate in the exam.

6 Remind students to check their work before they hand it in for individual feedback.

Answers

1 A true B false

2 C, B, A

3 Students' own answers

4 Paragraph 2: 1; Paragraph 3: 4

5 Sample answer

In today's world, there is tremendous scrutiny of sports heroes, with their decisions in sport and in their personal lives reported widely in the media.

Some people claim that what sportspeople do in their own time is their own business. However, it is clear that many young people are influenced by their actions and this should encourage them to use their position for the good of society.

When sports heroes behave badly, for example, if they demonstrate poor sportsmanship when losing or commit crimes, not only does it damage their own reputation, but it is also possible that in time, young people who admire the person will copy their negative behaviour.

Sport can be a good way of keeping young people out of trouble. It gives them something to do and helps them to work as a team. Famous sports people have an important role to play here to inspire young people.

In my opinion, therefore, sporting heroes should try their best to set a good example both on and off the field.

ADDITIONAL PRACTICE | **Maximiser** p.67, Writing 1–4 | **MyEnglishLab: Cambridge First**, Writing 14 *Text structure: The right references*; Writing 16 *Spelling and capital letters: Getting the details right*

Review ▶ p.97

Aim

- to revise structures and vocabulary covered in Unit 9

1–3 Ask students to complete the activities, circulating to provide assistance. Ask students to check in pairs before checking as a class on eText. Alternatively, set as a homework activity and then go through the interactive activities on eText to check.

Answers

1 1 B 2 C 3 A 4 D 5 C 6 A

2 1 ~~take~~ would take 2 ~~would book~~ book 3 ~~will practise~~ practised 4 ~~didn't have~~ wouldn't have 5 ~~can become~~ could have become 6 ~~wouldn't have offered~~ hadn't offered 7 ~~didn't become~~ wouldn't have become 8 ~~could afford~~ could have afforded

3 1 presentation 2 uncomfortable 3 enjoyable 4 precisely 5 successfully 6 preparation 7 helpful 8 dramatic

ADDITIONAL PRACTICE | **Online Testmaster** Unit 9 Test | **MyEnglishLab: Cambridge First**, Practice Test: Speaking

MyEnglishLab tip

Speaking Practice test activities

Students will need a partner for the MyEnglishLab Speaking Practice test activities and someone to act as 'examiner'. You can print the tasks for use in class if necessary. Students could do the practice test in groups of four, with one pair completing Parts 1–4 as candidates while the other pair act as examiners, time-keeping and noting down any good vocabulary/phrases the candidates use. After pairs swap roles, give them time to discuss the feedback on what they need to improve on.

Virtual friends

10

Vocabulary and listening focus ▶ p.98

Speaking

Aim

- to develop vocabulary related to friendship and to provide spoken practice

Warmer

Focus attention on the picture by magnifying it on eText and ask students to brainstorm qualities they think are important in a friend. Write students' ideas on the board. Save this page for use later in the lesson.

1 Check students understand *lose touch* (to gradually stop communicating with someone, e.g. *I've lost touch with all my old school friends*). Put students into pairs to discuss the questions, then elicit responses.

2 Tell students they are going to do a quiz to find out what kind of friend they are. Check students understand *favouritism* (treating one person or group better than others unfairly) and *lively* (full of energy), and elicit examples of *social networking*, e.g. Twitter, Facebook, Google plus, Orcut. Ask students to do the quiz in pairs, taking turns to ask the questions.

3 Refer students to page 158 to check their scores. Put them into small groups to discuss the results. Ask each group to report back to the class.

Answers

1–3 Students' own answers

Vocabulary

adjectives with *self*

4 Write the headings *Positive* and *Negative* on the board. Ask students to categorise the adjectives. Elicit answers and write the words under the correct heading on the board. Model pronunciation of the words. Then put students into pairs to discuss people they know and describe them using the adjectives. Tell students not to be negative about anyone in the class. Alternatively, students could describe celebrities or film characters.

5–**6** Students rank the features, and then work again with their small groups to find someone whose list is similar to theirs. Students then discuss what other features are important. You could display the brainstormed list from the warmer activity on the IWB while students do this. To finish, ask a student from each group to report back on their discussion. Discuss as a class what the three most important features of friendship are.

Answers

4 Positive: self-aware, self-confident, selfless, self-sufficient
Negative: self-centred, self-conscious, self-important, self-satisfied

5–6 Students' own answers

Additional activity: Friendship quotes

Choose a few quotes or proverbs about friendship from the internet and write them on the board. If you are using an IWB, you could type them up in advance. Ask students to read the quotes and discuss with a partner which they like best and why.

Possible quotes:

A best friend is someone who knows all about you and loves you anyway. (Elbert Hubbard)

Lots of your friends want to ride with you in the limo, but what you want is someone who will take the bus with you when the limo breaks down. (Oprah Winfrey)

Multiple matching (Part 3)

Aim

- to complete an exam-style listening task (Listening, Part 3)

Refer students to the **Exam Focus** on page 205 and turn to it on eText if you are using it. Read through it with students, making sure they understand everything. Leave it displayed on eText as a reference while students complete Activities 7–10.

7 Re-read strategy 1 and ask students to read the rubrics of Activities 7 and 8. Then re-read strategy 2 and ask students to first underline key words in the options. Check these as a class (see answers). Put students into pairs to compare statements A–H with their relationships with their best friends. Elicit some ideas as a class.

8 Before you play the recording, refer students back to strategy 3. Play the recording while students mark the option they think matches most closely. Read strategy 4 and the **Exam Tip** aloud, emphasising that this time, students should listen to check that the option they have chosen summarises each speaker's main idea. Play the recording again and then check answers.

9 Play the recording again while students note any matching paraphrases they hear. If students find this difficult, ask them to look at the audio script and find the paraphrases. Ask students if they predicted any of the paraphrases correctly. (You can photocopy page 130 or display it on the eText IWB.)

10 Ask students to think about the questions. Encourage them to include vocabulary from pages 98 and 99. Then put students into small groups to describe their friends. If they have access to photos of their friend (on a mobile device or social networking site, for example) encourage them to show it to their group as well.

Answers

7 Key words: A help each other B disagree C different personalities D only known each other … short time E didn't like each other F enjoy … same things G don't see each other often H got closer … got older

8 1 G 2 B 3 A 4 F 5 C

9 Suggested answers: A I'll always support her in whatever way I can and she'd do the same for me B we fight like brothers … about all sorts of things C he loves being the centre of attention whereas I'm quite shy F we have the same taste G I'd like us to spend more time together

10 Students' own answers

Additional activity: Writing

Ask students to write an article of 120–180 words about their closest friend, using the four headings in Activity 10 as a paragraph plan. Put students into different groups to read each other their articles and ask questions.

ADDITIONAL PRACTICE | **Maximiser** p.68, Vocabulary 1 | **Maximiser** p.68, Listening 1 | **Teacher's Book** p.149/180 Photocopiable 10A *Best friends* | **MyEnglishLab: Cambridge First**, Listening 17 *Listening to understand inferred information: Can we infer this?*; Listening 19 *Listening to identify the context: What exactly do they say?*

Grammar focus ▶ p.100

Conditionals

alternatives to *if*

Aim

- to review possible alternatives to *if* conditionals

Warmer: *Sheep out game*

Play *Sheep out* (phrasal verbs). Draw gaps on the board corresponding to the number of letters in one of the phrasal verbs below and draw a sheep (made up of head, body, two ears, four legs and a tail). Read the clue. Ask students to guess a letter. If it is correct, put it in the correct gap; if not, erase one part of the sheep. If students guess the phrase correctly before the sheep is erased, they win. After the word is revealed, elicit a few sentences using it.

Verbs (clues in brackets): *catch up* (spend time finding out what has been happening after you have not seen someone for a while), *keep in touch* (continue communicating with someone), *on my own* (by myself), *lose touch* (gradually stop communicating with someone).

1 Put students into pairs to read the examples and answer the questions. Check answers, then ask students to underline the alternatives to *if* in the quotes (*unless, even if, as long as, otherwise)*. Tell students that these phrases can indicate conditional phrases and hypothetical situations, but they have slightly different meanings to *if*.

2 Ask students to select the correct alternative, then compare with a partner before you check as a class.

3 Ask students to answer the questions in pairs, then go through the answers as a class. Refer students to the **Grammar Reference** on page 166 and turn to it on eText if you are using it. Go through it with the class, checking that students understand everything.

Answers

1 1 yes 2 no 3 yes 4 yes

2 1 Unless 2 Otherwise 3 even if 4 Provided that 5 whether

3 1 unless 2 whether 3 even if 4 provided that 5 otherwise 6 provided that

Additional activity: Personalisation

Write the following gapped sentences on the board and give students a few minutes to complete them so that they are true for them personally. Then put them into pairs to compare. Circulate, listening to the use of the alternatives to *if*, and noting down any inaccuracies. End with a short feedback session to correct any mistakes.

I try to ...... every day, otherwise I ....

Provided that I ......, I feel good.

Even if I try really hard to ......, I find it extremely difficult.

Unless I ......, I don't feel happy.

ADDITIONAL PRACTICE | **Maximiser** p.68–69, Grammar 1–3 | **eText IWB** Extra activity

Use of English

key word transformations (Part 4)

Aim

- to complete an exam-style transformation task (Reading and Use of English, Part 4)

Refer students to the **Exam Focus** on page 201 and turn to it on eText if you are using it. Read through it with students, making sure they understand everything. Leave it on eText while students complete Activity 4.

4 Do question 1 on the board as an example, talking through the strategies in the **Exam Focus**. Read strategy 1 again and ask a student to read the sentence and key word aloud. Elicit what is being tested (you need to use the right tense: first conditional, and move the phrase *when I get home*). Read strategy 2 and ask students to identify what kind of words need to be used with *unless* (the verb will need to be positive to keep the meaning the same). Read strategy 4 aloud and elicit the missing words (*unless I get home*). Read strategy 5 and get students to count the number of words to check it is between 2–5. Re-read both sentences aloud and ask students if the meaning is the same. Read strategy 6 and get students to re-check the spelling and meaning of the second sentence. Then read the **Exam Tip** aloud and ask students what they had to change in the example (the verb to positive; the position of the phrase *when I get home*). Continue to display the strategies on eText while students complete the task. When they finish, re-read the **Exam Tip** and ask students to discuss in pairs what they changed in each sentence. Then check answers, annotating on eText or the board.

Answers

4 1 unless I get home 2 even if he doesn't 3 long as it's not/it isn't 4 could/would/might have gone 5 provided (that) we don't 6 depending on whether there's/there is

Use of English focus

▶ p.101

Vocabulary

easily confused adjectives

Aim

- to identify and contrast easily confused adjectives

1 Tell students some adjectives are easily confused as they are similar but not identical in meaning. Ask students to complete the examples and compare with a partner before you check as a class. Make sure students understand *actual* (something that is real or exact).

Additional activity: pronunciation

Model the pronunciation of the words, or alternatively use the LDOCE CD-ROM with built-in audio to play the words. Ask students to listen and repeat, checking in particular that they are pronouncing /ʌ/ for the first vowel sound in *current*.

Answers

1 1 present/current 2 actual 3 current 4 usual
5 typical 6 common 7 individual
8 particular 9 unique

Multiple-choice cloze (Part 1)

Aim

- to complete an exam-style multiple-choice cloze task (Reading and Use of English, Part 1)

Warmer: Remembering the strategies

Put students in pairs and ask them to look at the multiple-choice cloze rubric and activity. Write the heading *Strategy* on the board, and the numbers 1–6. Ask students what strategy they think they should do first (after they have read the rubric) and elicit *read the title and text for general gist.* (Point out that this is also the **Exam Tip**.) Note this by the number 1 on the board. Then put students into pairs to see if they can remember the remaining strategies for this kind of task. Elicit answers and write students' ideas on the board, then refer students to the **Exam Focus** on page 200 to check.

2 Encourage students to work through the strategies they have listed in the warmer to complete the cloze. Students compare in pairs, then check as a class.

3 Elicit what Andy says about friends (people want undemanding companionship; too many friends make life complicated). Then put students into pairs to discuss whether they agree. Ask pairs to report back on their discussions.

Answers

2 1 C 2 D 3 D 4 C 5 B 6 C 7 D 8 A
3 Students' own answers

Speaking

Aim

- to provide spoken practice on the topics of friendship and leisure activities

4 Put students into pairs to discuss which activities are best done with friends and which alone. Elicit and write on the board some phrases to compare and contrast, e.g. *Y is much better done with friends, but/whereas X is best done alone, etc.*

Answers

4 Students' own answers

ADDITIONAL PRACTICE | **Maximiser** p.69, Use of English 1–2 | **eText Game**: Stepping stones (easily confused adjectives) | **MyEnglishLab: Cambridge First,** Vocabulary 12 *Comparing and contrasting: experiences and attitudes*

Reading focus ▶ p.102

Speaking

Aim

- to introduce the topic of friendship to prepare for reading the article and to provide spoken practice

1 Put students into small groups to discuss the questions. Check students understand that *social networking* refers to online sites such as Facebook and Twitter. Ask students to report back, then focus attention on the film poster for *The Social Network.* Elicit or explain that the film chronicles the origins and rise of Facebook.

Answers

1 Students' own answers

Multiple choice (Part 5)

Aim

- to complete an exam-style reading task (Reading and Use of English, Part 5)

Warmer: Remembering the strategies

Put students into pairs and focus them on the reading activity. Write the heading *Strategies* on the board and the numbers 1–8. Ask students what strategy they should do first (*read the instructions, title and subheading*). Note this by the number 1 on the board. Then put students into pairs to order the remaining strategies for this kind of task. Elicit answers and write students' ideas on the board, then refer students to the **Exam Focus** on page 202 to check.

2 Ask students to complete the activity. When they have finished, read the **Exam Tip** aloud and ask students to compare in pairs their answers and the paraphrases they found. Go through the answers as a class, elicit the part of the text/paraphrase that helped students answer each question (see answers below).

Answers

2 (paraphrases in text in brackets)
1 C (stating the obvious)
2 D
3 D (might say something they'll regret)
4 A (a way of exchanging information quickly and efficiently rather than being a social activity)
5 C (get rid of the social awkwardness that comes with trying to make a friend out of someone you don't know at all)
6 A (people are people whether online or not)

Speaking

Aim

- to provide spoken practice on the topic of friendship

3 Put students into pairs to discuss the opinions from the text and say whether or not they agree and why.

Answers

3 Students' own answers

ADDITIONAL PRACTICE | **Maximiser** p.70–71, Reading 1–4 | **eText IWB** Extra activity | **My English Lab: Cambridge First** Reading 15 *Text structure – pronouns and other short words for cohesion: Which is the right word?*

Vocabulary

compound adjectives: personality

Aim

- to form compound adjectives about personality and to use them in spoken practice

4 Elicit the first answer, then put students into pairs to complete the sentences. Brainstorm other compound adjectives, e.g. *open-minded, absent-minded, bad-tempered, well-behaved, tight-fisted, broken-hearted.*

5 Give an example using one of the compound adjectives, e.g. *He loses his temper very easily (quick-tempered).* Then students describe and guess in pairs.

Answers

4 1 like 2 quick 3 strong 4 level 5 old 6 kind
5 Students' own answers

ADDITIONAL PRACTICE | **Maximiser** p.71, Vocabulary 1–3 | **MyEnglishLab: Cambridge First**, Vocabulary 7 *Describing appearance*; Vocabulary 8 *Describing character*; Vocabulary 10 *Comparing and contrasting: people.*

Grammar focus ▶ p.104

Participles (*-ing* and *-ed*)

participle clauses

Aim

- to review the use of participles and to use them accurately in a gap-fill and spoken practice

Warmer

Start by displaying the title and picture from the article *Virtual people, real friends* (p.102) on eText and eliciting what students remember about the article.

1 Ask students to look at the extracts A–C from the article. Display them on eText if you are using it and ask a student to underline the present or past participle in each sentence on the board with the help of the class. Then for each phrase, read the participle aloud and ask whether it is active or passive, annotating the answer on eText.

2 Go through the extracts, comparing them to the equivalents in Activity 1 and eliciting responses to the questions. Ask students to turn to the **Grammar Reference** on page 171 and go through 14.1 with the class, on eText if using it.

3 Go through the example with the class. Then circulate as students complete the activity. Students compare their answers in pairs before you check as a class.

Answers

1 A claiming (active) B disapproving (active) C driven (passive)
2 A and B: pronouns are missed out (which/who). Present simple → present participle.
C: the auxiliary *be* is missed out.
3 1 bursting 2 developed 3 playing 4 cut 5 painted 6 speaking 7 designing

other uses of participles

Aim

- to review other uses of participles

4 Students work in pairs to match the examples 1–4 with the uses A–D. Check answers as a class. Ask students to turn back to the **Grammar Reference** on page 171 (go back to it on eText if using) and go through 14.2, checking that students understand everything.

5 Focus attention on the picture and elicit anything students know about the people in the picture. (Charley Boorman (right) is an English TV adventurer, travel writer and actor. He is well-known for his association with motorcycles and enthusiasm for biking. Ewan McGregor (left) is a Scottish actor best known for his roles in *Trainspotting* and *Star Wars*. Ask students to read the text quickly to find out why Ewan and Charley are such good friends.

6 Students complete the gap fill individually and then check their answers in pairs before you check as a class.

7 Students discuss the question in pairs, then repeat the activity with a new partner.

Answers

4 1 C 2 A 3 D 4 B

5 They have a lot of things in common.

6 1 going 2 saying 3 talking 4 becoming 5 amazing 6 hating 7 having 8 contented

7 Students' own answers

ADDITIONAL PRACTICE | **Maximiser** p.72, Grammar 1–2 | **Teacher's Book** p.149/182 Photocopiable 10B *Rejected words* | **eText IWB** Extra activity |

Speaking focus ▶ p.105

Listening

Aim

- to identify conversational strategies for use in an exam-style speaking task

Warmer

Focus attention on the exam task displaying it on eText and elicit names for the different age groups. Elicit or explain the new word *tween* (a blend of *between* and *teen*, used for 11–12 year-olds). Elicit the meaning of *toddler* (a very young child who is just learning to walk).

1 Play the recording and elicit the answers.

2 Ask students to read the extracts. Play the recording again, pausing as needed while students complete them. Play the recording again if necessary.

3 Put students into pairs to classify sentences 1–8. Do the first one with the class as an example if necessary. Elicit the answers. Display the audio script on eText and play the recording again, pausing after each extract for students to repeat, copying the tone and rhythm.

Answers

1 1 childhood 2 teenage years 3 college/university 4 motherhood 5 retirement

2 1 shall 2 could, with 3 Don't 4 Actually 5 Go on 6 just going 7 agree with 8 Do you think … too

3 A 1, 2 B 4, 6 C 3, 5, 7, 8

Grammar

emphasis with *what*

Aim

- to use *what* for emphasis in spoken practice

Display the **Grammar Reference** on page 168 on eText and go through it with the class. Underline the additions to each sentence when *what* is added (*what* at the beginning, and a form of *to be*). Leave the **Grammar Reference** on eText while students complete the activities.

4 Give students a few minutes to re-write the sentences in pairs. Then check as a class.

5 Ask students to re-write the sentences beginning with *what* with their partner. Check answers as a class.

Answers

4 1 Friends are really important to young kids.
2 You need to have friends to go out with at that age./At that age, you need to have friends to go out with.

5 1 What I used to love doing was going to theme parks.
2 What must be difficult is staying at home all day with a baby.
3 What is interesting is that men often take up sport as a way of making friends.
4 What people need is friends for every stage of their life.

Collaborative task (Part 3)

turn-taking

Aim

- to complete an exam-style speaking task (Speaking, Part 3) incorporating conversational strategies

Go through the **Exam Focus** on page 207 with students, displaying it on eText. Ask students what the most important tips are. Highlight their responses.

6 Read the **Exam Tip** aloud and elicit a few other possible phrases for interrupting politely, e.g. *If I could just come in here ...; Could I just add here that ...*. Remind students of the importance of tone (a higher-pitched, varying tone is more likely to sound polite than a low, monotone). Students complete the task in pairs, then swap partners and repeat for additional practice.

7 Put students into pairs to reach a decision. Remind them that they have a minute to do this and should not attempt to reach a decision too soon.

Answers

6–7 Students' own answers

Additional activity: Interrupting game

Write/type the following phrases on the board in a list:
Excuse me, I hate to interrupt, but could I take it from here?
If I could just come in here ...,
Would you mind if I took over from here?

Tell students they are going to practise interrupting politely. Put them into groups of 3–4 and tell them to turn to page 102. Tell them they are going to read the text *Virtual people, real friends* aloud. To demonstrate, nominate a student to start reading. Explain that the student on their left should interrupt, using one of the phrases on the board. That student then continues reading until they are interrupted. Students continue the game in their groups. Circulate, interrupting politely in each group until you are interrupted.

ADDITIONAL PRACTICE | **Maximiser** p.72–73, Speaking 1–4 | **MyEnglishLab: Cambridge** First Speaking II *Part 3 Inviting and responding to comments: Which phrase is better?*

Writing focus ▶ p.106

Speaking

Aim

- to provide spoken practice on the topic of friendship

Warmer: Discussion question

Ask students to think of two things that they remember about their first friend in their first school. Why do they think they became friends? Students discuss the question in pairs. Elicit some ideas.

1 Put students in pairs to discuss the question. Ask them to think about the different ways that friends are important at different stages of your life.

Answers

1 Students' own answers

Article (Part 2)

using a range of vocabulary

Aim

- to complete an exam-style writing task (Writing, Part 2)

2 Read the exam task aloud and elicit the kind of information that you might include in the article (details of where/how you met, how long you have known each other, why he/she is important to you). Refer students to **Writing Reference** on page 185 and go through the Useful language and *Dos* and *Don'ts* for writing an article.

3 Remind students that when they write an article, they want to catch the reader's interest. They need to think about different ways they can do this. Put students in pairs to do the activity. Elicit answers from the class. If using eText IWB, ask students to come forward and highlight different phrases.

4 Ask students to write a third paragraph for the article. Put them in pairs to compare their paragraphs. Ask some students to read their concluding sentence to the class. Which is the most dramatic/funniest/most surprising?

5 Read the **Exam Tip**. Before students begin to plan their own article, ask them to think about a particular moment when they were with their friend that can bring the friend to life. It could be the way they speak, the way they dress, the things that make them laugh, for example. They need to be able to explain this friendship to the reader. Give students a few minutes to plan their article before they start writing. Remind students that in the exam they will have 40 minutes for this task, and as well as spending some time on planning, they should allow themselves 5 minutes at the end to read through what they have written and check their work.

Answers

2 Students' own answers

3 **1** they add emphasis **2** set eyes on; struggling; rushed, grabbed, mass **3** (examples) straightaway, fascinated by, strange, fall out, ridiculous, talked

4 Students' own answers

5 Sample answer

My closest friend

When I first met Natalie, I didn't think we would get on, but she turned out to be one of my closest friends at college. The first thing I noticed about her was her hair. It is bright red and she has pale skin, so her appearance is very striking. The next thing I noticed was that she talked extremely fast. We had all just arrived at our hall of residence and no one knew anyone else. A lot of us were feeling shy and a little homesick. She was rushing around, trying to organise some social event. I admired her energy, but I was a little afraid of her at first.

Then one day, she knocked on my door when I wasn't feeling well. She made me a hot drink and we chatted for ages. It was such fun to talk to someone who looks at life in a completely different way. I think we get on because we are not at all alike. It is a friendship that has lasted to this day. She's always the first person I talk to if I have a problem or a decision to make and she always helps me to sort it out.

ADDITIONAL PRACTICE | **Maximiser** p.73, Writing 1–5 | **MyEnglishLab: Cambridge First**, Writing 13 *Linking ideas: Holding the story together*; Writing 17 *Spelling and punctuation: Make it right*

MyEnglishLab tip

Uploading resources

If you have additional resources you would like to make available for students online, you can add them to the resources folder in MyEnglishLab. Like all MyEnglishLab resources, you have control over whether they are visible to or hidden from students at any one time.

Progress test 2 ▶ p.107

Aim

- to revise structures and vocabulary covered in Units 6–10

Set the tests as a homework activity, then go through the interactive activities on eText to check answers.

Answers

1 1 Even if 2 Provided that 3 whether 4 otherwise 5 As long as 6 if

2 1 B 2 A 3 D 4 B 5 A 6 C 7 B 8 D

3 1 That woman waving to us is one of my work colleagues. 2 That's the path leading to the sea. 3 I saw your brother waiting for a train. 4 I found the money hidden under my bed. 5 I'm living in a flat owned by an old friend. 6 Shall we book the flight to Rome leaving at 6p.m. from Heathrow?

4 1 He must have gone to France because I saw him a few minutes ago. can't 2 Tom has done so a lot of cycling that he is very fit. such 3 We were warned driving slowly because of the icy roads. to drive
4 I'm sure he'll phone as soon as he'll get there. he gets
5 I ordered a fish risotto, that was delicious. which
6 The boss wanted to know why was I resigning. I was
7 Next Sunday at midday, my daughter will get married. is getting/will be getting 8 I might go with him if I hadn't been so busy at work. might have gone **OR** I might go with him if I hadn't been so busy at work. am not 9 If we don't make a decision soon, they will be selling all the tickets. will have sold
10 My father suggested her that she went to work for him. to her 11 Here's the article I told you about, wrote by my sister. written 12 I asked them don't speak in the library. not to speak 13 Louise may leave already, but I'll check if you like. may have left
14 I'll come, whether I have enough money. if
15 If I weren't a teacher, I'll want to be a doctor. I would want

5 1 lost 2 over 3 get 4 Job 5 competitive 6 out 7 script 8 growth 9 Applicants 10 on 11 flight 12 in order to 13 over 14 telling 15 tour

6 1 B 2 A 3 D 4 D 5 B 6 A 7 B 8 C

7 9 have 10 even 11 Unless 12 of 13 be 14 for 15 other 16 something

8 17 useless 18 successfully 19 training 20 choice 21 employment 22 managers 23 unpleasant 24 complaints

9 25 providing (that) he isn't/ he's not 26 whether or not 27 such a lot of 28 apologised for breaking/ having broken her 29 suggested (that) we go/ suggested (that) we went/suggested going/suggested (that) we should go 30 warned us not to swim/ warned us against swimming

ADDITIONAL PRACTICE | **Maximiser** p.74–75, Use of English | **Online Testmaster**, Unit 10 Test, Progress Test | **MyEnglishLab: Cambridge First**, Vocabulary 3 *Phrases with 'make' and 'do'*; Vocabulary 4 *Phrases with 'get'*

Living on the edge

11

Reading focus ▶p.110

▶p.110

Gapped text (Part 6)

Aim

- to complete an exam-style gapped text task (Reading and Use of English, Part 6)

1 Magnify the picture on eText and elicit what the person in the picture is doing (mountaineering/mountain-climbing) and where they might be. Put students into small groups to discuss the questions. Ask groups to think of at least three benefits and three risks for young people going on adventures like this.

2 Draw students' attention to the gaps in the text and the missing sentences and elicit the task type (a gapped text). Write the heading *Strategy* on the board and the numbers 1–9. Ask students to discuss in pairs what strategies they should use for this task type. Elicit answers and write students' ideas on the board, then refer students to the **Exam Focus** on page 202 to check. Leave the **Exam Focus** displayed on eText while students complete the tasks. Students read the title and introduction. Elicit what kind of person Jordan might be (see answer). Check that students know Everest is the highest mountain in the world and is located in the Himalayas in Nepal. Then tell students to read the main text quickly and ask them if anything about Jordan surprised them.

3 Read the rubric aloud. Focus on the first gap as an example on the board, working through strategies 3–6 in the **Exam Focus**. For strategy 3, read aloud the sentences before and after the gap and elicit what kind of information would fit (information about another side of his 'double life'). For strategy 4, underline any words that give clues, e.g. *more intense*. For strategy 5, focus attention on sentences A–G and ask students to look for any references towards this other side of life (D). Write *D* in the gap and refer to the **Exam Tip** and strategy 6. Ask students to complete the task. Circulate, referring students back to the **Exam Tip** and the other strategies. Put students into pairs to compare answers. Elicit which sentence students have left over. Demonstrate strategy 8 by reading the sentences before and after each gap and inserting the extra sentence(s) to check they don't fit. Finally, go through the answers as a class.

Answers

1 Sample answers: Benefits: gain confidence/increase self-belief, make friends on the journey, have some amazing memories, easier to do physical adventures while young, have a break. Risks: safety, might distract young people from other commitments (career, family, etc.), often quite expensive.

2 Sample answers

1 risk-taker, unusual, inspirational, dedicated, adventurous, crazy

2 the support he gets from his family (para 1), the time he has spent in hard training (para 2), that Jordan didn't appear to be very competitive as a child (para 6)

3 1 D 2 G 3 A 4 C 5 B 6 F

ADDITIONAL PRACTICE | **Maximiser** p.76, Vocabulary 1 | **Maximiser** p.76–77, Reading 1–3

Speaking

Aim

- to provide spoken practice on the topic of risk and achievement

4 Ask students to discuss the questions with their partner, encouraging them to use turn-taking strategies. Revise these if necessary (see Coursebook page 105). Circulate and encourage students to extend their answers. If time allows, students can repeat the activity with a different partner, for extra practice. Finish by eliciting a few responses for each question.

Answers

4 Students' own answers

Additional activity: Useful websites

Students might be interested in reading more about Jordan Romero. They can visit his blog at **http://www.jordanromero.com/weblog/** or find articles about him on other websites:

Vocabulary

using prefixes to work out meaning

Aim

- to review the meaning of common prefixes and to practise using them to work out meaning

5 Students match the prefixes to the meanings. Check answers as a class.

6 Give students a few minutes to think of some words and questions using the prefixes. Then put students into pairs to ask and answer the questions. Alternatively, students could circulate around the classroom asking and answering one question each with someone, then finding a new partner.

Answers

5 1 dis-/im- 2 re- 3 pre- 4 hyper-/over- 5 tri- 6 inter-

6 Students' own answers

Alternative activity

Divide the class into groups of four students and assign each group one or two of the prefixes from Activity 5. Ask them to make a list of words with those prefixes and then write two discussion questions for each one. Each group member should write down a copy of the questions. Put students into new groups with one person from each of the original groups. Students take turns to ask their discussion questions to the other members of the group.

ADDITIONAL PRACTICE | **Maximiser** p.77, Vocabulary 1–2 | **eText IWB** Extra activity | **MyEnglishLab: Cambridge First**, Reading 18 *Text structure: What's the discourse structure?*; Vocabulary 9 *Describing action*

Grammar focus ▶ p.112

Mixed conditionals

Aim

- to review the structure and use of mixed conditionals

Warmer

Elicit what students remember about Paul Romero from the article on page 111 and note the key words on the board. Give the students five minutes to skim the article again and see what further information they can find to add to the brainstorm on the board (he was married to Karen; is the father of Jordan; is part of Team Jordan racing team; has been a professional adventure racer for over ten years; was diagnosed with a rare knee disorder (bone disease) as a child but recovered; is hyper-competitive and driven).

1 Ask students to underline the verb forms in the sentences and get one student to underline them on eText if you are using it.

2 Tell students that a *mixed* conditional is one in which one clause refers to the past and one part refers to the present. Ask students to re-read the sentence pairs, and elicit which ones are *mixed*.

3 Elicit the answer. Ask students to read the **Grammar Reference** on page 167 for more information. Turn to it on eText and go through the examples with the class.

4–**5** Ask students to complete the activities, then compare in pairs before you check as a class. Refer to the **Grammar Reference** on page 167 to clarify any points that arise.

Answers

1 1 A If Paul hadn't had a bone disease, he wouldn't be so driven. B If Paul hadn't had a bone disease, he wouldn't have been so driven.

2 A If Paul hadn't been an extreme athlete, Jordan might not have climbed Everest. B If Paul weren't an extreme athlete, Jordan might not have climbed Everest.

3 A Paul might still be cycle racing if he hadn't had the knee disorder. B Paul might have raced cycles if he hadn't had the knee disorder.

2 1 A 2 B 3 A

3 1 A 2 B 3 A

4 1 had seen 2 wouldn't feel/be feeling/have felt 3 'd spoken/spoke/could speak 4 wouldn't be 5 had spoken/could have spoken 6 enjoyed 7 might earn/might be earning 8 would play/would be playing/might play

5 1 If my car wasn't/weren't so old, it wouldn't have broken down. 2 If I hadn't spent so much money in the sales, I wouldn't be broke. 3 If I hadn't taken him to that Liverpool match, he wouldn't play/be playing football all the time. 4 If my aunt didn't live in Moscow, I wouldn't have learnt Russian. 5 I wouldn't know so many people if Paula hadn't introduced me to them. 6 If I could get/could have got/had been able to get a job at home, I wouldn't have gone to live abroad.

Speaking

Aim

- to provide spoken practice of mixed conditionals

6 Remind students to use the contraction *I'd* instead of *I would,* and elicit the pronunciation of the weak forms of *have* in pronunciation of *I'd have* and *I wouldn't have.* Then put students into pairs to discuss the questions. Ask a few students to report back on what their partner said.

Answers

6 Students' own answers

Additional activity: Voxopop voicethread

Voxopop is a voice-based e-learning tool that allows you to set up a talk group for your class where you can post audio messages or questions and ask students to listen and respond with audio messages and listen to others' responses. It only takes a few minutes to sign up and set up a talk group at **http://www.voxopop.com/**. Make sure you set up the discussion as private if you don't want people outside your class to access it. You could post one (or more) of the discussion questions in Activity 6 to your talk group, then email (or display) the link for students to access. This could be done in class time if you have access to computers and headsets, or as a homework activity. Voxopop only works if you have Flash player installed on your computer.

ADDITIONAL PRACTICE | **Maximiser** p.78, Grammar 1–3 | **Teacher's Book** p.150/183 Photocopiable 11A *Party on* | **eText IWB** Extra activity

Use of English focus

▶ p.113

Vocabulary

verbs, nouns and adjectives

Aim

- to recognise some common patterns for forming verbs from nouns and adjectives

1 Put students into pairs to look at the verbs and discuss the question. Elicit answers.

2–**3** Have students complete these activities then check with a partner before you check as a class.

Answers

1 1 adjective 2 noun 3 noun

2 educate → education → educative/educated/educational

terrify → terror → terrifying

strengthen → strength → strong

criticise → critic → critical

endanger → danger → dangerous

3 adjectives (verb forms in brackets): dry (dry) frozen (freeze) hot (heat) just (justify) low (lower) modern (modernise) separate (separate) sure (ensure)

nouns (verb forms in brackets): blood (bleed) cheat (cheat) experience (experience) length (lengthen) memory (memorise) threat (threaten)

ADDITIONAL PRACTICE | **Maximiser** p.78, Vocabulary 1–2

Word formation (Part 3)

Aim

- to complete an exam-style word formation task (Reading and Use of English, Part 3)

Warmer: Remembering the strategies

Write the heading *Strategy* on the board and the numbers 1–5. Ask students to discuss in pairs the strategies they think they should use for this activity. Elicit the strategy they think they should do first after reading the rubric: *read the title and text for general gist.* Note this by the number 1 on the board. Then elicit the remaining strategies in order (referring to the **Exam Focus** on page 201 of the Coursebook for the answers) and writing them on the board.

4 This corresponds to strategy 1. Show students the title of the article on eText or write the title *Walk of a lifetime* on the board and ask students to predict what the article might be about. Then give students one minute to skim the article, to find out why Simone's walk was the 'walk of a lifetime'.

5 Go through the example (0) with students, talking through strategy 2. Remind students they should allow 8–10 minutes for each part of the Use of English section. Give them about 10 minutes to complete the gap-fill.

When students have finished, focus attention on the **Exam Tip** and ask them to read the article through again to check that their answers make sense and the words are spelt correctly. Students then compare their answers in pairs before you check as a class.

6 Put students into pairs or small groups to discuss the question. If students find it difficult to think of an achievement, write some possible categories on the board to help prompt ideas, e.g. *overcoming an obstacle, winning a prize, completing something, travelling somewhere, helping someone.*

Answers

4 It was a walk to the North Pole.

5 1 determination 2 ensure 3 safety 4 intention 5 inexperienced 6 successfully 7 supportive 8 engineering

6 Students' own answers

ADDITIONAL PRACTICE | **Maximiser** p.79, Use of English 1 | **eText Game**: Noughts and crosses | **MyEnglishLab: Cambridge First**, Vocabulary 15 *Topic: Holidays*

Listening focus ▶ p.114

Speaking and vocabulary

Aim

- to develop vocabulary related to adventure sports and to provide spoken practice

1 Focus attention on the photos and elicit the sports (sky-diving, extreme mountain biking, martial arts). Students discuss the questions in pairs. Elicit a few answers for each one with the class.

2 Write on the board the headings *Adjectives describing sports* and *Adjectives describing people.* Ask students to copy the headings and work in pairs to put the adjectives under the correct heading. Check answers and point out that the adjectives describing sports all end in *-ing*.

Answers

1 Students' own answers

2 Sports: breathtaking, demanding, exciting, exhausting, terrifying, worthwhile

People: adventurous, brave, determined, irresponsible, skilful

Additional activity: Discussion questions

Have you ever done something terrifying?

Tell your partner about a breathtaking place you have visited or would like to visit.

Do you consider yourself an adventurous person?

What is something that you find exhausting?

What do you consider to be the difference between being adventurous and being irresponsible?

Sentence completion (Part 2)

Aim

- to complete an exam-style sentence completion task (Listening, Part 2)

Warmer: Remembering the strategies

Write the heading *Strategy* on the board and below, numbers 1–6. Ask students to discuss in pairs the strategies they think they should use for this activity. Elicit the strategy they think they should do first (after they have read the rubric) and elicit: *read the sentences, highlight key words* and *think about what is missing*. Note this by the number 1 on the board. Point out that this is also the **Exam Tip** on this page. Then elicit the remaining strategies in order one by one, referring to page 204 of the Coursebook for the answers), and writing them on the board in students' own words.

3 Give students a minute to read the text and elicit the answer. Then demonstrate strategy 1 on the board with the first gap by reading aloud the sentence around the gap, eliciting the type of word that goes in the gap (noun) and underlining the key words (*main attraction*). Ask students to speculate as to what might be the main attraction of mountain biking. Ask students to follow the same strategy with gaps 2–10, then to compare their answers in pairs.

4 Re-read strategies 2–3, then play the recording while students complete their sentences. Then re-read strategy 4 before playing the recording a second time. Finally, ask students to re-read the sentences and check their spelling and grammar (strategy 5), then compare their answers in pairs. Check as a class.

Answers

3 Andrew thinks risk-taking is a good thing.

4 **1** freedom **2** mud **3** (safety) equipment
4 fighting **5** horse-riding **6** alive **7** age
8 energy **9** business **10** driving

Speaking

Aim

- to provide spoken practice on the topic of risk

5 Put students into pairs for the discussion. Check students understand the terms *risk-taker* (someone who does things with risks to achieve something) and *risk-averse* (not liking to take risks).

Answers

5 Students' own answers

ADDITIONAL PRACTICE | **Maximiser** p.79, Listening 1 | **MyEnglishLab: Cambridge First**, Listening 18 *Hearing the difference between similar sounds: What did they say?*

Vocabulary focus ▶ p.115

Adjectives and verbs with prepositions

Aim

- to develop knowledge of *adjective/verb + preposition* combinations and to understand how preposition combinations can help choice in a gap-fill exercise

Warmer: Brainstorm

Show students the picture of the Danger sign on eText and elicit the meaning of *avalanche* (a large mass of snow, ice and rocks that falls down the side of a mountain). Put students into small groups and ask them to make a list of other disasters they can think of. Ask groups to share their lists, writing the ideas on the board. If necessary, elicit the words *flood, flooding, tsunami, volcanic eruption, explosion, storm, hurricane, tornado.*

1 Do the first sentence as an example on the board, eliciting that *involved* doesn't fit because the preposition would be *in/with*, not *to*. Tell students that looking at prepositions to help eliminate options is a very useful strategy for all gap-fill activities in the exam, so learning *adjective* and *verb + preposition* combinations is very important.

2 Give students a few minutes to write their own sentences, then put them into pairs to discuss them. Circulate, noting down any errors with prepositions. On the board, write a few sentences with the errors you heard, changing the details to avoid embarrassing any particular student and elicit corrections.

3 Point out that the prepositions in the box can be used more than once. Students complete the exercise then compare answers in pairs before you check as a class.

Answers

1 1 involved 2 timid 3 determined 4 keen

2 Students' own answers

3 1 about 2 on 3 to 4 in 5 from 6 with 7 on 8 to 9 on 10 on

Additional activity: Discussion questions

Write these sentences on the board and ask students to discuss them in pairs then tell the class something they learnt about their partner.

Are you keen on the idea of sky-diving? Why/Why not?

Have you ever had to deal with a dangerous situation?

Do you often complain about things that irritate you or do you keep them to yourself?

ADDITIONAL PRACTICE | **Maximiser** p.79–80, Vocabulary 1–2

Phrasal verbs with *off*

Aim

- to develop knowledge of phrasal verbs with *off*

4 Tell students that phrasal verbs often have a more formal one-word verb equivalent. Ask a student to read the first sentence and elicit the phrasal verb to replace *delayed* (*put off*). Students complete the activity, checking with a partner or using dictionaries to help.

Answers

4 1 put off 2 back off 3 called off 4 told off 5 see us off 6 gone off 7 wore off 8 cut off

ADDITIONAL PRACTICE | **eText Game**: Pelmanism (phrasal verbs)

Speaking

Aim

- to give spoken practice using phrasal verbs with *off*

5 Ask students to read the questions and think about their own answers, then put them into pairs to discuss. Students can swap partners and repeat.

Answers

5 Students' own answers

Grammar focus ▶ p.116

Hypothetical meaning

wish and *if only*

Aim

- to use *wish, if only* and other expressions to convey hypothetical meaning

Warmer

Display the picture of the skateboarder on the IWB. Ask students if skateboarding is popular where they live and whether they have ever tried it or would like to.

1 Give students time to read the question and options, then play the recording once. Elicit the answer. Refer students to the **Grammar Reference** on page 169 and go through it with students.

2–3 Put students in pairs to work through the questions then check as a class, referring back to the **Grammar Reference** as necessary. Focus attention on the **Language Tip**. Elicit some examples where *if only* might be appropriate, e.g. *If only my alarm had gone off (I wouldn't have missed the exam).; If only someone had reminded me it was his birthday (I wouldn't have forgotten).*

4 Give students a few minutes to complete the sentences. Then ask students to compare with their partner. Elicit from students any wishes they had in common with other pairs.

Answers

1 C

2 1 yes, yes 2 yes, no 3 yes, no 4 yes, yes

3 1 D 2 C 3 B 4 A

4 Students' own answers

other expressions with hypothetical meaning

5 Tell students there are some other expressions used to convey hypothetical meaning. Ask students to select the alternatives then compare their answers with a partner. Check answers as a class, then ask students to underline the phrases which have been used to convey hypothetical meaning (*Suppose, it was as though, would rather, It's time*).

6 Students complete the sentences then compare their answers in pairs before you check as a class.

7 Put students into A/B pairs for the role play situations on pages 158 and159. Students could replay the situations with a new partner for extra practice.

Answers

5 1 are thinking about not going 2 had 3 I don't want you to 4 Let's have

6 1 went 2 had given 3 didn't take 4 realised

7 Students' own answers

ADDITIONAL PRACTICE | **Maximiser** p.80, Grammar 1–2 | **Teacher's Book** p.151/184 Photocopiable 11B *Just supposing* | **eText IWB** Extra activity

Speaking focus

Long turn (Part 2)

responding to your partner's photographs

Aim

- to complete an exam-style speaking task (Speaking, Part 2)

1 Elicit the sports shown in the photographs (boxing, sailing). Ask students to discuss in pairs which they would least like to do, then ask for a show of hands to see which sport is least popular. If any students have tried these sports, invite them to share their experiences.

2 Elicit what students remember about the Long turn (Part 2) in Speaking, Part 2. Then turn to the **Exam Focus** on page 206 to check, displaying it on eText if using. Read the rubric, task and questions aloud. Then play the recording and get students to discuss their answers in pairs before discussing as a class.

3 Read the question aloud and ensure students understand they need to write down phrases they hear for each function. Play the recording again, then ask students to look at the audio script and underline the phrases. (You can photocopy page 132 or display it on the eText IWB.)

4 Read the rubric aloud then play the recording. Elicit student responses about what Leo said and whether they agree with him.

5–6 Ensure students understand the task, referring back to **Exam Focus** on page 206 if necessary. Then ask students to complete the task in pairs. Read the **Exam Tip** aloud. Encourage students to time the follow-up question response and to aim for 30 seconds. Tell them that they can practise it several times to get the timing right. Students can then repeat the activity with a new partner, swapping roles for extra practice.

Answers

1 Students' own answers

2 1 Yes 2 Students' own answers

3 1 both photos show …; in a similar situation, they are both …; In a way it's harder for …; whereas …; But although …; compared to
2 I think, I'd say, I'd imagine
3 fit, well-trained, completely alone, fearless, determined, a little bit crazy

4–6 Students' own answers

ADDITIONAL PRACTICE | **Maximiser** p.80–81, Speaking 1–2 | **My English Lab: Cambridge First**, Speaking 14a *Focus on stress and intonation: Find the stressed words*; Speaking 14b *Responding to pictures: Practice*

Writing focus ▶ p.118

Speaking

Aim

- to provide spoken practice on the topic of reviews

1 Put students in pairs to discuss the questions. Elicit examples of anything they have done or decided not to do (watch a film, buy a product) as the result of reading a review. Have they ever reviewed products on a website? Do they trust what they read?

Review (Part 2)

expressing personal opinions

Aim

- to complete an exam-style writing task (Writing, Part 2)

2 Read the exam task aloud and elicit the kind of information that you might include in a film review (type of film, summary of the plot, details of actors, scenery, music, whether they liked the film or not and why).

3 Give students a few minutes to read the model review. Then ask them to complete the activity and check answers as a class. Refer students to the **Writing Reference** on page 193 and display it on the eText IWB if using. Ask students to look at the sample answer A and think about how it could be improved. What other details would they like to know about the film? What would make them want to go and see it? Elicit suggestions from the class.

4 Check students understand the meaning of *cast*, *script* and *cinematography*. Then put them in pairs to do the activity. Check answers as a class.

5 Check students understand the meaning of the adjectives. Elicit synonyms for some of the adjectives in the box, for example *exciting*, *frightening*, *outstanding*, *stunning*. Students put the words under the headings. Check answers as a class. Elicit as many possible words and phrases for each of the headings and encourage students to make a note of them.

6 Ask students to read through the task. Elicit suggestions for different types of shops that might be reviewed (for example, fashion boutique, bookshop, gift shop, florist, music store, games store, toy shop). Write up the headings on the board and brainstorm words and phrases that might be used to describe each of them. Read the **Exam Tip** aloud and remind students of the importance of making sure they make a recommendation (either positive or negative) at the end of their review. Suggest they spend a few minutes planning their review before they start writing.

7 Once students have completed their reviews, ask them to check their work. They could exchange their reviews with a partner and check each other's work.

Answers

1–2 Students' own answers

3 1 B 2 A 3 D 4 C

4 the cast, music, director, story, cinematography, location

5 (examples) 1 stunning, disappointing, convincing, entertaining, impressive, exciting, outstanding 2 impressive, outstanding 3 stunning, disappointing, complicated, entertaining, impressive, frightening, exciting 4 fast-paced, disappointing, confusing, complicated, entertaining, exciting 5 fast-paced, witty, entertaining

6 Sample answer

Katy's Corner

Katy's Corner is a small corner shop at the end of our local high street. When I go out to do my shopping on a Saturday morning, I always make time to go in and look around. It is a gift shop run by Katy, a woman in her 60s. The shop has a lovely atmosphere. It smells of fresh flowers and there is soft music playing. The walls are covered with colourful pictures and cards. It is very welcoming.

If I am looking for a present, I am sure to find something suitable. There is something for everyone. There are toys for children of all ages, as well as scarves, jewellery and all kinds of gifts. Katy makes a lot of the jewellery herself, so it is not something you will find anywhere else. Some of the jewellery can be quite expensive, although it's well worth the money, but most of the other gifts are not expensive. Perhaps the nicest thing about the shop, though, is Katy herself. She is very friendly and enthusiastic. I would suggest you go there just to meet her. She doesn't mind how long you spend looking around, and she doesn't try to sell you something you don't want. Sometimes I just go in for a chat.

7 Students' own answers

ADDITIONAL PRACTICE | **Maximiser** p.81, Writing 1–5 | **MyEnglishLab: Cambridge First,** Writing 11 *Expressing opinion: Sort out what they wrote*; Writing 18 *Punctuation: Make it right*

Review ▶ p.119

Aim

- to revise structures and vocabulary covered in Unit 11

1–3 Ask students to complete the exercises, then check in pairs before checking as a class on eText. Alternatively, set as a homework activity and then go through the interactive activities on eText.

Answers

1 1 wishes she had learnt 2 would rather you wore 3 it's time you went 4 felt as though they 5 train wasn't/train hadn't been 6 wouldn't have been

2 1 from 2 in 3 in/at 4 on 5 on 6 off 7 for 8 of 9 on 10 to 11 with 12 from

3 1 irresponsible 2 terrifying 3 memorable 4 critical 5 success 6 strength

ADDITIONAL PRACTICE | **Online Testmaster**, Unit 11 Test | **MyEnglishLab: Cambridge First,** Mock Test: Reading and Use of English

MyEnglishLab tip

Mock Reading and Use of English paper

For this paper, suggest to students that they allow 75 minutes to complete Parts 1–7 as a block, to get a feel for the progression in the exam.

Crime scene

Listening and vocabulary focus ▶ p.120

▶ p.120

Speaking and vocabulary

Aim

- to develop vocabulary related to crime and to provide spoken practice

Warmer: Brainstorming: *crime*

Tell students that this unit is about crime. Focus attention on the picture and elicit the words *prison* and *jail*, (*gaol* also possible in British English), *criminals* and *to commit a crime*. Brainstorm any other words that students associate with the topic of crime.

If students have computers and an internet connection, you could consider using online collaborative tools which allow users on many computers to draw or type simultaneously on a document. Go to **http://cooltoolsforschools.wikispaces.com/Collaborative+Tools** where you can find a selection of tools to try out.

1 Put students into pairs to discuss the questions, then elicit a few responses for each question.

2 Give students time to read the sentences and put them in order. Then put students into pairs to compare their answers. Encourage them to use turn-taking strategies in their discussion. Elicit the noun forms of *protect, punish, discourage* and *rehabilitate* (protection, punishment, discouragement, rehabilitation).

3 Students read the crimes and punishments. Check that they understand *armed* (carrying weapons, especially a gun), *curfew* (a law that forces people to stay indoors after a particular time at night) and *a fine* (money that you have to pay as a punishment). Elicit the collocations *a heavy/hefty fine*. Highlight the collocation *serving a prison sentence*. Students match the crimes and punishments in the way they think is most suitable, then compare their ideas with a partner. Elicit some answers and see if the class can agree on which punishments suit which crimes.

Answers

1–3 Students' own answers

Sentence completion (Part 2)

Aim

- to complete an exam-style sentence completion task (Listening, Part 2)

Elicit what students can remember about Listening, Part 2, then turn to the **Exam Focus** on page 204 and go through it with students, on eText if using. Check that students understand everything.

4 Read the rubric aloud and ask the question to the class, eliciting responses.

5 Focus attention on the gap-fill text *Prison hotels* and give students a few minutes to skim the text for gist. Then play the recording while the students complete the sentences.

Read the **Exam Tip** aloud. Ask students if they needed to change any of the words on the recording to fit the sentence and whether any words were difficult to spell. Then play the recording again for students to check and complete their answers. Check as a class.

6 Students discuss the question in pairs. Write this discussion question on the board: *What standard of accommodation should prisoners expect today?*

Answers

4 Students' own answers

5 1 reality tourism 2 school 3 photo/photograph 4 (black) tea 5 silent 6 service 7 Tarceny 8 beds 9 staff 10 49–69 euros

6 Students' own answers

ADDITIONAL PRACTICE | **Maximiser** p.82, Listening 1–2 | **MyEnglishLab: Cambridge First**, Listening 14 *Listening for detail: Completely right or completely wrong?*

Vocabulary

crime

Aim

- to develop vocabulary related to crime

7 Elicit the meanings of the words in the box in a criminal context. Students then complete the sentences. Check that students understand the words *burglar* (someone who goes into houses, shops, etc. to steal things) and *defendant* (the person in a court of law who has been accused of doing something illegal). Students check answers in pairs, then check as a class.

8 Go through questions 1–3 as a class. For question 2, elicit any other verb/noun combinations that follow the same pronunciation change as *suspect,* e.g. *research, decrease, increase, survey, torment.*

9 Put students into small groups to discuss recent crime stories in the news. If you think your students might struggle for ideas, brainstorm a few recent news stories as a class, then put students into groups to discuss them.

Answers

7 1 arrest 2 witness 3 suspect 4 sentence 5 suspect 6 witness 7 fine 8 arrest 9 fine 10 sentence

8 1 yes
2 in some cases the stress is different: ˈ*suspect* (n) *susˈpect* (v), ˈ*convict* (n) *conˈvict* (v)
3 *fine* is also an adjective; *sentence* is also a noun (a group of words); *arrest* can mean *stop*; *suspect* can mean *think* (e.g. *I suspect you're right*).

9 Students' own answers

collocations with *catch, follow, reach*

Aim

- to develop knowledge of collocations with *catch, follow* and *reach*

10 Ask students to complete the sentences, then check their answers in pairs. Check as a class, then ask students to write three sentences using the collocations. Students can share their sentences in small groups.

Additional activity: Discussion questions using collocations with *catch, reach, follow*

Write the following questions on the board and put students into small groups to discuss them.

What tips would you give to friends finding it hard to reach an agreement about something?

When it comes to fashion, do you care about following trends?

Do you ever set targets for yourself, for example with study or exercise? How do you celebrate when you reach them?

Answers

10 1 reach 2 follows/followed 3 caught 4 catch 5 reaching 6 following

ADDITIONAL PRACTICE | **Maximiser** p.83, Vocabulary 1–2

Grammar focus ▸ p.122

Modal verbs

obligation, prohibition and necessity

Aim

- to review the structure and use of modal verbs for obligation, prohibition and necessity and to complete an exam-style word transformation task (Reading and Use of English, Part 4)

Warmer

Display the picture of police officers on eText. Divide students into three groups and assign each group one role: police officer, prison officer or prisoner. Give the groups about five minutes to make a list of the kinds of activities they think the people would do over a typical week. Then ask a reporter from each group to read their list and ask the rest of the class if they have any ideas to add.

1 Students read the statements and decide who said each one. Students check their answers in pairs then as a class.

2 Ask students to match A–E to the statements in Activity 1. Go through the answers as a class. Focus students on the **Language Tip** and examples. Elicit the past form of sentence 5 in Activity 1: *I must try and stay positive until I am freed.* (I had to try and stay positive until I was freed.) Then turn to the **Grammar Reference** on page 170 (on eText if using) and go through it with the class.

3 Students complete the activity then check with their partner. Check answers with the class, and elicit the pronunciation of *mustn't* /mʌsənt/.

4 This activity is in the style of Reading and Use of English, Part 4. Remind students to use between two and five words for this and not to change the word given. Students complete the activity, then check their answers in pairs before you check as a class.

Answers

1 **1** b **2** a **3** c **4** c **5** c **6** a

2 **1** B **2** C **3** D **4** C **5** A **6** E

3 **1** don't have to **2** mustn't **3** had to **4** have to

4 **1** needn't have **2** aren't allowed to open **3** mustn't talk **4** don't have to **5** has to collect **6** he need to get

Speaking

Aim

- to provide spoken practice of using modal verbs for obligation, prohibition and necessity

5 Students work in small groups for the discussion. Ask each group to report back to the class on their discussion.

Answers

5 Students' own answers

Alternative activity

As an alternative, or for additional practice, ask students to discuss the same four categories in Activity 5 (what people have to do, mustn't do/aren't allowed to do, are allowed to do and needn't do/don't have to do) in one of the following situations:

- in class
- at a swimming pool
- on a plane.

Additional activity: Obligation, prohibition and necessity in the past

Ask students to discuss their childhood using the modal verbs in this lesson. They should talk about things they had to do, things they were/weren't allowed to do and things they didn't have to do.

ADDITIONAL PRACTICE | **Maximiser** p.83, Grammar 1–3 | **Teacher's Book** p.152/185, Photocopiable 12A *All part of the job* | **eText IWB** Extra activity | **MyEnglishLab: Cambridge First**, Use of English 18 *Modal verbs: Two are right, one is wrong*

Speaking focus ▶ p.123

Vocabulary and speaking

cybercrime

Aim

- to develop vocabulary related to cybercrime and to provide spoken practice

Warmer: Cybercrime introduction

Tell students that they are going to be discussing the topic of cybercrime. Write *cyber* on the board and elicit the meaning (computer-related) and any words students know that use this prefix. Write up any suggestions on the board and include *cyberspace* (a term used to describe the imaginary location of internet and interactions on the internet, e.g. *You didn't get the email? Must have got lost in cyberspace!*), *cybercafé* (an alternative word for internet café), *cyber safety* (internet safety), *cyber bully* (someone who bullies others online, for example sending them cruel messages or posting offensive statements about them) and *cybercrime* (crime that occurs on or through the internet).

Elicit any cybercrime stories or scams students have heard of. (For example, someone receives a fake email from the bank asking for their account details and pin number, which is then used to withdraw money from their account.)

Put students into pairs or small groups and give them a few minutes to brainstorm any other words they can think of that are related to the topic of cybercrime. If necessary, you could elicit a few examples first, e.g. *computer hacking, credit card, virus*. Then elicit ideas from each group and write them on the board, checking students understand each word.

1 Elicit the meaning of *cybercrime* (criminal activity that involves the use of computers or the internet). Put students into pairs to discuss the questions, then elicit a few answers for each question.

2 Students work in pairs to complete the activity. Check the answers as a class.

3 Elicit some responses from the class.

4–**5** Put students into small groups to discuss the questions. Remind them to use language for disagreeing politely and to use turn-taking strategies. Either elicit some phrases or review the phrases from Activity 2 on page 105 and Activity 3 on page 80. Write the phrases on the board or leave them on eText as a prompt during the discussion.

Answers

1 Students' own answers

2 1 C 2 D 3 E 4 B 5 A

3–5 Students' own answers

Discussion (Part 4)

Aim

- to complete an exam-style discussion task (Speaking, Part 4)

Elicit what students remember about Part 4 of the speaking paper, then ask them to turn to the **Exam Focus** on page 207 and talk through it, displaying it on eText if using.

6–**7** Put students into groups of four (two pairs). Tell students that they are going to help each other – pairs are going to take turns to listen and offer feedback while the other pair in their group answers some exam-style questions.

Read the **Exam Tip** aloud. Allow about five minutes for the first pair in each group to discuss Question 1, then about two minutes for the other pair to offer feedback under the headings. Then get pairs to swap roles for Question 2. Remind students of the **Exam Tip** and ask for some specific examples that students used for the first two questions. The groups then continue to work through the remaining questions. Finish by eliciting from students what they found they did well and what they found most difficult (from A–C). Make a note of this for further practice. Students could work in new pairs/groups and repeat the activity for further practice.

Answers

6–7 Students' own answers

Alternative activity: Recording in pairs

If students have access to recording devices, e.g. computers or mobile phones, they could record themselves (in pairs) discussing each question. This will work best if there is a quiet area where each pair can go to avoid interference on the recording. After they have recorded their discussions, students can listen to their own recording and make notes on the criteria in A–C. Students can then join together with another pair to share what they noticed about their own discussion.

ADDITIONAL PRACTICE | **Maximiser** p.84, Speaking 1 | **eText Game**: Sheep out (*cybercrime*) | **MyEnglishLab: Cambridge First** Speaking 19 *Part 4 Assessment: True or False?*

Reading focus ▶ p.124

Speaking

Aim

- to provide spoken practice on the topic of crime fiction and to introduce the topic of the reading text

1 Display the questions on eText and check that students understand *fiction* (books and stories about imaginary people and events; collocations include *crime fiction, historical fiction, romantic fiction*), *novel* (a long written story in which the characters and events are usually imaginary) and *genre* (a particular type of art, writing, music, etc.). Students discuss the questions in pairs. Elicit a few ideas for each question to finish.

Answers

1 Students' own answers

Multiple choice (Part 5)

Aim

- to complete an exam-style reading task (Reading and Use of English, Part 5)

Elicit what students can remember about Reading and Use of English, Part 5 then turn the **Exam Focus** on page 202 and go through it with students on eText.

2 Refer students to strategies 1–2, and give them a few minutes to skim the text.

Continue to display the strategies in the **Exam Focus** on eText as a prompt while students complete the task. Students complete the activity then compare answers in pairs. Check as a class and ask students which of the strategies they find most useful for this task. Elicit a range of answers.

Answers

2 **1** C **2** C **3** D **4** C **5** B **6** B

Speaking

Aim

- to consolidate understanding of the text and to provide spoken practice

3 Students discuss the questions in small groups.

Answers

3 Students' own answers

Vocabulary

verbs

Aim

- to develop understanding of action verbs in the text

4 Students complete the matching activity, then compare answers in pairs before you check as a class.

5 Tell students that they are going to play a game called *Two truths and a lie*. Give students about five minutes to write their sentences, then put them into pairs to read their sentences to each other and guess which one is untrue. This is a good activity for students to swap partners and repeat.

Answers

4 **1** follow through **2** spin **3** stalk **4** cling to **5** intervene **6** bully **7** brandish **8** set aside

5 Students' own answers

ADDITIONAL PRACTICE | **Maximiser** p.84–85, Reading 1–3 | **Maximiser** p.85, Vocabulary 1 | **eText IWB** Extra activity | **MyEnglishLab: Cambridge First**, Reading 10 *Understanding text purpose when reading: What's the writer doing here?*

Grammar focus ▶ p.126

have/get something done

Aim

- to review the structure and use of the phrase *have/get something done*

Warmer: Discouraging burglars

Check students understand the meaning of *break-in.* (an act of entering a building illegally and by force, especially in order to steal things, e.g. *Since the break-in we've had all our locks changed.*) Elicit possible words for someone who breaks in (*burglar, robber, thief*).

Tell students that you are going to read aloud five suggestions to discourage burglars. Ask students to write the numbers 1–5 and tell them they should note the gist of each suggestion, emphasising that they should not write every word.

Read the following suggestions aloud, pausing briefly after each one.

1 Always make sure your doors and windows are securely locked.
2 An automatic light near the door that detects movement can be a deterrent.
3 If you are going on holiday, consider asking someone to housesit for you, or at least to collect the post.
4 Get to know your neighbours so that they can keep an eye out for anything unusual.
5 Install an alarm system, preferably a monitored one, so that if someone tries to break in there will be a quick response.

Ask students to compare their notes in pairs. If you think students have found this difficult, you could read the suggestions again. Elicit the five ideas from the class, re-reading the suggestions if necessary and clarifying any questions students may have.

Ask students to work with their partner to discuss each item and whether or not they already do it. Then ask each pair to think of two more possible suggestions to add to the list. Elicit these and write them on the board.

1 Put students into pairs and ask them to read the dialogue aloud, taking the parts of Dan and Zara. Then elicit answers to the questions.

2 Complete the rule on eText or on the board. Read the **Language Tip** with the class and make sure students understand everything.

3 Students complete the sentences, then compare their answers in pairs. As you check the answers as a class, ask some students to read the mini-dialogues aloud in pairs.

4 Give students a few minutes to make their lists, encouraging them to think of three more things each. Put students into pairs or small groups to discuss their lists. Circulate and make sure that students are using *have/get something done* correctly.

Answers

1 1 had some computers stolen
2 got the rooms fingerprinted

2 *have* or *get* + object + past participle of the verb

3 1 have just had it painted **2** get it looked at
3 have it cut **4** get your eyes tested
5 got a friend to make it **6** had it taken

4 ✓: report the crime to the police, buy a guard dog, stop their credit cards, clean the house, find their insurance policy

✗: change their locks, repair broken windows, install an alarm

ADDITIONAL PRACTICE | **Maximiser** p.86, Grammar 1 | **eText IWB** Extra activity

Use of English focus ▶ p.127

Vocabulary

phrasal verbs with *go*

Aim

- to develop knowledge of phrasal verbs with *go*

Warmer

Either zoom in on the box of phrasal verbs on eText or write them on the board. Ask students to discuss in pairs whether they know the meanings of any of them and to form sentences. Invite students to share and write some of their sentences on the board. Do not worry too much about meaning as long as the sentences are accurate at this stage, as you will revisit them after Activity 1.

1 Complete the first sentence on the board as an example, then get students to complete the remainder in pairs. Elicit the answers with the class. If you did the warmer with the class, ask students to compare the meanings of the phrasal verbs in sentences 1–8 with the meanings on the board and elicit whether they are the same or different meanings. Other meanings could be verified with a dictionary such as the *Longman Dictionary of Contemporary English* (Online/App/Paper).

2 Students take turns to ask and answer the questions in pairs.

Answers

1 1 going on 2 go on/go ahead 3 gone off 4 gone down/gone off 5 went off 6 went off 7 went off 8 went over

2 Students' own answers

Additional activity

Try a *Speak for a minute* challenge, where students have to keep talking about a topic or question for one minute. You could give students topics, or they could choose questions/topics from other units of the book. The activity could be done in pairs initially and then if students feel up to the challenge, some could try it in front of the class. Students can encourage their partner to continue by using the phrasal verb *go on.*

ADDITIONAL PRACTICE | **Teacher's Book** p.153/186 Photocopiable 12B *Cops and robbers*

Open cloze (Part 2)

Aim

- to complete an exam-style open cloze task (Reading and Use of English, Part 2)

Elicit what students can remember about Reading and Use of English, Part 2 then turn to the **Exam Focus** on page 201 and go through it with students on eText.

3 Magnify the picture and heading on eText and elicit a few predictions about what the text is about. Read Question 3 aloud and give students one minute to skim the text for the answer.

4 Ask students to complete the gap fill, then read the **Exam Tip** and encourage students to re-read the text, checking that their answers make sense and their spelling is accurate. Put students into pairs to compare, then finish by eliciting answers as a class.

5 Students discuss the question in pairs.

Answers

3 People want to visit the places connected with famous fictional crimes.

4 1 be 2 like 3 over 4 so 5 for 6 most 7 by 8 the

5 Students' own answers

ADDITIONAL PRACTICE | **Maximiser** p.86, Use of English 1–2 | **MyEnglishLab: Cambridge First**, Use of English 3 *Spelling in context: What's the right spelling?*

Writing focus ▶ p.128

Report (Part 2)

making recommendations

Aim

- to identify key features of a report and to complete an exam-style writing task (Writing, Part 2)

1 Ask students to read the exam task and elicit what the report is to be about (improving security) and the two ways to do this (installing lockers and installing security cameras). Before they read the student's report, elicit possible benefits of each. Then put students in pairs to read the report to check whether their ideas were included and to answer the questions. Check answers as a class.

2 Remind students that reports are written in a formal style. Refer them to the **Writing Reference** on page 184 and go through the Useful language. Elicit other possible expressions for making recommendations. Then ask students to turn back to page 128 and do the activity. Check answers as a class.

3 Point out to students that for each sentence there is one or sometimes two verbs that could be used to replace *recommend* in each sentence. Elicit answers.

4 Give students time to read through the task. Write the headings *Advantages* and *Disadvantages* on the board. Elicit points for and against banning mobile phones and write them on the board. Remind students that whether they are going to make a recommendation for or against banning mobile phones, they should give points for both sides of the argument.

5 Read the **Exam Tip** and ask students to look again at the recommendations that they noted in Activity 4. Are they expressed appropriately? Give students thirty minutes to write their answers. Ask them to turn to page 179, or display on the IWB if using eText IWB. Ask students to go through the checklist and check through their work before they hand it in.

Answers

1 **1** yes **2** Yes. *I dropped my laptop in the canteen and broke it.* This is irrelevant because it's not related to the main point. *But another solution would be to prevent students from bringing valuables into the canteen.* This is irrelevant because it is adding extra information which does not answer the question. **3** yes

2 **2** to spend **3** spends **4** is spent, should be spent, be spent

3 **1** suggest/ advise **2** suggestion/advice **3** suggest **4** advised/suggested

4 Students' own answers

5 Sample answer

The purpose of this report is to recommend the best way of dealing with the problem of mobile phone thefts in the college. It has been suggested that students should be banned from bringing their mobile phones into college.

Advantages

There are several advantages to banning mobile phones from college. A ban would:

- cut the number of thefts.
- solve the problem of students losing their phones.
- reduce the amount of distraction in class when students are often checking their phones rather than listening to the teacher.

Disadvantages

There are also significant disadvantages to a ban. It would:

- be very difficult to enforce a ban as phones are small and easily hidden.
- prevent useful communication between students and their teachers, who often use text messages to inform their students about changes to class venues or timetables as well as homework.

Recommendations

Mobile phones have become a very important form of communication, not only between students, but also between students and teachers. It would cause more problems than it would solve to try to ban them from college. I would recommend instead putting up notices around the college to warn students about the danger of theft and advising them to take care of their valuables.

ADDITIONAL PRACTICE | **Maximiser** p.87, Writing 1–4 | **MyEnglishLab: Cambridge First**, Writing 10 *Suggesting and recommending: What goes with that?*

Review ▶ p.129

Aim

- to revise structures and vocabulary covered in Unit 12

1–3 Ask students to complete the exercises, circulating to provide assistance. Ask students to check in pairs before checking as a class on eText. Alternatively set as a homework activity and then go through the interactive activities on eText to check.

Answers

1 **1** A **2** B **3** C **4** D **5** C **6** A

2 **1** needn't have gone/didn't need to go
2 weren't allowed to
3 you mustn't/can't/don't speak without
4 get Harry to check
5 have a newspaper delivered
6 have my wedding dress made

3 **1** theft **2** description **3** suspiciously **4** lawyer **5** convictions **6** decision **7** guilty **8** criminal

ADDITIONAL PRACTICE | **Maximiser** p.88–89, Use of English | **Online Testmaster** Unit 12 Test | **MyEnglishLab: Cambridge First**, Mock Test: Writing

MyEnglishLab tip

Mock Writing paper

For the Mock Writing paper, students write their tasks on separate pieces of paper. Collect these in to provide individualised feedback using the Writing marking guidelines on page 194.

Who are you again?

Reading focus ▶ p.130

Multiple matching (Part 7)

Aim

- to complete an exam-style reading task (Reading and Use of English, Part 7)

Warmer

Ask: *Do you find it easier to remember names or faces? Have you ever had a situation where you recognise someone but they don't recognise you, or vice versa?* Put students into pairs to discuss the questions, then ask pairs to report back to the class.

1 Give students a few minutes to put the faces in order, then put them into small groups to discuss the questions. Ask one student from each group to summarise their discussion for the class.

2 Elicit what students can remember about Reading and Use of English, Part 7, then ask them to turn to the **Exam Focus** on page 203 to check. Display the **Exam Focus** on eText if using it and go through it with the class. Refer to strategy 1 and ask the students to read the title and subheadings. Tell them that these offer important clues to help prepare them to understand as much as possible under pressure. Refer to strategy 2 and give students a couple of minutes to skim each text. Refer to strategy 3 and on the board, highlight key words in Question 1 as an example (*location, biggest clue*). Give students time to read the questions and underline the key words. Refer to strategies 4 and 5 and get students to scan for information about location being a clue (highlighted in the text – *I usually depend on venue*). Then ask students to do the same with the remaining sentences. Re-read strategies 6–7 and the **Exam Tip** and give students time to decide which is the exact answer to each question. Students compare their answers in pairs then check as a class.

Answers

1 Students' own answers

2 1 C **2** B **3** A **4** D **5** B **6** A **7** C **8** D **9** B **10** C

Speaking

Aim

- to consolidate understanding of the text and to give spoken practice

3 Students discuss the questions in small groups. Ask one student from each group to report back to the class on their discussion.

Answers

3 Students' own answers

ADDITIONAL PRACTICE | **Maximiser** p.90, Vocabulary | **Maximiser** p.90–91, Reading 1–3 | **eText IWB** Extra activity | **MyEnglishLab: Cambridge First**, Reading 2 *Reading for gist: Choose the headings*; Reading 7 *Understanding attitude and opinion: What is their view?*

Vocabulary

phrasal verbs with *come*

Aim

- to learn and practise using phrasal verbs with *come*

Warmer

Ask students to scan the article *Identity Crisis* for a phrasal verb with *come*. (*I probably* come across *as rather a cold person* – Laura). Elicit the meaning, then share the following examples from the LDOCE: If someone comes across in a particular way, they seem to have particular qualities, e.g. *He comes across as a very intelligent, sensitive man; She sometimes comes across as being rather arrogant.*

Elicit any other phrasal verbs with *come* that students know, writing them on the board and eliciting meaning and examples.

4 Students match the phrasal verbs, then check their answers in pairs before you check as a class.

5 Put students into pairs to write five questions using the phrasal verbs. Explain that they both need to write down the questions. Then ask students to swap partners and ask their new partner the questions.

Answers

4 **1** A **2** C **3** D **4** G **5** F **6** E **7** H **8** B

5 Students' own answers

ADDITIONAL PRACTICE | **Maximiser** p.92, Vocabulary 1 | **eText Game**: Noughts and crosses (phrasal verbs with *come*)

Grammar focus ▶ p.132

Modal verbs

ability

Aim

- to review modal verbs used to express ability

Warmer: Fancy dress guess

Write the following sentence on the board: *We had to dress up for the party*. Elicit the two possible meanings of the phrasal verb *dress up* in this sentence (to dress nicely for a special occasion, or to wear a costume/disguise/fancy dress, usually for a party or carnival). Write the following questions on the board and ask students to discuss them in pairs:

At what sorts of occasions do people wear fancy dress in your country?

Do you enjoy dressing up? (the second meaning above)

Elicit a few ideas from the class, then tell students that you are going to describe a costume and they are going to guess what you were dressed up as. Read aloud the following description or make up one of your own: *I was wearing brown, leather boots and a checked shirt tucked into blue jeans. I wore a belt with a large buckle and a red bandana around my neck. To finish off my costume, I was wearing a hat with a brim.*

Ask for guesses of what you were dressed up as (a cowboy). You may like to re-read the description or write it on the board and check students understand *buckle*, *checked*, *bandana* and *brim*. Next, ask students to work with their partner to think of a costume and write a description of it, which they will read to someone else to guess. If you have an able class, they may prefer to do this individually. Circulate, helping with vocabulary as necessary. Useful vocabulary may include: *cape*, *wings*, *wig*. If students are working in pairs, both students in each pair should write down a copy of their description. Separate the pairs and form new groups, ideally of 5–6 students. Students take turns to read their description aloud and others guess what their costume is.

1 Give students a couple of minutes to read the extracts, then elicit the answer.

2 Read the rubric aloud, then give students a few minutes to complete the questions before checking as a class. Focus attention on the **Language Tip** and elicit further examples for each point, e.g. C: *I've known how to cook since I was a child;* D: *I would love to succeed in starting my own business one day;* A: *I managed to finish all my work on time.* Then refer students to the **Grammar Reference** on page 170 for further information. Turn to it on eText if using and go through it with students, checking that they understand everything.

3 – 4 While the students work through the questions, circulate to provide help as required. Ask students to compare their answers in pairs, then check as a class.

5 Ask students to complete the sentences in a way that is personally true to them. Put students into small groups to share their sentences, then ask students to report back on what they learnt about the others in their group.

Answers

1 **a)** B is a 'super-recogniser' **b)** A is 'face-blind'

2 A 5, 6 B 7 C 3, 4 D 2 E 1

3 1 were able to 2 could/were able to 3 be able to
4 could have caught 5 've been unable to
6 to be able to

4 1 wasn't able/was unable to finish
2 could play football better/played football better than
3 succeed in running
4 could have taken
5 was able to cook

5 Students' own answers

ADDITIONAL PRACTICE | **Maximiser** p.92, Grammar 1 | **eText IWB** Extra activity

Speaking focus ▶ p.133

Speaking

Aim

- to give spoken practice on the topic of memories

1 Focus attention on the photos and elicit what students think the people are doing (writing/keeping a diary/journal, looking at/browsing digital photos on a computer). Then, put students into pairs to discuss the questions. Elicit a few responses for each question.

Answers

1 Students' own answers

Vocabulary

useful phrases for Part 2

Aim

- to learn some useful phrases for Speaking, Part 2

2 Students match the expressions 1–6 to the reasons A–F, then check in pairs before you check as a class. Check students know how to pronounce the phrases and drill them with the class, giving students an opportunity to listen and repeat each one.

3 Give students five minutes to do this and then elicit responses, recording useful expressions on the board.

Answers

2 1 C **2** B **3** A **4** F **5** E **6** D

3 Sample answers

A Did you mean …? You wanted me to …?

B What I'm trying to say is …; To put it another way …; I guess I mean …

C Something they have in common is that …; One similarity is that …

D The first photo is of …, whereas the second …; I think the biggest difference is that …

E He/she could be …; It looks like …; I'd say …

F It's a sort of …; I think it's something for …

ADDITIONAL PRACTICE | **Teacher's Book** p.154/187 Photocopiable 13A *Useful expressions*

Long turn (Part 2)

Aim

- to complete an exam-style speaking task (Speaking, Part 2) and to reflect on areas to improve

Elicit what students remember about the Long Turn task, then go through the **Exam Focus** on page 206 with students, on eText if using.

4 – 5 Put students in pairs and ask them to nominate a Student A and Student B. Tell them that Student A should read the task aloud as the Examiner and then give Student B about one minute to answer, after which Student A should say *Thank you* to indicate the time is up. Then Student B will read the follow-up question aloud for Student A to answer. Students then swap roles for the photos on page 156.

6 Give students a few minutes to reflect on and discuss the questions.

7 Students tell their partner two things they did well and two things they could improve. Then ask students to swap partners and try the task their partner did for extra practice, keeping in mind the feedback they were given.

Answers

4–7 Students' own answers

ADDITIONAL PRACTICE | **Maximiser** p.92–93, Speaking 1–4 | **MyEnglishLab: Cambridge First**, Speaking 6 *Part 2 Accuracy: Pick the right word*; Speaking 7 *Part 2 Describing pictures: Which picture is being described?*

Vocabulary focus ▶ p.134

Expressions with *mind*

Aim

- to develop vocabulary with expressions with *mind*

Warmer: A lot on your mind

Write the following sentence on the board: *Throughout dinner, she looked deep in thought as if she had a lot on her mind.* Underline the phrase *she had a lot on her mind* and elicit the meaning (if something is on your mind, you keep thinking or worrying about it). Ask students if they can think of any other phrases that use the word *mind*. Elicit ideas and write them on the board.

1 Students read the sentences and choose the correct meaning, then compare their answers in pairs. Check answers as a class and ask students which expressions are new to them.

Answers

1 **1** A **2** B **3** B **4** A **5** B **6** A **7** B **8** A

Speaking

Aim

- to give spoken practice using expressions with *mind*

2 Give students a few minutes to plan their answers, then put them in pairs to discuss. Circulate while students are working and check they are using the expressions correctly.

Suggested answers

2 **1** I'm in two minds whether to …
2 My mind went blank./It slipped my mind.
3 put my mind at rest/take my mind off …
4 I need to take my mind off …

Verbs with similar meanings

Aim

- to compare and contrast verbs with similar meanings

Warmer: 'I'll think about it' dialogue

Write the following dialogue on the board:

A: ....
B: I'll think about it.
A: ....
B: I told you, I'll think about it.

Put students into pairs and ask them to speculate about what A might be saying. Encourage them to think of at least three different scenarios. Then ask each pair to choose one of their scenarios and write the dialogue, which they will then read for the class with some expression.

If you have a very able class, you could ask them to perform one of their scenarios without writing it down first. If you have a very small class, students may share more than one of their scenarios, swapping parts A and B. Finally, elicit the meaning of *think* in the dialogue (consider) and tell students that in this lesson they are going to compare and contrast a range of verbs with similar meanings related to thinking.

3 Students complete the activity individually. Then ask them to compare their answers in pairs before you check as a class.

4 Students complete the activity individually. Then ask them to compare their answers in pairs before you check as a class.

5 Elicit answers as a class. Read the **Language Tip** and elicit additional examples for each use of *think*, e.g. *I'm thinking of/about taking up tennis; What did you think of the colour?; What do you think about the new policies?; I can't stop thinking about the dream I had last night.*

Answers

3 1 store 2 recall 3 reflected 4 reminded

4 1 believe 2 judge 3 considering 4 thinking 5 believed/thought 6 consider 7 judge 8 thinking

5 1 1, 4, 7, 8
2 2, 6, 7

ADDITIONAL PRACTICE | **Maximiser** p.93, Vocabulary 1–3

Use of English focus ▶ p.135

Multiple-choice cloze (Part 1)

Aim

- to complete an exam-style multiple-choice cloze task (Reading and Use of English, Part 1)

Warmer: Hoarding

Elicit the meaning of *hoard* (to collect and save large amounts of stuff such as food, money, etc, especially when it is not necessary to do so). Ask students to discuss in pairs whether they are hoarders or whether they find it easy to part with old belongings.

Elicit what students remember about Reading and Use of English, Part 1, then go through the **Exam Focus** on page 200 with students (on eText if using) to check.

1 Give students a minute to read the text quickly to find out what problem the writer describes. Elicit the answer. Remind students that this relates to strategy 1.

2 Refer students to strategies 2–3 and focus on the first gap (0). Read the sentence with each of the options A–D in turn and elicit which one fits. Do the second gap (1) as another example with the class by eliciting some predictions of what could fit in the gap without looking at the options. Then go through the options A–D for (1), reading each one aloud in the sentence and elicit which one fits. Check with the class that the chosen word fits with the words either side of the gap.

Ask students to complete the remaining gaps, keeping the strategies in the **Exam Focus** displayed on eText for reference during the activity.

3 Students discuss the answers (and reasons) in pairs. Check answers as a class.

4 Give students a few minutes to discuss, then ask a few students to report back on what their partner said.

Answers

1 C

2 1 A 2 D 3 A 4 B 5 D 6 B 7 C 8 B

3–4 Students' own answers

ADDITIONAL PRACTICE | **Maximiser** p.94, Use of English 1 | **MyEnglishLab: Cambridge First**, Vocabulary 11 *Comparing and contrasting: Objects*

Listening focus ▶ p.136

Multiple choice: short extracts (Part 1)

Aim

- to complete an exam-style listening task (Listening, Part 1)

Warmer

Focus attention on the picture. Elicit what the man is doing (hiking in a remote place). Ask students if they have ever been to a remote place away from civilisation. Ask students to share their experiences in small groups. Ask each group to tell the class who in their group has had the most interesting experiences.

Elicit what students remember about Listening, Part 1 and then refer them to the **Exam Focus** on page 204 to check. Go through the **Exam Focus** with students on eText if using, checking they understand everything.

1 Ask students to read the questions and underline key words (see answers). Play the recording twice, then elicit answers. If students have found the task challenging, open the audio script on eText and refer to it as you go through the answers.

Answers

1 1 C 2 B 3 B 4 C 5 A 6 C 7 C 8 B

Key words:
1 woman, difficult, learning Chinese
2 say about them
3 travelling alone, disadvantage
4 he thinking of doing … leaves university
5 woman, leaving a message
6 why woman doesn't enjoy parties
7 woman, how feel about problem
8 why like photo

ADDITIONAL PRACTICE | **Maximiser** p.94, Listening | **MyEnglishLab: Cambridge First**, Listening 6 *Listening to understand inferred information: What's going on?*; Listening 9 *Listening to understand attitude: What did they say?*

Speaking

Aim
- to provide spoken practice

2 Students discuss the questions in small groups.

Answers

2 Students' own answers

MyEnglishLab tip:
Exam links

Each exercise in MyEnglishLab has a tip text included. This usually links the exercise with the skills and part of the Cambridge First Exam that it provides practice for. Encourage students to click on the 'tip' before they try the activity.

Vocabulary

expressions with *time*

Aim
- to develop knowledge of expressions with *time*

3 Write *Time flies* on the board. Ask if students have heard this expression before and what it means (time passes very quickly). Then ask them to match the sentences with the responses.

4 Put students into pairs to discuss the questions, then elicit a few responses.

Answers

3 1 A 2 C 3 D 4 B

4 Students' own answers

ADDITIONAL PRACTICE | **Maximiser** p.95, Vocabulary 1

Grammar focus ▶ p.137

Reflexive pronouns

Aim
- to review how reflexive pronouns are used in English and to practise using them

1 Display the first sentence group on eText if you are using it and elicit the difference in meaning. Repeat with the remaining sentence pairs. Then read the **Language Tip** aloud. Elicit extra examples for the first point, e.g. *I've bought myself* (NOT ~~me~~) *a new mobile for my birthday. He sends himself reminders so he never forgets a birthday.* Elicit some example sentences with intransitive verbs, such as *I remembered his birthday; I relaxed by taking a long bath.*
Then ask students to turn to the **Grammar Reference** on page 173 and talk them through it, displaying it on eText if using.

2 First review the reflexive pronouns *myself, yourself, himself/herself/itself, ourselves, yourselves, themselves.* Then circulate while students complete the activity. Students compare their answers in pairs, then check answers as a whole class.

3 Do the first question with the whole class as an example, then ask students to complete the activity individually. Students check their answers in pairs before you check as a class.

4 Put students into pairs, then give them about ten minutes to write some advice while you circulate, checking reflexive pronouns.

5 Ask each pair to share a piece of advice from their list. Or, if you have a small class, you may like to ask every pair to share their full list.

Answers

1 1 A Florence told Florence (reflexive)
B Florence told another woman
C Florence told another woman, and this was unusual (herself is used for emphasis)

2 A They both took responsibility for losing the photos.
B Suzy blamed Sam, and Sam blamed Suzy.

3 A I went there – not another person
B No one came with me.

2 1 himself 2 ourselves 3 him 4 myself
5 (-) 6 me 7 herself 8 him

3 1 The president of the bank himself apologised for losing my money.

2 I (myself) never have a problem remembering numbers (myself).

3 Even Einstein himself occasionally made mistakes with numbers.

4 I think you should tell him yourself.

4–5 Students' own answers

ADDITIONAL PRACTICE | **Maximiser** p.95, Grammar 1–2 | **Teacher's Book** p.154/188 Photocopiable 13B *Reflexive revelation* | **eText IWB** Extra activity

Writing focus ▶ p.138

Speaking

Aim

- to introduce the topic of apologies in preparation for the writing task and to provide spoken practice

1 Focus attention on the picture and ask students what they think might have happened. Put students in pairs to discuss the questions, then elicit a few responses for each.

Answers

1 Students' own answers

Informal email (Part 2)

▶ p.138

Aim

- to complete an exam-style writing task (an informal email) using appropriate phrases

Ask students to turn to the **Writing Reference** on page 182, and display it on eText if using. Read the task aloud, then give students a few minutes to read the letter. Talk through the *Dos* and *Don'ts* with the class, checking that students understand everything.

2 Students choose the correct word in the phrases then compare their answers with a partner before you check as a class.

3 Students identify the phrases that can be used in an informal email. Check answers as a class.

4 Students match the phrasal verbs with the correct meanings. Check answers as a class.

5 Read the rubric and the **Exam tip** aloud and ask students to find intensifiers that collocate with *sorry* and *disappointed*. Remind them that it is useful to learn these fixed phrases.

6 Give students a few minutes to discuss the task in pairs and decide what information to include and in which paragraph. Ask each pair to make brief notes. The writing activity could be set as a homework activity. Alternatively, give students about 35 minutes to complete it in class.

Answers

2 1 owe 2 can't, forgetting 3 extremely
4 must 5 give 6 avoided 7 out of 8 up to
9 fault 10 won't 11 terribly 12 cause

3 3, 5, 7, 8, 9, 10, 11

4 1 not my responsibility – wasn't up to me (8); impossible to avoid – can't get out of (7) 2 informal writing

5 awfully, deeply, enormously, extremely, incredibly, terribly

6 Students' own answers

7 Sample answer

Hi Sam,

I'm extremely sorry to say that there is a problem with looking after Bonzo in August. Unfortunately, those are the dates that my uncle is coming over from Australia and staying with us. I'm afraid that we're all going to visit my grandmother for a few days for a big family reunion. When we made the arrangement about Bonzo, I thought my uncle was coming over in September. I've just found out that he has changed his plans, and now it won't be possible to get out of the family reunion.

I hope that it won't be too difficult for you to find someone else to look after Bonzo, he is such a lovely dog. I could ask some friends if they would be able to look after him, if you like. Would he be happy in a house where there are other dogs? Let me know what you think. I hope this doesn't cause you too much inconvenience.

Hope to see you soon,

Love,

Sally

Additional Activity: Perform a dialogue

In pairs, students prepare a short dialogue (about 6–8 lines) about one of the situations mentioned in Speaking Activity 1. Assign each pair one of the situations to ensure that a good range of situations is covered. While they are preparing the dialogues, display the language from Activity 2 on eText as a prompt. Students can then perform their dialogues for the class. If students are very shy about performing in front of the class, they could alternatively record their dialogue as a radio play/short video and then play it through the IWB.

ADDITIONAL PRACTICE | **Maximiser** p.95, Writing 1–2 | **MyEnglishLab: Cambridge First,** Writing 7 *Informal functions in writing: Sort out this muddle*

Review ▶ p.139

Aim

- to revise the structures and vocabulary covered in Unit 13

1–3 Ask students to complete the activities, circulating to provide assistance. Ask students to check in pairs before checking as a class on eText. Alternatively, set as a homework activity and then go through the activities on eText to check.

Answers

1 **1** couldn't **2** able **3** able **4** unable **5** could **6** know **7** ability **8** managed **9** unable **10** couldn't

2 **1** A **2** B **3** B **4** B **5** C **6** B **7** A **8** C

3 **1** did/had done it (by) themselves
2 blamed herself for (causing) the
3 reminds herself of/about
4 apologised for being
5 is/was thinking of becoming
6 considers himself (to be)

ADDITIONAL PRACTICE | **Online Testmaster**, Unit 13 Test, | **MyEnglishLab: Cambridge First,** Mock Test: Listening

Say what you mean

14

Listening and vocabulary focus ▶ p.140

Speaking

Aim

- to introduce/review vocabulary related to speech and gestures and to provide spoken practice

Warmer: Different accents

Ask students if they have heard any different accents in English. If you have an IWB, open the site **http://accent.gmu.edu/browse_atlas.php** where you can browse the world map and click on flags in many countries to hear a standard paragraph being read out with a representative accent of that region. Choose three or four places to listen to, e.g. the place you are in, London, Edinburgh, Sydney, Texas.

1 Put students into pairs to discuss the questions, then elicit a few responses for each from the class.

2 Check that students understand the words for each gesture by inviting them to do each one. Then discuss the question as a class.

3 Give students a few minutes to discuss the questions with their partner, before brainstorming a few ideas as a class.

Answers

1 Students' own answers

2 **1** that they don't care/don't know **2** surprise
3 agreement/disagreement (In some cultures e.g. India, nodding your head from side to side means 'no'. It can express frustration, too.)
4 show that they are hoping for good luck **5** impatience or annoyance

3 Students' own answers

ADDITIONAL PRACTICE | **Maximiser** p.96, Vocabulary 1

Multiple matching (Part 3)

Aim

- to complete an exam-style listening task (Listening, Part 3)

Elicit what students remember about Listening Part 3, then refer them to the **Exam Focus** on page 205 to check. Go through the strategies with the class, on eText if you are using it.

4 Refer to the strategies and remind students to do strategies 1 and 2 before you play the recording. Then play the recording. Read the **Exam Tip** aloud, then play the recording again for students to check and complete their answers. Students can compare their answers in pairs before you check as a class.

5 Elicit some phrases to use for sharing opinions and write them on the board e.g. *I'm absolutely convinced that ...; I think generally ...; I'm not sure about ...; I'm in two minds about ...; I definitely disagree with ...*, etc. Put students into pairs to discuss their opinions with their partner. Ask the class if any of the statements were contentious for them and elicit a few opinions.

Answers

4 Speaker 1 H Speaker 2 B Speaker 3 A Speaker 4 G Speaker 5 C

5 Student's own answers

ADDITIONAL PRACTICE | **Maximiser** p.96, Listening 1–2 | **MyEnglishLab: Cambridge First**, Listening 4 *Listening for gist: Spot the gist*

say, speak, talk and *tell*

Aim

- to compare and contrast the uses of *say, speak, talk* and *tell*

Warmer

Write *say, speak, talk* and *tell* on the board. Tell students that although these four words are similar, they are used in slightly different ways. Put students in pairs and ask them to write four sentences, each containing one of the words (the tense can be changed). While they do this, circulate and note down any errors you hear. Students will refer back to these sentences later in the lesson.

6 Ask students to complete the sentences, then compare their answers with a partner before you check as a class.

Additional activity

You may like to refer to the BBC Learning English website **http://www.bbc.co.uk/worldservice/learningenglish/radio/specials/1535_questionanswer/page34.shtml**, where a student has written in to ask what the difference is between *say, speak* and *tell*. A teacher replies with a recording that could be played through the IWB. Alternatively, students could read the audio script, which also appears on the page.

7 Students complete the table. You could invite students to use the *Longman Dictionary of Contemporary English* (Online/App/Paper) to help complete the table. Students compare their answers in pairs, then check as a class.

8 Students choose the correct verbs for expressions 1–6. Check answers, then give students a few minutes to match the expressions with the meanings A–F. To finish, ask students to look again at the sentences they wrote in the warmer and make any necessary corrections. Ask some students to share their sentences with the class.

Answers

6 **1** speak **2** says **3** tell **4** say **5** say **6** talking

7 *tell:* the difference, a joke, lies, (someone) a secret, a story, the truth

talk: rubbish, sense, to yourself

8 **1** saying D **2** speak F **3** say C **4** say E **5** speaking B **6** speaks A

Additional activity

Ask students to re-read the collocations in Activities 7 and 8 and underline any that are either new for them or that they can imagine being particularly useful. Students write three questions containing one of these collocations, then work in small groups to ask and answer their questions.

Sample questions: *Is it always best to tell the truth in every situation? Can you tell us a joke? Do you ever talk to yourself?*

Ways of speaking

Aim

- to review and expand vocabulary related to ways of speaking, and to provide spoken practice

9 Elicit what each word means, demonstrating if necessary, then ask students to complete the sentences. Check answers as a class and make sure that students understand the difference between *mumble* (to say something too quietly or not clearly enough, so that other people cannot understand you) and *mutter* (to speak in a low voice, especially because you are annoyed about something, or you do not want people to hear you).

10 Ask the pairs to make a list of at least three situations for each question.

Answers

9 1 yelled 2 whisper 3 mutters 4 mumble

10 Students' own answers

ADDITIONAL PRACTICE | **Maximiser** p.97, Vocabulary 1–3 | **Teacher's Book** p155/189 Photocopiable 14A *Speak up*

Grammar focus ▶ p.142

it is, there is

Aim

- to compare and contrast the uses of *it is* and *there is*

Warmer: Snacks discussion

Tell students that the context for this lesson is *customs* (as in habits or traditions) and that they are going to start by discussing the custom of snacks.

Elicit the meaning of the word *snack.* (*Verb = to eat small amounts of food between meals or instead of a meal, e.g. I'm trying not to snack between meals. Noun = a small amount of food that is eaten between main meals or instead of a meal, e.g. I grabbed a quick snack. Drinks and light snacks are served at the bar.*)

Then write the following questions on the board and ask students to discuss them in pairs:

Do people generally snack in your country? What are the most popular snacks?
What were your favourite snacks as you were growing up?
Do you think snacking is a healthy habit?

If students are studying abroad, this could be an ideal opportunity to share some information about typical snacks in the local country, or to bring a typical snack to class for students to try.

1 Ask students to work in pairs to discuss and choose the correct pronouns, then check as a class. Ask students to turn to the **Grammar Reference** on page 170 and display it on eText if you are using it. Talk students through the **Grammar Reference**, checking that they understand everything.

2 Complete the first sentence with the class as an example, then ask students to complete the rest in pairs. Elicit the answers.

3 Elicit some ideas. Ask if any of the customs are true in the students' own countries.

4 Ask each student to make a list of four customs. Then put students into small groups to describe their customs.

Answers

1 1 It 2 There 3 There 4 It 5 It 6 It

2 1 It is 2 It is 3 There 4 There is

3 Suggested answers:
1 Argentina 2 Saudi Arabia 3 China 4 Japan

4 Students' own answers

Key word transformations (Part 4)

Aim

- to complete an exam-style cloze task (Reading and Use of English, Part 4)

5 Elicit what students remember about Reading and Use of English Part 4 in the exam, then refer students to the **Exam Focus** on page 201 to check. Read the **Exam Tip** aloud.

Allow about twelve minutes for students to complete the exercise as an exam practice. Then focus students' attention on the **Exam Tip** again and ask them to read their answers to check that the key word remains unchanged and to check that all answers are 2–5 words (including the key word.) Students compare their answers in pairs, then check as a class.

Answers

5 1 it was great to see/seeing 2 there's going to be
3 it's/was wonderful (that) 4 there used to be
5 there was no need 6 it might be

ADDITIONAL PRACTICE | **Maximiser** p.97, Grammar 1–2 | **eText IWB** Extra activity

Speaking focus ▶ p.143

Interview (Part 1)

Aim

- to complete an exam-style speaking task (Speaking, Part 1)

1 Ask students to work in pairs to tick the things they should do in Part 1 in the Speaking test.

2 Ask students to check their answers by reading the **Exam Focus** on page 206.

3 Give students about five minutes to write their questions, circulating to provide help, and encouraging students to write open questions.

4 Students work in small groups to practise asking and answering each other's questions.

Answers

1 In Part 1, candidates would be expected to answer personal questions.

2–4 Students' own answers

Additional activity:
Which was the most interesting question?

Ask each group to decide which was the most interesting question from their group (if you have a class with fewer than three groups, ask them to select the two most interesting questions). Write these questions on the board (checking they are accurate) and give students a few minutes to discuss the questions that were not from their own group. Finish by eliciting a few answers for each of the questions on the board.

Long turn (Part 2)

Aim

- to complete an exam-style speaking task (Speaking, Part 2)

5 Focus attention on the photos and exam task (magnify these in eText if using). Then ask students to tick the boxes indicating what they need to do. Check as a class, then refer students to the **Exam Focus** on page 206 for more information.

6 Read the **Exam Tip** aloud, then put students into pairs for the activity. Each pair should decide who is Student A and who is Student B and then take turns to do the task. Encourage the student acting as the examiner to time the other student and to say *Thank you* when the time is up.

Answers

5 ✓: 1, 2, 4, 7

6 Students' own answers

ADDITIONAL PRACTICE | **Maximiser** p.98, Speaking 1–2 | **MyEnglishLab: Cambridge First**, Speaking 3 *Part 1 Assessment: Who is the examiner describing?*; Speaking 4a *Part 1 Giving complete answers: Choose how to fill the gap*; Speaking 4b *Responding to pictures: Practice*; Speaking 8 *Part 2 Assessment: Put the examiner's comments together*

Reading focus ▶ p.144

Speaking and vocabulary

Aim

- to introduce the topic of dogs and vocabulary associated with dogs in preparation for the reading text and to provide spoken practice

1 Ask students to discuss the question in pairs. Finish by eliciting a few responses and checking that students understand all of the vocabulary.

Answers

1 Students' own answers

Gapped text (Part 6)

Aim

- to complete an exam-style reading task (Reading and Use of English, Part 6)

Elicit what students remember about Reading and Use of English, Part 6, then refer them to the **Exam Focus** on page 202 to check.

2 Tell the students you will give them 15 minutes to read the instructions and complete the task as an exam practice. If students have questions about vocabulary, encourage them to guess the meanings from context. When students have finished, read the **Exam Tip** aloud and give students a few minutes to check that the text makes sense and that they haven't used a sentence more than once.

3 Students compare their answers in pairs, then check as a class.

Answers

2 1 F 2 A 3 G 4 D 5 E 6 C

3 Students' own answers

Speaking

Aim

- to provide spoken practice on the topic of pets

4 Students discuss the questions in small groups. Ask one student from each group to tell the class about their discussion.

Answers

4 Students' own answers

ADDITIONAL PRACTICE | **Maximiser** p.99, Reading 1–3 | **eText IWB** Extra activity | **MyEnglishLab: Cambridge First**, Reading 13 *Text structure – comparisons and connections: What's the connection?*

Vocabulary

idioms: animals

Aim

- to expand vocabulary of animal idioms

Warmer

Write on the board *to kill two birds with one stone* and elicit the meaning (to solve two problems with one solution). Ask if students have a similar equivalent in their language. Elicit any other animal idioms they know in English or in their own language.

5 Ask students to read and match the sentences and responses. They can work in pairs, then check as a class.

6 Encourage students to make four sentences about their own lives using some of the idioms. Put students in small groups to share their sentences.

Answers

5 1 F 2 E 3 B 4 A 5 C 6 G 7 D 8 H

6 Students' own answers

Additional activity: Useful websites

There are several good websites for animal idioms. The website *Idiom Connection* has definitions and examples of many animal idioms (divided by animal) and an online quiz at

http://www.idiomconnection.com/animal.html#BQ
http://www.idiomconnection.com/animal.html .

On *YouTube*, there is a three-minute video series by BBC Learning English in which a teacher explains common animal idioms, including:

dog idioms: **http://www.youtube.com/watch?v=33V_fE5Mde4**

horse idioms: **http://www.youtube.com/watch?v=AX0T2oxv0Jo**

insect idioms: **http://www.youtube.com/watch?v=BiiXVGa1axg&feature=relmfu** .

ADDITIONAL PRACTICE | **Maximiser** p.100, Vocabulary 1 | **Teacher's Book** p.156/190, Photocopiable 14B *Context and Meaning* | **eText Game**: Sheep out (animal idioms) | **MyEnglishLab: Cambridge First**, Use of English 6 *Idioms: Getting it exactly right*

Grammar focus ▶ p.146

Subject/Verb agreement

Aim

- to practise making verbs agree with subjects

Warmer

Students discuss with their partner what they remember about *Inside a Dog's World* on page 144.

1 Ask students to choose the correct option in each sentence then check with a partner. Check as a class.

2 Students work through the activity in pairs, then check as a class. Display the **Grammar Reference** on page 175 on eText if you are using it and go through it with the class, checking that students understand everything.

3 - 4 Ask students to complete the activity then compare their answers in pairs before you check as a class. Then ask students which fact they found most surprising.

5 Give students a few minutes to complete the sentences while you circulate and then put students into small groups to share their sentences.

Answers

1 **1** bothers **2** are **3** think **4** gets **5** seems **6** is **7** is

2 **1** C **2** F **3** G **4** E **5** B **6** A and D **7** D

3 **1** have **2** it **3** is **4** understand **5** has **6** knows **7** has **8** are

4 **1** are **2** have **3** seems **4** prefer **5** have **6** is **7** has **8** is

5 Students' own answers

ADDITIONAL PRACTICE | **Maximiser** p.100, Grammar 1–2

Use of English focus

▶ p.147

Open cloze (Part 2)

Aim

- to complete an exam-style Use of English task (Reading and Use of English, Part 2)

Warmer: Picture match

Before class: Find pictures on the internet of the following animals: a bonobo ape, dolphin, whale and parrot and save them on a slide that can be opened on your IWB, eg. Activestudio slide, Smart Notebook slide. Type the name of each animal individually on the slide so that the names are free moving and not lined up with any particular picture. Hide these with a screenshade so that the pictures are visible but not the words. Save the slide.

In class: Open the slide and elicit any names of the animals students know. Then, reveal the names and ask a volunteer student to match them on behalf of the class. Ask students to discuss the following question in pairs: *How do you think each of these animals communicates?* Finish by eliciting ideas for each and writing them on the board.

Elicit what students remember about Reading and Use of English, Part 2, then refer students to the **Exam Focus** on page 201 to review what is required in this section of the exam. Display it on eText and go through it briefly with the class.

1 Emphasise that students should read the article but not fill in the gaps yet. Remind students of the value of skim reading for gist in the exam before answering the questions. Students discuss the questions in pairs, then check with the class.

2 Students complete the gaps. Then, read the **Exam Tip** aloud and ask students to fill in any blanks they have left and to check in pairs that their answers make sense and are spelt correctly.

3 Elicit the answers and write them on eText. Ask students to circle the answers related to subject/verb agreement.

4 Students discuss the questions in pairs. During this discussion, you could display your pictures of animals from the warmer as an additional prompt.

Answers

1 **1** Kanzi is an ape that can understand some human language.
2 Some think animals can't speak because they haven't enough tongue control; others believe it is because they haven't got the necessary gene.
3 The species which can copy sound because they might be able to tell us more about how human language developed.

2 **1** is **2** from **3** While/Whilst/Although **4** in **5** each **6** such **7** of **8** into

3 answers 0, 1

4 Students' own answers

ADDITIONAL PRACTICE | **Maximiser** p.100, Use of English 1

Writing focus ▶ p.148

Essay (Part 1)

proofreading

Aim

- to provide practice of proofreading and to complete an exam-style writing task (Writing, Paper 1)
- Put students in pairs and ask them to write five statements on a sheet of paper on the topic of 'young people and technology' with the following stems: *I think that young people are …; The government should …; Chatting online is …; It's rude when …; It's surprising that …*
- Ask them to exchange their statements with another pair and check for mistakes in grammar or spelling and return them to the original pair. Ask students to keep the statements to refer to later. Elicit examples of words students typically spell incorrectly and how to check for them. Ask if they use any particular techniques (mnemonics, pronouncing silent letters, etc.).

1 Explain that each sentence contains a spelling mistake. See how quickly they can identify the mistakes. Students match the mistakes to types A–D. Check answers in pairs before going through as a class.

2 Put students in pairs to discuss the questions. Elicit opinions of the statements from the class. Ask them to look back at the statements they completed. Are there any other ideas that they think should be included in the topic of 'young people and technology'?

3 Ask a volunteer to read the task aloud and if using eText IWB, display on the IWB. Students read through the essay to identify errors. Give them a time limit of five minutes to do this, reminding them that this is the time they should be setting aside in the exam to check their own work. Check answers as a class and elicit response to the content of the essay.

4 Ask students to turn to page 160 and read through the task. Brainstorm some suggestions for the third point and write them on the board (guide dogs/dogs for the blind, dogs as companions for old people, dogs to help disabled people or people with learning difficulties, sheep dogs, for example). Set a time limit of thirty-five minutes to plan and write the essay.

5 Read the **Exam Tip** aloud and explain that students now have five minutes to check their work before they hand it in. Alternatively, put students in pairs to check each other's work.

Answers

1 **1** C definitely **2** A government **3** B necessary **4** D friends **5** C dependent **6** A surprising **7** A answer **8** D receive

2 Students' own answers.

3 **1** extremely **2** arrangements **3** believe **4** because **5** hurtful **6** suffering **7** technology **8** beneficial

4 Students' own answers

5 **Sample answer**

Dogs are the most useful animals to humans. Do you agree?

There is no doubt that dogs are extremely useful animals for humans. They can serve as guard dogs to protect people and their property. They bark if a stranger approaches, and if they see that their owner is in danger, they will rush to defend them. In many ways, this is better than having an alarm.

Dogs are also used by the police. They have a strong sense of smell and can help find illegal drugs, for example. They are also involved in finding people who are missing or rescuing people from danger. These dogs need very special training.

Some dogs work to support people who are blind or deaf. They act as their eyes and ears. Guide dogs can make a huge difference to the lives of their owners, allowing them to live more independent lives.

These are only a few examples of the different ways that dogs help humans. Over the years dogs have developed a very special relationship with humans. As well as working for humans they are also good companions. For all these reasons, I agree that dogs are the most useful animals.

ADDITIONAL PRACTICE | **Maximiser** p.101, Writing 1–4 | **MyEnglishLab: Cambridge First**, Writing 19 *Assessing: What does the examiner think?;* Writing 20 *Assessing: Who are they judging?*

Progress test 3 ▶ p.149

Aim

- to revise structures and vocabulary covered in Units 11–14

Set the tests as a homework activity and then go through the interactive activities on eText to check the answers.

Answers

1 1 There 2 are 3 There 4 are 5 has 6 likes 7 have 8 is 9 it 10 There

2 1 B 2 A 3 C 4 C 5 A 6 B 7 B 8 C

3 1 over/through 2 off 3 in 4 off 5 on 6 in 7 of/in 8 through 9 over/in 10 off 11 into 12 ahead/through/on 13 down 14 in 15 of

4
1 If Sarah had listened to her parents she <u>will</u> never have become a world champion. (would)
2 If my father <u>doesn't</u> speak Russian, he wouldn't have got the job in Moscow. (didn't speak/hadn't spoken)
3 If I had saved more money I would <u>been</u> able to go on holiday next month. (be)
4 If I were younger I <u>work</u> much harder. (would work/would be working)
5 If only that car <u>doesn't</u> cost so much, I would buy it. (didn't)
6 I wish my brother <u>help</u> me more with my homework. (would help/helped)
7 Suppose we <u>will not</u> go to the party this evening. (didn't)
8 I'd rather you <u>come</u> home before midnight. (came)
9 You aren't allowed <u>using</u> Facebook in the college library. (to use)
10 It was a waste of time doing all that research. We <u>needn't to do</u> it. (needn't have done/didn't need to do)
11 They have just <u>have</u> their car stolen. (had)
12 We're getting a friend <u>looked</u> after our house while we're away. (to look)
13 After trying several times we <u>could finally get</u> tickets for the show. (were finally able to get/finally got)
14 I need to remind <u>me</u> of my passwords. (myself)
15 You shouldn't blame <u>myself</u> for losing your wallet – it wasn't <u>my</u> fault. (*either* me, my *or* yourself, your)

5 1 C 2 D 3 B 4 A 5 B 6 C 7 A 8 A

6 9 few 10 until 11 which 12 as 13 used 14 his 15 had 16 on

7 17 impossible 18 competitors 19 successful 20 especially/specially 21 visual 22 imagination 23 helpful 24 effective

8 25 aren't allowed to 26 needn't have called 27 would rather I didn't 28 wishes he could/he were able to/he was able to 29 reminded him to text her 30 didn't manage to/couldn't manage to

ADDITIONAL PRACTICE | **Maximiser** p.102–103, Use of English | **Online Testmaster** Unit 14 Test, Progress Test 3 | **MyEnglishLab: Cambridge First**, Mock Test: Speaking; Vocabulary 5 *Phrases with 'have'*; Vocabulary 6 *Phrases with 'take'*

MyEnglishLab tip:
Mock Speaking paper

Students will need a partner for these activities and someone to act as 'examiner'. You can print the tasks for use in class if necessary. Students could do the mock test in groups of four, with one pair completing Parts 1–4 as candidates while the other pair act as examiners, time-keeping and noting down any good vocabulary/phrases the candidates use. After pairs swap roles, give them time to discuss the feedback on what they need to improve on.

Audio scripts

Unit 1, Speaking, Activity 4

01

1 How do you usually relax when you have some free time?

2 What do you do when you stay in? Where do you go when you go out?

3 Do you like being in a large group or would you rather be with a few close friends?

Unit 1, Speaking, Activity 5

02

Speaker 1: I usually find watching TV quite relaxing but it depends on my mood.

Speaker 2: I tend to stay in on weekdays though I sometimes have friends round.

Speaker 3: Playing the guitar is good fun.

Speaker 1: Doing yoga helps me to switch off.

Speaker 2: I'm really into computer games.

Speaker 3: I go out for a pizza now and again.

Unit 1, Speaking, Activity 9

03

1 Yes, a sister.

2 I'm hoping to go on an activity holiday in this country and learn water-skiing and other things, but my parents want me to go to the beach with them in Spain.

3 His name is Thomas and I've known him all my life. He's the person I'd phone if I had any problems because he's always there for me and he gives me good advice. I'm really fond of him and I think we'll always stay in touch.

4 I'm sorry. Would you repeat the question, please?
OK, thanks. Well, some people think it's a bit boring, because there isn't a lot to do in the evenings, but I love it. It's near the mountains, but also not too far from the beach.

Unit 1, Listening, Activity 2

04

Speaker 1: I suppose I've always been mad about music. I used to listen to my dad's favourite rock bands from the sixties but now I'm just into the same stuff as my friends – hip hop mainly. Some people I know always want to be different so they'll only listen to new bands that no-one's heard of. It's just a way of showing off, I think. My group of friends are always sharing music files and telling each other about new discoveries. I've found a lot of new bands that way. But it's the music I'm interested in, not the personalities of the band members – so I don't usually bother with Twitter or Facebook.

Unit 1, Listening, Activity 4

05

Speaker 2: Some people I know aren't prepared to pay anything for music, and that's fine. But I think you miss out a lot that way. I like to keep up with what's happening and Twitter's good for that. Artists'll tell you when they've got a song coming out, and when their next gig'll be on Facebook, too. I listen to music on my phone all day and I watch music videos before I go to sleep. I suppose you could say my taste in music's quite narrow but not everyone can like everything, can they?

Speaker 3: It doesn't matter to me what music my friends like. I think you can have other things in common with people besides music. I'm going out with a girl who has completely different tastes to me and we're quite happy! I used to pay for downloads but it's getting easier to get all the music I want for nothing. So I haven't actually bought anything for a long time. But I spend quite a lot on going to gigs. Small gigs are more fun than large ones. I usually go with a group of friends and it's really sociable.

Speaker 4: Whatever I'm doing, I'm listening to music. There's never a silent period in my day. I couldn't live without my iPod. I used to be obsessed with music videos but now I find they're all the same. At home I like playing music really loud. I'm lucky because my parents don't seem to mind. They've influenced me a lot. When I was growing up, my mum would often play seventies music and dance around the kitchen. I think that's what's made me so open to all kinds of music.

Speaker 5: I like being one of the first to discover a new band. I think artists are at their most creative when they're just starting out, so you probably won't be familiar with what's on my mp3 player. Once a band's become really famous and everyone's listening to them and following them on Twitter and Facebook, I start to lose interest. I try to see as much live music as I can because it's a completely different experience to watching a video. Often I'll download an album after I've seen the band play live.

Unit 2, Use of English, Activity 6

06

sociable
comfortable
lovable
predictable
reliable
adventurous
cautious
generous
realistic
dramatic
pessimistic
sympathetic
practical
emotional
personal
thoughtful
harmful
hopeful
meaningful

Unit 2, Listening, Activity 3

07

P = Presenter M = Max

P: As the youngest of four children, I know my older brothers and sisters always thought I had a much easier time. I didn't use to do as many jobs around the house and my parents were more relaxed about letting me do things as I got older. But has this affected my personality in any way? Our reporter, Max Berry, has been listening to psychologists at Southfield University who are doing some research into what's known as 'the birth order effect' - how your position in a family can affect your life. They've been asking people whether they believe there's any truth in this. Max, what can you tell us?

M: Well Esther, it seems that the vast majority of people believe that the oldest child's always the most successful in later life. But apparently, there's a lot of evidence to show that it's actually middle children who have the best chance of leading happy, as well as successful, lives. People also believe that the youngest child always has a problem learning to be responsible and independent, which again isn't supported by any real facts.

Unit 2, Listening, Activity 4

 08

P = Presenter M = Max

P: So, is it true, for example, that oldest children perform best in intelligence tests?

M: Well, yes. There are lots of studies which prove this to be the case. One explanation for this might be that parents often encourage the oldest child to help their younger brothers and sisters to learn new skills, especially learning to read, and this actually helps the older child become more confident and independent.

P: Interesting. So what other characteristics do oldest children have?

M: Some psychologists believe that first-borns like me often take life too seriously and worry too much. They may feel under pressure to be the best all the time, though I must say that isn't something that's ever been a problem for me. But as a young child, I do remember hating my younger brother and thinking that he was my parents' favourite, and this is something that's quite common in oldest children.

P: What about youngest children, like me?

M: Well, in families where there are three or more children, the baby of the family's often treated as just that – a baby. They're allowed to grow up more slowly. But their good points are that they're likely to question everything and to be imaginative and artistic. Just like you, Esther.

P: Are there any factors which increase the 'birth order effect' in some families?

M: According to some psychologists, it seems that in families where there are either two boys, or two girls, the birth order effect is stronger. But it can have hardly any impact on large families, or where siblings aren't close in age. Although some people believe the birth order effect is so important that it should influence really important decisions such as our choice of marriage partner.

P: So, if you're the oldest, should you marry someone who's also the oldest in their family?

M: Well, it's been suggested that two first-born children will have to work very hard to make a marriage a success, but that it'd be much easier for two third-born children because they're likely to be more relaxed. And two middle children will probably want to compete with each other, so it could be difficult for them to get on well.

P: That does make things complicated! But surely birth order isn't the most important thing which affects people's personalities?

M: Absolutely not. Before you start to examine every aspect of your life in relation to whether you were born first, middle or last, a word of caution. The influence this can have when we are children doesn't necessarily last as we become adults. Our relationships outside our family can have just as much influence on the development of our personalities.

P: Right. So it might be wise to resist blaming your brothers and sisters for everything that's gone wrong in your life! Thanks very much …

Unit 2, Grammar, Activity 2

09

Speaker 1: I've always found my nephew really cute, but it took me ages to have the confidence to be on my own with him without feeling nervous. I hadn't been around babies before so I found it a bit scary, but it's fine now.

Speaker 2: I get on well with most of the family but one of my cousins is a bit weird. He's so argumentative . It's not worth talking to him really because he just disagrees with whatever anybody says. It's a good thing he doesn't live that near.

Speaker 3: My mum got married again a few years ago and my stepfather has a daughter. Luckily, she's about the same age as me and we both love riding, so it's great to have something in common.

Speaker 4: I don't see my grandad that much as he lives hundreds of miles away. We'd like him to come and live nearer. He's quite old now but when I was younger we used to support the same football team so we always had loads to talk about on the phone.

Speaker 5: I was quite surprised when my sister married Charlie, because he's very different from her other boyfriends. But actually he's a really nice guy to have as a brother-in-law and I've promised to give him tennis lessons.

Unit 2, Speaking, Activity 2

10

A = Alana F = Federico

A: I think the relationship with a twin sister would be very important because you would probably be very close and tell her stuff you wouldn't tell other people.

F: Yes, that's very true. Even if I argue with my brother, we're still very close. But don't you think grandparents have a big influence on your life, too, because …

A: I suppose so, but it depends how often you see them. I didn't see mine very often but I did learn a lot from them and they were very patient and kind to me.

F: So were mine, even if there was a generation gap. What's your view on the father/son relationship?

A: I'm not sure, but I imagine perhaps they would share hobbies together, like, er, well, learning to drive or playing football together.

F: I suppose so. My father was much older than most fathers but I suppose it depends on your personality, too and if you have things in common.

A: I see what you mean. If you get an inspirational teacher, they have a huge effect on your life, too. I know somebody who took up, er, drama and became an actor because of the encouragement a teacher gave them.

F: Then there's …

Unit 3, Listening, Activity 5

11

I've always been interested in making lots of money and I always believed I'd be successful. My father was very proud that I'd been to university – the first in my family to do so, and I think he hoped I'd become a banker or a lawyer, and not a fruit seller like him. But instead I saw an opportunity to make money from sports shoes, which were becoming fashionable in the early 1980s, and from a humble start on a market stall my business grew rapidly. I took a lot of risks and faced an uncertain future, especially as the economic situation wasn't good at that time, but somehow I still knew things would work out. The company kept growing; by 1990 I had one hundred and twenty shops, and just before I sold the business in 1998, this figure had grown to two hundred and fifty, with over seven thousand employees.

I made £268 million from the sale and, obviously, I'd now made all the money I could ever need. I decided to take time out and enjoy myself. I spent loads of money on a yacht and luxury homes but I didn't find this lifestyle satisfying; so I decided to do something useful. I got interested in education and invested in training programmes that taught children about business. I thought this would give them the opportunity to do what I'd done.

After a while, I was bored and wanted to work again. But I didn't need any more money for myself so I decided to give the money I made to charity. I visited Africa for the first time in 2004 and saw I could offer business advice and financial support to farmers who were in difficulty. They were given small loans which, in the vast majority of cases, they were able to pay back on time.

I started thinking, and realised that the £3,000 I would spend on a suit was a fortune to most people. Even £100 could make a huge difference to someone. It was a chance to get out of poverty. So about five years ago, I started lending small amounts of money to people all over the world who had nothing, and who wanted to start their own business.

Recently, I've been involved in projects that help village communities in Africa to help themselves. We've been able to build new schools, improve access to water and invest in farm machinery. The first of these projects to be completed was a hospital in a small town in Malawi. Seeing that finished and operational was the most satisfying experience of my life – far more important to me than any business deal.

I feel very privileged to be able to help people in this way. I think it's taught me what's really important in life –

now I appreciate my family so much more and I'm not as interested as I used to be in holidays or expensive clothes. But in order to finance these projects, I need to spend about 70 per cent of my time working. Now I'm mainly involved in property companies, and it's the money I make from these that I spend on development projects in Africa.

I would advise anyone who's earning millions to give most of it away. Initially I was only interested in the security money could bring, but now it means something else to me. It means freedom to do what I want with my life. I'm much happier now than I was twenty years ago. I do understand that not having enough money can be very worrying, but it's important to realise there's a limit to how much you actually need for yourself.

People often ask me how much money I intend to give away. I don't know the answer to that exactly, but what I do know is that I wouldn't feel right if I ended up leaving a lot of money to my kids. I don't think a yacht or a Ferrari would bring them happiness – I'll make sure they have enough to buy a house, but I want them to work and earn their own money. It's important to be independent.

Unit 3, Grammar, Activity 1

12

1 I'm not as interested as I used to be in holidays.

2 Building the hospital was the most satisfying experience of my life.

3 I'm much happier than I was twenty years ago.

Unit 3, Speaking, Activity 3

13

In both pictures there are people doing something which is very important to them. In the first picture the people look very happy because they are celebrating success. It looks like a graduation ceremony. In the second picture the man looks as if he's very proud of his car because he's taking very good care of it. It looks like hard work. He probably spent a lot of money on it and it looks like it's very valuable.

I'd say that both pictures show an achievement but the first picture is celebrating an experience whereas the second picture shows someone who values an expensive thing. The graduation photo is more special because it's something you can remember for your whole life. The car can be sold or it could be damaged in an accident – it's not something that lasts in the same way. While the man might really love his car, his passion is something he does on his own. The girl in the graduation photo seems happier because she's sharing her success with her family and friends. She looks like she's having more fun than the man.

Unit 4, Listening, Activity 3

14

P = Presenter L = Leo

P: Today on the travel programme, we're reviewing a book called *Following in Shackleton's Footsteps* by Henry Worsley. It tells the story of Worsley's recent expedition to the South Pole exactly one hundred years after Shackleton's famous failed expedition of 1908. It's been chosen by my guest, Leo Stone, himself the veteran of several polar expeditions. Welcome to the programme, Leo.

L: Thank you.

P: First of all, can you tell us about Worsley and his team?

L: Sure. The really unusual thing about this trip is that Worsley and his team are all related to members of Shackleton's team. Worsley is a descendant of Shackleton's captain, Frank Worsley.

P: So they had some unfinished family business.

L: Exactly. Worsley took the compass Shackleton used and his diary all the way to the South Pole. Apparently this trip had been a lifelong ambition for him. Shackleton'd had to turn back before reaching the South Pole and Worsley wanted to finish the journey.

P: Amazing. Did the trip take a long time to organise?

L: Yes. It took them five years to prepare for this trip. They had to find the money, which was no easy task. As you can imagine, the costs involved were enormous. Then there was the physical training. You'd think this would be the hardest part, but Worsley'd been in the army so he was used to this kind of thing. And one of the team members had run a few marathons, so they were all relatively fit. It was actually the mental challenge that Worsley's team struggled with most; having to get their heads around a nine hundred mile journey.

P: So was the trip any easier for the twenty-first century team?

L: In some ways, yes. But they still had to walk for ten hours a day with all their equipment. And then they had to put up their tent and cook a meal in what Worsley describes as a 'frozen hell'. But Shackleton was travelling into the unknown with only a compass to guide him, while Worsley's team had a map and modern navigation equipment.

P: And did they experience any of the same problems?

L: They did. For example, Worsley and his team had to spend two days in their tent because high winds made it impossible to continue, which Shackleton also endured. But it was worse for Shackleton because they were also very low on food at that point. And one of Shackleton's men fell seriously ill, which luckily the twenty-first century team was spared.

P: Did Worsley feel confident that he would reach the South Pole?

L: Yes, but he faced some very tough moments. Like Shackleton, Worsley's team went up the Beardmore Glacier, which was incredibly dangerous with huge crevasses everywhere. And just when Worsley thought it couldn't get any worse, they reached the Antarctic plateau. This proved to be even tougher going than the glacier. It's the coldest, driest place on earth and both teams experienced symptoms of altitude sickness. It was when he came face to face with the brutality of conditions there that Shackleton began to doubt he'd ever reach the Pole.

P: Which part of the book did you enjoy the most?

L: The climax of the book is definitely when Worsley and his team arrived at the place where Shackleton decided to turn back. They arrived there on the hundredth anniversary and the excitement and sense of joy is really inspiring and memorable – better even than the part where they get to the Pole itself or the huge sense of relief at arriving back safely. There're some amazing photos, too.

P: Do you think Shackleton deserves his reputation as a great hero?

L: Yes, I do. I've always really admired Shackleton, and anyone who doesn't know anything about him should definitely read this book. His decision to turn back to save his men took great courage. That's why I think he's such a hero. He never did reach his goal and it was Roald Amundsen who finally made it to the South Pole in 1911. There are so many lessons we …

Unit 4, Speaking, Activity 3

15

A: So which two skills do you think would be the most useful?

B: Top of the list for me would be finding water and making a shelter because without these things you can't survive.

A: I'd put making a fire above making a shelter. I think learning to make a fire would be the highest priority for me because a fire can keep you warm and you can also use it to boil water so that it's safe to drink and for cooking.

B: That's true. So out of these five skills, making a fire and finding water would be the most useful.

Unit 5, Listening, Activity 4

16

My name is Sarah Willis and I'm a food historian. Have you ever wondered what our lives would be like without cooking and how easy it would be to survive in the wild eating only raw food? Well the answer is that humans are not very good at eating food that hasn't been cooked and would find it almost impossible to survive on the diet of a chimpanzee, for example. Chimpanzees do eat a lot of fruit, which would be OK for us, not just bananas but all sorts of berries too, which account for 60 percent of their diet. But the remaining 40 percent is made up of other plant food, which wouldn't really be suitable for human consumption. These plants don't contain sugar so they're bitter rather than sweet like berries. The other problem with the chimpanzee diet is that human teeth aren't strong enough to chew the huge quantities of plants that we'd need and our stomachs just wouldn't be big enough to digest it all.

But long ago, before people discovered cooking, our human ancestors must have had a diet that was quite similar to a chimpanzee's. They would have spent an awful lot of time chewing plants and raw meat in order to digest it properly. They might spend eight hours a day finding things to eat and then about six hours actually eating their food. Which didn't leave them much time for any leisure activities. So when people started cooking, life began to get a lot better. They had more time for other things and the food also tasted much better. But as well as that, cooking made it possible to preserve meat for longer, which meant they could save some food for the next day in case they didn't manage to find any.

No one knows exactly when people started cooking. But a lot of scientists believe the discovery of cooking was a really important development. They think that because of cooking, our mouths gradually became smaller and the brain became much bigger. These changes happened over thousands of years, of course. And as well as bringing about physical changes, some scientists believe the activity of cooking also introduced significant social change. They say that cooking food meant that everyone in the family ate at the same time, so it's where the tradition of sitting down together and having a family meal may have begun. But there were new risks involved too. For the first time, people had to wait until the food was cooked before they could eat. This delay between catching or finding the food and then eating it meant there was a stronger possibility it might get stolen. So the female cooks had to be protected against potential thieves by the men who were also responsible for the hunting and gathering of food.

Until a few years ago, it was thought that cooking was a relatively recent development but now tests indicate that our ancestors started cooking in Africa a very long time ago. Scientists have discovered that fire may have been used for this purpose over one million years ago, which is far earlier than was previously thought.

Scientists do know that people began cooking routinely during the last ice age around twelve thousand years ago. Cooking food was a good idea in the extreme cold because it gives more energy than raw food so cooking helped people survive this harsh environment.

Unit 5, Speaking, Activity 4

17

OK, well obviously both photos show restaurants but the similarity ends there, I think. The one on the right is a much more special kind of place. It's probably really expensive and the food will be more adventurous and interesting than in the other photo. The photo on the left shows a self-service restaurant so the atmosphere will be more casual and the food is probably more basic, such as burgers or pizza.

I'd imagine the young people at the expensive restaurant are there because they are celebrating a special occasion and they wanted to do something different. But actually, they would probably prefer to be eating in a less formal situation, like in the other photo. The people in the fast food restaurant probably go there because it's cheaper, they can eat quickly, and they don't have to dress up.

Unit 6, Speaking, Activity 4

18

Examiner: Roberto, which do you think you need more of, luck or talent, to succeed in the arts?

Roberto: I think a lot depends on luck. You need the opportunity to succeed and not everyone gets the right opportunity even if they're really talented. Then there are lots of examples of people who are really famous and successful but not very talented. I think these people need to have a lot of ambition and determination as well as luck. Would you agree with that, Beata?

Beata: I'm not sure. Basically, you're saying you don't really need talent to succeed. But you can't become successful without any talent at all.

Roberto: Yes, I suppose you are right. You don't need a lot of talent to succeed but you do need a lot of luck.

Unit 6, Listening, Activity 1

19

Extract 1

It's one of my favourite plays so I was really excited about seeing it again. But I must warn you – it's quite different from any other production I've seen. And on the whole it works. The futuristic set is stunning, very cleverly contrasted with the present-day jeans and hoodies. The specially composed music is a welcome addition and really helps to create a threatening atmosphere. But for some reason most of the action takes place in semi-darkness, so I just wish I'd been able to see everything more clearly.

Unit 6, Listening, Activity 3

20

Extract 2

A: OK. So shall we meet outside the theatre at 6.30? That'll give us time to have a coffee first.

B: But it starts at 6.45 – really early – and it won't finish until ten. I'll be starving by then!

A: Well, we could meet a bit earlier and grab a pizza or something. There are a few places to eat nearby.

B: Yeah. If we meet at six, that should give us enough time – it's not like we've got to queue for tickets or anything.

Extract 3

For all you Josh Willard fans – exciting news. Josh's new film, which is set in nineteenth century Scotland, has its premiere next week and Josh will be here in London to attend. Josh, who famously doesn't do many interviews, will appear on Channel 3's *Live Tonight*, so make sure you don't miss him talking to Ned Bryan. Then it's back to New York where he'll be starring alongside Natasha Reynolds in *The Holly Tree* at the District Theatre from the end of April …

Extract 4

The comedy festival will be held again in Lenbury this year, but with a few changes to last year's programme. The organisers have decided that this year it'll be held in the third weekend in July instead of the first. The main stage is also moving from the Lenbury Theatre to a tent in the park to provide more seats, although the theatre'll still be used for smaller gigs. This means more tickets'll be available for the main events.

Extract 5

A: So, Maria, is it true you're going to retire soon?

B: Yes. I'm going to be thirty-five soon, so it's getting harder and harder for me physically, and I'm still recovering from that last back injury I had. But the main reason's that I need to spend time with my little boy. He's only two and he's growing up so fast. I don't want to miss it.

A: So you don't enjoy being on tour any more?

B: It's not that I don't enjoy it. It's just not practical any more. It'll actually break my heart to give up dancing in public.

Extract 6

A: So, as usual, The View will be the biggest contemporary art event of the summer – not in terms of the number of artworks on display, but in the variety of art on show.

B: That's right. Everything from landscape to abstract and mostly young artists who are just beginning to make a name for themselves.

A: Although there are one or two big names as well, which'll be an added bonus for art lovers.

B: Yes, indeed. It's a shame, though, that a permanent venue can't be found for it. The museum's a bit old-fashioned and I don't think the displays are very imaginative.

Extract 7

I'm really excited about the play. It's the first time I've worked with this director and that's always quite challenging. I'm not sure if it'll be a big success or not because it is quite a depressing subject and people might not want to spend an evening in the theatre watching something that they may well find upsetting. But I think it's an important subject and theatre is all about exploring all aspects of life. So I do hope people will support it.

Extract 8

A: Who do you think will get the main part?

B: I expect it'll be Zoe. She's a good singer and dancer, but it could be Molly. I thought she did a good audition, too. Mr Panton says he's going to tell us in class on Thursday.

A: When are you starting rehearsals?

B: On Friday. It's going to be really hard work because performances start in three weeks.

A: I'll help you learn your lines, if you like.

B: Thanks. That'd be very helpful.

Unit 6, Grammar, Activity 4

21

1

A: What are you doing this weekend?

B: I'm going to the dance festival in the park. It's on all weekend.

A: Oh, I'd really like to go but my brother's moving house and I have to help him.

B: That's a shame!

A: Never mind. I'm sure you'll enjoy it.

B: Yes. It should be fun especially as I think the weather'll be good.

2

A: Hi Ben! Are you going to the film festival at the weekend?

B: Yes, on Saturday. I'm going to buy the tickets online today.

A: How much are they?

B: Only £15. I'll get you one if you like.

A: That would be great. What time does it start?

B: At 7.30. But I'm going to leave home early, at six o'clock because of the traffic. I'll pick you up on my way, if you like.

Unit 7, Speaking, Activity 2

22

Well, I'm not absolutely certain what the place on the right is but it could be an underwater hotel. The other one seems to have been built in the trees and is a hotel, too. The underwater hotel looks quite luxurious, whereas the treehouse appears to be more basic; but it's eco-friendly and it would definitely be less expensive to stay at.

It must be an interesting experience to stay at both of them, although I'd imagine the treehouse might not be such fun in bad weather. The hotel under the sea must feel a bit weird and scary at first, I think. Having said that, it would be wonderful to watch the fish without having to get wet.

Of the two, I think the treehouse would be more enjoyable to stay in because, although the underwater one would be the experience of a lifetime, guests would probably always be wondering what would happen if something went wrong.

Unit 7, Speaking, Activity 4

23

1 Well, I'm not absolutely certain what the place on the right is.

2 It could be an underwater hotel.

3 The other one seems to have been built in the trees.

4 The underwater hotel looks quite luxurious.

5 The treehouse appears to be more basic.

6 It would definitely be less expensive to stay at.

7 It must be an interesting experience to stay at both of them.

8 I'd imagine the treehouse might not be such fun in bad weather.

Unit 7, Listening, Activity 2

24

breathtaking	mysterious
inspirational	peaceful
luxurious	remote
magnificent	spiritual

Unit 7, Listening, Activity 4

25

E = Examiner P = Presenter O = Olivia

E: You will hear a journalist interviewing a travel writer, called Olivia Rees about a place called Shangri-La.

P: Today we turn to Shangri-La. The word Shangri-La is now a synonym for an earthly paradise and is used all over the world as a name for hotels, restaurants and holiday homes. But the name actually comes from a novel called *Lost Horizon* by James Hilton. This was published in 1933 and enjoyed huge popularity at the time. What made it so popular, Olivia?

O: Very little was actually known about Tibet in those days; it was a remote and mysterious place. But in the years leading up to the Second World War, people were only too keen to forget their troubles and read a fantasy about somewhere that was peaceful and harmonious.

P: The story of *Lost Horizon*'s about a group of travellers who get lost, isn't it?

O: Yes. Their plane crashes in Tibet. Luckily, they're found by guides who lead them up a steep mountain to the valley of Shangri-La. The location of the fictional lost valley is never precisely given. But on its last fateful flight the plane appears to be heading northwest to Afghanistan across the Himalayas, and Hilton clearly imagined that it landed somewhere in the west of Tibet, for which no detailed maps existed.

P: And how does he describe Shangri-La?

O: It's a very special place; like nowhere else. He describes how in Shangri-La there's no war or violence and people don't believe in material wealth. The monastery in Shangri-La has a magnificent library containing the world's greatest works of literature in every language – a place where all the wisdom of humanity is contained. This monastery's built in the shadow of a white mountain, which Hilton describes as 'the loveliest mountain on Earth' – so perfect it hardly seems to be real. And the weather in Shangri-La enables the inhabitants to live for over one hundred and fifty years. So it's like an earthly paradise.

P: What do we know about the author, James Hilton?

O: James Hilton had been inspired by articles published in *National Geographic* magazine during the 1920s by early travellers to Tibet. These provided fascinating, detailed descriptions of the scenery and the Buddhist way of life there. Hilton himself actually travelled no further than the British Library to research the location of *Lost Horizon*. But many, many people have since travelled to the region to try and find exactly where Shangri-La is set and to discover more about Buddhism.

P: Was Hilton the first person to imagine a place like this?

O: Well, actually, Hilton would have been aware of the ancient Tibetan legend of Shambhala. According to this legend, Shambhala was a kingdom, cut off from the outside world, where the people also lived in peace and harmony and which was also dominated by a magnificent white mountain. I don't think these similarities are accidental or show that Hilton had run out of ideas. It's clear he was very attracted by Tibetan values and wanted to include an authentic Tibetan idea of how a perfect society should be run.

P: There is a place actually called Shangri-La, isn't there?

O: Yes. In 2002, the county of Zhongdian renamed itself Shangri-La in order to attract investment in the tourist industry. This provides a better living for the inhabitants of Zhongdian and means they're no longer so reliant on the tea trade for survival. Thousands of tourists visit every year to see the monastery which they believe could've been the inspiration for Hilton's monastery in Shangri-La, but no one can be sure this is true

P: How similar is modern-day Shangri-La to Hilton's?

O: There's a relaxed pace of life and things seem very peaceful but visitors to modern-day Shangri-La may find it doesn't live up to their expectations, as there are several major differences. For one thing, there's no mountain which matches Hilton's perfect mountain. And for another, you won't find anyone much over the age of one hundred living there.

Unit 8, Listening, Activity 2

26

Speaker 1: In my work as a counsellor, I'm already seeing a huge increase in the number of victims of cyber-bullying on social network sites and this is a trend that can only get worse. To deal with bullying or other problems that can occur online, social networking counsellors will support people in their cyber-relationships using the same counselling skills we use today. The only difference is that, because we'll be online, it'll be easier for people to contact us when they need us – in the evenings, for example. This may mean that we'll have to change our working patterns and work out of office hours.

Speaker 2: I work as a robotics engineer for a company that makes robots to perform operations in hospitals. Robots are increasingly being used in this field, and it's a trend that'll continue to grow. We'll eventually get to a point where all operations are performed by robots, as they're perfect for doing highly-skilled work. Building robots is slowly becoming more affordable. This means that routine operations like bypass surgery will be cheaper in the future because highly-skilled, highly-paid surgeons won't be needed as much. This'll be good news for patients who are waiting for operations.

Speaker 3: The company I work for is currently developing spaceships for leisure space travel. We aim to have six spaceships taking people on trips into space, each able to carry six passengers. I'm working as a test pilot at the moment, but eventually my role will be to recruit airline pilots and train them in the skills they'll need to become spaceship pilots. We're expecting there to be a lot of public interest in our service, even though it'll only be something very wealthy individuals can afford. But it'll be the experience of a lifetime and something a lot of people will be willing to pay for.

Speaker 4: We've been operating virtually for a few years now and it's a trend that's likely to continue across the globe. We have a team of virtual lawyers, all specialising in employment law, who just charge for their advice, without adding on costs for expensive office rents and other expenses. Already, we've made legal services more affordable for people. Being accessible on the internet has encouraged people to contact us, who before wouldn't have considered hiring a lawyer. So I can see that, instead of spending most of my time with clients from the banking industry, I'll be dealing with people from all sorts of companies.

Speaker 5: Vertical agriculture, where vegetables are grown on shelves in giant glasshouses, is the answer to feeding an increasing population, especially in towns and cities where space is so limited. Vertical farmers will be able to get food from the farm to the supermarket in under two hours; quite different to today, where some food takes at least a day to reach its destination. People'll soon get used to this and start to expect a really fresh product. There are lots of other advantages, too, which I've discovered on my vertical farm: er, there's no pollution, we don't use pesticides, all the water we use is recycled and we don't have to worry about the weather.

Unit 8, Speaking, Activity 3

27

1 Actually, I'm not sure about that.

2 I agree up to a point but …

3 I suppose so.

4 That's just what I was going to say!

Unit 8, Grammar, Activity 1

28

1

Boss: So how are you getting on with the report, Amy?

Amy: I've done most of it but I still need to get some information from the sales team in Brazil before I can finish it.

Boss: OK. Good. Remember to keep it brief. Don't write loads of detail and summarise the data in graphs if you can. No one has time to read very long reports.

Amy: Don't worry, it won't be more than four pages long.

2

OK, so, it's your dream job and you know they're interviewing at least ten other people. Who wouldn't be nervous? But remember experienced interviewers want you to do your best and aren't there to catch you out, so try to forget about being nervous. One thing that can really help with the nerves is being sure of your facts. So memorise key information about where you worked and for how long. Also, find out as much as you can about your prospective employer. And ask one or two questions to show you've done your homework.

3

Angela: I've just had JPS on the phone and they say they've left three messages for me but that I haven't phoned them back. Why wasn't I given the messages?

Mike: Oh dear. Well, I haven't taken any calls from JPS. They must've rung yesterday when I was out of the office on my training course.

Angela: OK, Mike. Sorry. But I really must find out who took those calls. We can't afford to upset such an important customer.

Mike: No problem, Angela. I'll look into why the messages weren't passed on if you like.

Unit 8, Grammar, Activity 1

29

I = Interviewer L = Lauren

I: Lauren, how did you hear about this job?

L: Well, I spotted the advert while I was on the internet. I think it's something I'd be good at.

I: Being an entertainment co-ordinator will involve looking after very young children. Have you had much experience of doing this?

L: Well, I look after my niece and nephew every month and I'm taking them on a cycling holiday tomorrow.

I: Well, you might be unlucky, I'm afraid, because I've heard that it's going to rain.

L: Oh, I'm sure we'll still have a lot of fun.

I: Well, you sound very positive, and this is one of the qualities we're looking for. Anyway, enjoy your weekend!

L: Thanks.

I: Lauren, thanks for coming. We'll write soon, but don't worry if you don't hear anything for a few days.

Unit 9, Speaking, Activity 2

30

Interviewer: What do you think makes some people more successful at sport than other people?

A: I'm sorry, did you say successful?

Interviewer: Yes, that's right.

A: Thanks. Well, it's difficult to say, of course, but I suppose a lot depends on your personality: whether you are self … erm … I mean sure of your ability.

B: Yes, and also really, really want to win. You have to be … erm … hungry. What I'm trying to say is, you need to be very determined.

A: But it's not enough if you … you need the ability in the first place otherwise it doesn't matter how you are … or rather, how ambitious you are.

B: Maybe, but some people say if you practise a lot …

A: Yes but it isn't enough. There is also … right, a … you need a good body, for example, good health and you also need …

Unit 9, Speaking, Activity 4

31

Do you mean …?

I'm sorry, did you say …?

So, what you're saying is …?

OK, let me see.

Well, it's difficult to say, of course, …

As far as I know, …

Right, …

I mean …

What I meant was …

What I'm trying to say is …

… or rather, …

Unit 9, Listening, Activity 2

32

What is it that makes a champion? How much is sporting achievement down to the ability you're born with and how much to effort? And what part does luck play in the difference between winning and losing? Most top sportspeople claim that their success is down to dedication, ambition and long hours of practice. Luck is rarely mentioned; unless they happen to lose, and that's sometimes blamed on something they couldn't control, like the weather.

Unit 9, Listening focus, Activity 3

33

E = Examiner P = Presenter M = Max

E: You're going to listen to a radio interview with a sports writer called Max Wilson about luck in sport.

P: What is it that makes a champion? How much is sporting achievement down to the ability you're born with and how much to effort? And what part does luck play in the difference between winning and losing? To discuss these questions with me is sports writer Max Wilson. What's the answer, Max?

M: Most top sportspeople claim that their success is down to dedication, ambition and long hours of practice. Luck is rarely mentioned, unless they happen to lose, and that's sometimes blamed on something they couldn't control, like the weather.

P: One thing that's clear is that records go on being broken year after year. But is this because athletes are bigger and stronger than they were twenty, fifty, a hundred years ago? Or is it because sportspeople are getting more talented?

M: Well, experts say physical changes develop over a much longer time span. So it must be that people are practising longer and harder, and striving to achieve more. Sure, improvements in running shoes, tennis rackets and other technological advances play their part, but they can't account on their own for the differences in standards.

P: Could it be that sportspeople are able to achieve more these days because their talent is recognised and nourished at a younger and younger age?

M: That's certainly true of incredibly successful tennis clubs like Spartak, in Moscow. In recent years, this club's created more top twenty women players than the whole of the United States. But a seemingly exceptional natural talent in a young child is often only the product of hours and hours of expert tuition and practice, and the child is unlikely to continue to make progress at such a fast rate.

P: This is something that's discussed in Matthew Syed's book, Bounce, I believe?

M: Yes, he examines the relationship between talent, success and luck. Matthew was a British number one and top international table tennis player during the late 1990s. He lists several factors which he believes contributed to his success and which had very little to do with his own talent. Matthew says his first piece of good fortune was that when he was eight, his parents decided to buy a full-size, professional table-tennis table, which they kept in the garage, as a way of keeping their boys occupied and out of trouble. Matthew says he was also lucky that his older brother loved the game as much as he did and was happy to fight out endless battles in the garage.

P: But he was also a member of a really good club.

M: Absolutely. Matthew and his brother were lucky enough to be spotted by one of the leading table tennis coaches in the country, Peter Charters, who ran the Omega club. He also happened to be a teacher at Matthew's primary school. The Omega club wasn't a big or well-known club in those days but the tiny group of members could play whenever they liked, day or night, even though there was only one table and it was freezing in winter and incredibly hot in summer.

P: I see. So how important was the Omega club in Matthew's success?

M: Very important. The Omega club members began having considerable success and started to attract a lot of attention. The street where Matthew lived, Silverdale Road, contained an astonishing number of the country's top players, including both the men's and women's future Commonwealth champions. Was this inevitable, given the quality of the coach, the talent of the players and the location of the Omega club, or was it, as Matthew argues in the book, just a combination of lucky events? If he hadn't lived in Silverdale Road, he would have gone to a different school and he wouldn't have met Peter Charters, nor become a member of the Omega club.

P: Do you think Matthew Syed is right about the importance of luck?

M: Interestingly, a ten-year investigation into what makes people lucky or unlucky has concluded that people do make their own luck. Obviously, Matthew couldn't have succeeded without some raw talent, but he also took full advantage of the opportunities given to him, and this is what ultimately made him so successful. Lucky people are better at taking chances and finding ways to improve their situation. Unlucky people are less likely to take risks and don't like change. If there are lessons to be learnt …

Unit 10, Listening, Activity 8

 34

Speaker 1: Our friendship is now mainly conducted on the phone and by text. That's OK and we're still very close but I'd like us to spend more time together. We can have conversations about anything from politics to music to family problems. We love to have a good debate but generally we see eye-to-eye on everything. I suppose that's why we get on so well. When we first met, we used to go out together all the time but now I travel a lot for my job and she just got promoted so, unless we're very organised, it can be hard to arrange to go out. As long as we plan ahead, it's fine.

Speaker 2: We grew up together, went to the same school, spent holidays together when we were kids. He's got to know my parents, and brothers and sisters, and grandparents over the years – so he's almost part of the family. Like having another brother. And we fight like brothers, too, about all sorts of things; politics, music and sport, mainly. Watching sport on TV with him is a nightmare. Sometimes he makes me change my mind about something, so it's good in a way, because he helps me to see things from a different point of view. And he makes me laugh a lot too, which is really important.

Speaker 3: Even if we haven't seen each other for a few months, we can catch up really easily. We've got such a strong connection. Our relationship's built on trust – she knows I'll always support her in whatever way I can and she'd do the same for me. She's the best listener I know. She understands what I'm talking about even though her life is so different. I'm single and she's married. I work in a huge office and she works in her family's business. But we're not always serious; we do have a laugh together, too.

Speaker 4: We met at college at a party when we were both studying law. We have the same taste in music and films so he's the one I call if there's a gig on or a film I want to see. Or he calls me. Sometimes we go out to eat as a foursome with our girlfriends, other times it's just a boys' night out. He loves football as much as I do but he supports a different football team, so that's one thing we don't do together. Otherwise we'd end up arguing. We usually get to see each other about once a week but we text each other all the time, too.

Speaker 5: I suppose people sometimes wonder why we're such good friends. For example, he loves being the centre of attention whereas I'm quite shy. But apart from that, I think we've got a lot in common. I mean, we have a lot of shared experiences. We do the same job. We're both married with a young child and we've both lived in the same town for a few years. I'd really miss him if he moved away. I've got used to him being around. I like just being able to call him up at short notice to see if he wants to go out.

Unit 10, Speaking, Activity 1

35

A: OK, shall we begin?

B: Yes. We could start with childhood. What's really important to young kids is their friends, don't you think?

A: I suppose so, although maybe not so much if they have brothers and siblings to play with.

B: That's true, and they're still quite close to their parents at this age. Maybe friends are more important when you're teenagers, then.

A: Definitely, especially if you're quite shy. That's why they text each other a lot and go on Facebook and so on. But what you need to have at that age as well is friends to go out with.

B: Yes, and as well as that to give you confidence because at that age it can be difficult. When you're older – between nineteen and twenty maybe – they're not so …

A: Actually, … oh sorry …

B: No, that's OK. Go on.

A: I was just going to say that at college, friends are very important too. Otherwise you'd be very lonely.

B: It must also be lonely if you're looking after a baby though and you're at home every day on your own. Would you agree with that?

A: Yes, I've got no experience of this but I'd imagine that friends are essential or you'd go mad! Do you think friends are as important for men too?

B: Probably not so much. They probably don't need them as much. I'm not sure. Although I think men like doing sport together and when you have … er … when you retire from your job it must be good to have someone to go out with and do things.

Unit 11, Listening, Activity 4

36

Some people are 'risk-takers' and enjoy taking unnecessary and sometimes stupid risks, while others are 'risk-averse' and avoid taking the smallest risk at all costs. As someone who enjoys extreme mountain biking, I'm definitely a risk-taker. A lot of people find that quite hard to understand and wonder how I can enjoy something that they think's frightening and dangerous. Well, I'd like to get the facts straight and reassure people about extreme sports. I don't do extreme biking for the fear or the speed. It's the freedom I love. There are no rules and no winners and losers in this kind of sport. You're really only competing against yourself and the weather. I prefer it when it doesn't rain but I do like the conditions to be challenging, especially when there's loads of mud everywhere, which makes the surface really slippery.

Having said that, I don't go out biking to get hurt, and I haven't ever had a serious injury – and I hope I never will. There's a lot of emphasis on health and safety in all extreme sports, even though there are a few crazy people who ignore all the advice. Each sport keeps developing all kinds of equipment to help improve safety – from headgear to harnesses – and that makes extreme sports much safer than they used to be in the past.

It annoys me that a lot of people are so negative about extreme sports and say that we're irresponsible for taking so many risks. There've always been risks in sports. For example, when I played rugby at school it was basically just an organised form of fighting. There were injuries all the time. But it helped us to deal with negative emotions and it tired us out. I think that's why rugby was taught in schools in those days. And today people still get injured by doing traditional sports as much as they do from new extreme sports. Anyway, I'd say the most dangerous sport isn't snowboarding or free-running, but horse-riding. I bet the statistics show that's true.

But I'm not arguing that risk is a bad thing. So long as people take safety seriously, I think everyone needs to be more adventurous. I feel quite strongly that using all your skill and strength to meet a challenge gives you the greatest sense of being alive. There's nothing quite like it.

And another thing that people don't understand about risk-taking is that the hormones the body releases when it's experiencing stress – adrenaline's the one everyone's heard of – can actually help you to live longer; whereas being cautious and always playing it safe can cause some people to age faster, and to catch colds and flu more frequently. You could argue that doing extreme sports is actually less dangerous than sitting at home watching TV!

Anyway, my philosophy is never to worry about what might happen. If I did that, then I'd end up doing nothing and going nowhere. Don't use up lots of energy on worrying, is what I say. And that's true about any kind of activity, not just ones which involve physical risk. Whatever you're terrified of – speaking in public, or going on a journey – you should just go ahead and do it. What you'll probably find is that it wasn't nearly as bad as you'd expected.

And I believe doing extreme sports doesn't just benefit the individual, it benefits society as a whole. Society needs risk-takers for scientific developments. Otherwise we'd never have sent astronauts into space. Risk-taking is really important in business, too – you can't be a success without it.

So, basically, risk-taking is a good thing. And the kinds of people who participate in extreme sports have a need to seek excitement and stimulation. Doing extreme sports is a positive way of meeting that need. If I couldn't do extreme biking, maybe I'd get involved in some other risky behaviour – something more negative and destructive like dangerous driving, for example – which could end up doing a lot more harm.

Unit 11, Grammar, Activity 1

37

I was pretty good at skateboarding and I used to love going to the park with my two sons. The problem was that, as my sons got older, they didn't want me hanging out with them. I always wished I'd had a skater friend my own age. I was lonely and self-conscious. I wasn't worried about having an accident because I was always careful and wore protective clothing and a helmet, but I felt it was time I stopped. And then last year they opened a brand new skate park, and I said to myself 'If only I hadn't given up. If only I could start again!' But I've lost confidence. I wish I was twenty years younger, and I wish my wife wouldn't tell me I need a new hobby all the time.

Unit 11, Speaking, Activity 2

38

Examiner: Layla, here are your photographs. They show people taking risks in different situations. I'd like you to compare the two photographs and say which person you think is taking the most risks, and why.

Layla: OK. Well, both photos show sportspeople who have to take risks while doing their chosen sport. The boxer faces risks of injury every time he has a fight. There's also the risk of permanent, long-term brain damage. The yachtswoman is in a similar situation because she has to rely on her skill to avoid getting into danger or being injured. Both the boxer and the yachtswoman have to be extremely fit and well-trained. They're probably both aware of the risks they're taking. In a way, it's harder for the yachtswoman because she's completely alone, whereas the boxer has a team of people to help and support him. I think you'd have to be quite fearless and determined but also a little bit crazy to want to do dangerous sports like these.

But although the possible dangers to the yachtswoman are serious, she has all kinds of technology available to her to help her avoid dangerous situations, so I'd say that she's taking less of a risk than the boxer. I'd imagine the chances of her getting injured out at sea are quite small compared to the boxer, who probably gets injured every time he has a fight.

Unit 11, Speaking, Activity 4

39

Examiner: Which of these activities would you prefer to do, Leo?

L: To be honest, I've never thought about doing either of them. But I'd choose sailing because it's out in the open air, you're surrounded by sea and sky and it must be a wonderful feeling.

Unit 12, Listening, Activity 5

40

You'd think a prison would be the last place anyone would willingly spend money to stay in, but you'd be wrong. Former prisons all over the world've been opening their gates to paying guests. Some've been converted into luxury hotels, but others, like the Karosta Prison in Latvia, are left almost unchanged, with none of the usual comforts, thanks to the rise in popularity of what's become known as 'reality tourism'. Unlike luxury tourism, people're given the chance to have an authentic and challenging experience.

Constructed in 1905 as a jail for sailors who didn't obey orders, Karosta Prison was taken over in the 1970s by the USSR's secret service, the KGB. Today, it's a hotel with a difference. The extreme package offers the opportunity to experience life as a prisoner for a few hours. Too extreme you may think, but hundreds of people actually choose to stay here every year. Admittedly, most are on trips organised by their school, but there're growing numbers of business-people who come here on team building exercises. Not too many on their honeymoon, I suspect.

I recently spent one night as a guest in Karosta prison. The extreme package started at 9 p.m. when the prison guards lined everybody up in the courtyard and shouted out orders. The experience felt so real, it was sometimes too difficult to remember that the guards were really actors and that we were only role-playing.

Before we were taken to our cells, we had to put on a prison uniform and then one of the guards took a photo of each of us to put in our prison document. I half-expected them to take our fingerprints too, but that didn't happen. After that it was 'dinner' – which consisted of a hunk of dry bread and black tea. If you wanted coffee or a cold drink, too bad. We were then shut in our cells for the night. There were four people in every cell, so we weren't alone, but we were given strict instructions to keep silent, unless given permission to speak.

After a very uncomfortable few hours, we were finally allowed to leave, which all of my cell mates did, along with almost everyone else, without waiting for breakfast. As the advertisement says, the service is 'unfriendly and unwelcoming', which sums it up nicely. For me it was a memorable night, but not one I'd wish to repeat in a hurry. But at least it didn't cost much, at only ten euros. If this appeals to you, then go to www.Tarcenytours.com. That's: T-A-R-C-E-N-Y T-O-U-R-S. They offer a three-day tour of Latvia which includes one night's stay at Karosta.

The Alcatraz prison hotel, near Frankfurt in Germany, is also located in a former prison and is named after the famous Alcatraz prison near San Francisco. Guests have the option of choosing one of the basic cell rooms, which are very small, or one of the rather better 'comfort' rooms, which have private showers. Although the cells are clean and cheerful, there's still some discomfort; the beds, which are original and made by prisoners, are very narrow and there're still bars on the windows.

But if it's an authentic prison experience you're looking for, then the Alcatraz probably isn't for you. The staff are the most striking difference. Here, they couldn't be more friendly and welcoming; not at all what a convict would've expected here in the past.

The cost of staying at the Alcatraz is comparable to other budget hotels in the area, although I would've expected to pay a bit more. Prices range from forty-nine euros for a single to sixty-nine euros for a double in the smaller cell rooms, while the larger rooms cost about twenty euros per night more.

If you've experienced a night in a prison hotel, we'd love to hear from you. Contact us at www dot ...

Unit 13, Listening, Activity 1

41

Extract 1

A: I'm thinking about taking up Chinese. But it's very hard to learn, isn't it?

B: Well, if you just want to learn conversational Chinese, then it's not that bad. So I'd recommend you do what I did and forget writing until you can speak. The biggest challenge for me's been learning the sounds, but that's true for most learners. Once I had some idea of how words're pronounced, the rest was much more straightforward. For example, Chinese doesn't have articles and the verb system's simpler than most European languages.

Extract 2

A: How do you get on with your new colleagues?

B: Er, it's not like in my last job. There, it was completely different. It was hard to get anything done because there was so much gossip going on. It's much easier to concentrate here and I prefer that, although the atmosphere in the office isn't as much fun. It's not that they're unfriendly, it's just they're a lot more serious and focused. They don't like being distracted from what they're doing, so in the office I'd only ever bring up something that's related to the project we're working on.

Extract 3

A: You don't prefer travelling alone to travelling with someone else, do you? I'm not sure I'd like it.

B: Oh, it's fine, really. I like the fact that you don't have to make compromises about where to go or what to eat. You can make all the decisions yourself. The only thing is that when you come back, you haven't got anyone to talk to about the trip. And it's nice to have someone to remember things with.

A: What about if you're feeling ill or when things go wrong?

B: Well, you meet people while you're travelling and someone's always there to help you sort things out. People are generally very kind.

Extract 4

A: So, do you have any idea what you might do when you leave university?

B: I'd been considering doing a journalism course and getting a job with a conservation magazine. But I'm in two minds about it. Perhaps I'm not quite ready for that yet. I'd like to get more experience first of working with endangered species somewhere like Borneo.

A: You wouldn't get paid for that, would you?

B: That's the problem. But I reckon I could do that straight after I leave for a few months and then apply for a job in a zoo. I'd have lots of useful experience then.

A: That sounds like a good plan.

Extract 5

Listen, I'm really sorry but I won't be able to get home to pick you up, as I've been held up in a meeting. But don't worry because everything's arranged. I've got a taxi booked at two o'clock to take you to the station. There's some money on the shelf in the kitchen to pay the fare. So you *will* be ready, won't you? And don't forget to clean your shoes. I'm hoping to get out of this meeting in about half an hour and then I'll meet you there. If I don't see you before the interview starts, just do your best and try to relax. And good luck.

Extract 6

A: Emma! What are you doing outside by yourself? Aren't you enjoying the party?

B: Not really. Parties aren't really my thing. And it's so hot and crowded in there.

A: I know what you mean. But parties are a great way to meet new people, aren't they?

B: Yes, I suppose so, but then it's almost impossible to have a conversation when the music's so loud. And if you're not into dancing there's not much point. So I think I'll head home soon. It's getting late anyway.

A: I don't think I'll stay much longer either. I've got an early start in the morning.

Extract 7

I was in a hurry, queuing to buy a train ticket but, when it was my turn to pay, I just couldn't remember the pin number for my credit card. My mind'd gone totally blank! I'd never forgotten it before. Luckily, I was with a friend, so he paid instead. I've only got one card and I've used it hundreds of times, but my brain had deleted it for no reason whatsoever – I thought I was losing my mind! I still can't understand why that happened. Since then I keep reminding myself what the number is and I've kept it stored on my phone.

Extract 8

A: Oh, this one was taken at Jane's twenty-first birthday party. Wow – doesn't time fly?! That was a great party.

B: Oh yes, I'd forgotten all about it. It's a shame – nobody has such fun parties any more. But look at what we're wearing! I think I've still got that dress.

A: I'm not surprised you haven't worn it for a while. But that hairstyle suits you.

B: I think it makes me look middle-aged, and I like yours better the way it is now, too.

A: So, you think we've improved with age. That's good.

Unit 14, Listening, Activity 4

42

Speaker 1: I'm from the north of England. I live on the south coast and work in an office where there aren't any other northerners. My colleagues're always commenting on my northern accent. Everyone can understand what I say, but I get fed up when they copy the way I pronounce certain words, like 'bath' instead of 'bath' and 'bus' instead of 'bus'. They don't mean to be rude but it gets really annoying. But there's no way I'd want to try and sound like a southerner. An accent represents where you come from and it's a big part of what makes you who you are. Anyway, it'd be boring if we all sounded exactly the same.

Speaker 2: As an American woman living in London, I often notice people rolling their eyes when there's a group of loud Americans on the train. I don't think this is anything to do with their accents. It's just American tourists aren't aware that they should lower their volume when they're outside the States and this could possibly be because they have a different attitude to privacy. British people find this annoying because they don't tend to talk much on public transport. The exception to this are groups of young women, who can be very loud. But the Americans aren't actually being rude or arrogant. They may even be hoping that you'll join them in the conversation.

Speaker 3: I work for a customer service helpline so I have to talk to customers all over the country on the phone. I've got used to understanding all their different accents. I enjoy interacting with customers but sometimes I'm tired of talking by the time I get home. It's important to be polite and cheerful all the time and some managers think women find this easier because they think we're naturally good at chatting and building relationships with people. But I disagree with this; some of my male colleagues are brilliant with customers, while some female colleagues really struggle.

Speaker 4: I think men may be more aware of the importance of non-verbal communication, such as facial expressions and body language. This could be because they need to learn whether another male is aggressive or not. It's not a skill many women take much notice of, but these little clues can tell you an awful lot about someone's personality – in the same way their accent can tell you where they're from. When I was preparing for a job interview recently, I was advised not to touch my throat because apparently this shows that you aren't feeling confident or may not be telling the truth.

Speaker 5: Personally, I have a weakness for the way the French speak. There's just something about it – whether the Frenchman's speaking in his native tongue or in English. And I think a lot of my women friends feel the same way. But interestingly, I read an article which said that Japanese people love the way Scottish people speak, in particular people from Glasgow. In a study, a group of Japanese people listened to different accents from around Britain and North America and it was Glaswegian they liked best. This is really surprising because most British people find people from Glasgow quite hard to understand. The article didn't say which one they liked the least.

Contents

Teaching notes

If this is the answer, what's the question?

Aim

to practise talking about yourself and giving personal information

Exam link

Speaking: Part 1

Activity type

answering questions and identifying questions from the answers other students give

Classroom dynamics

individual and teams

Time taken

25 minutes

When to use

after Speaking Focus Activity 10 on page 7

Preparation

Make one copy of the activity and cut into cards.

Procedure

1 Give each student one of the cards and ask them to read it carefully. They should not show it to anyone else. Note that if you have more than 24 students, some will need to 'double up'. If you have fewer than 24 students, you will not need all of the cards.

2 Divide your class into two teams, Team A and Team B.

3 Explain that they are going to take turns to answer the question on their card. Another student in their team is going to guess what the question is. They will do this as follows:

- One student in Team A chooses another student in their team. They then give the *answer* to the question on their card, *but they must not say what the question is*. They should avoid one word answers and their answer should be 20–30 seconds long.
- The student they chose then tries to decide what the *question* was that prompted that answer. Note that they do not need to give the exact wording of the question. You should decide if the question they give is acceptable.
- If that student is able to identify the question, Team A wins 1 point.
- Play then alternates between Team A and Team B until all the students have given the answer to their question. Keep a record of the scores on the board.
- The winning team is the team with the most points.

4 If you have 12 students or fewer in your class, you could choose to do a second round with the rest of the cards, repeating the steps above.

Over to you

Aim

to practise simple and continuous forms in the present, *would* and *used to* for past habit

Exam link

Reading and Use of English: Gapped text (Part 6)

Activity type

completing a text using appropriate sentences

Classroom dynamics

pairwork

Time taken

20 minutes

When to use

after Grammar Focus Activity 3 on page 13

Preparation

Make one copy of the activity for each pair of students in your class. Cut into three sections: the gapped description, and the Student A and Student B cards.

Procedure

1. Divide your class into pairs and give each pair a copy of the gapped text. Explain that it is a description of a person, but there are lots of missing sentences.
2. In their pairs, students should read through the description and briefly discuss what sort of information might go in the gaps. Allow them about three or four minutes for this. You can then extend this into a whole-class discussion, with students sharing their ideas about the missing information. You could also ask them to focus on some of the words in the description and ask them what they might refer to, e.g. Who does *her* refer to in the second sentence? What do you think *some* refers to in the fifth sentence?
3. Give each student in each pair a Student A or Student B card and ask them to look at the sentences. Tell them they should *not* show their sentences to their partner.
4. Explain that they are going to complete the description with their sentences. They will do this as follows:
   - When a gapped sentence is preceded by (A), Student A should look for an appropriate sentence on their card. They should then *read* that sentence to Student B, who writes it in the gap. When a gapped sentence is preceded by (B), Student B chooses and reads out the appropriate sentence and Student A writes it down. They should spell any unusual words and say if there is any punctuation within the sentence.
   - The winning pair is the first pair in the class to complete the description correctly. Alternatively, it is the pair with the most complete sentences after 15 minutes.

Answer key

1. He's always listening to it on the radio.
2. My mum is always complaining that he plays it far too loud.
3. Of course, he usually ignores her.
4. As a result, they're always arguing!
5. He likes *JTV*, which is dedicated to reggae, and *Life!*, which specialises in dance music.
6. However, his favourite one is *Rock Universe*, which shows all the latest rock videos.
7. When he finds a song he likes, he downloads it onto his MP3 player.
8. He's probably got over five thousand songs stored on it.
9. He listens to part of one, then moves on to the next.
10. He's probably getting really good at recognising songs from the first few notes!
11. He used to go to a concert once a week, sometimes twice.
12. And he would queue for hours to get a ticket to see a band he really liked.
13. He would wait outside the theatre after each concert, hoping to meet them.
14. Unfortunately, most of them used to ignore him!
15. He plays the guitar, and he's learning to play the drums.
16. In fact, he's practising as I speak.

2A Dialogue pairs

Aim
to practise adjective forms

Exam link
Reading and Use of English: Word formation (Part 3)

Activity type
playing a board game in which sentence pairs are matched and completed with an appropriate adjective

Classroom dynamics
groups of four, divided into teams of two

Time taken
15–20 minutes

When to use
after Use of English Focus Activity 7 on page 17

Preparation
Make one copy of the activity for each group of four students in your class. You will also need dice (one per group) and counters (two per group).

Procedure

1. Write on the board: *It's a lovely day today, isn't it?* Ask your students to call out suitable responses. Then write on the board: *I disagree, it's really .... and I think it's going to rain.* Ask which words might fit in the gap, e.g. *cold*, *windy*, *humid*, etc.

2 Now divide your class into groups of four and give each group a copy of the activity, a die and two counters. Ask each group to divide into pairs and each pair to place a counter on any one of the shaded spaces.

3 Explain that the sentences in the shaded spaces form the *first* part of a short dialogue. The sentences in the white spaces are the *second* part of each dialogue. The aim is to collect as many complete dialogues as possible. They do this as follows:

- Both pairs look at the sentence that their counter is on. They then look for the follow-on sentence that forms the second part of the dialogue.
- Pairs then take it in turns to roll their die and move towards their follow-on sentence. They can move across the board horizontally or vertically (but they *cannot* cross the black spaces). They can move in any direction on one throw. For example, if they throw a five, they can move two spaces right, then three spaces up or down. They must throw an exact number to land on their follow-on sentence.
- When they land on their follow-on sentence, students must complete it with an appropriate adjective form of one of the nouns in the box at the top of the activity sheet. In some cases they will need the prefix *un-* or the suffix *-less*. The pair should then read out the completed dialogue. If the other pair thinks there is a mistake, the group should ask you. If a mistake has been made, tell them so, but don't give them the correct answer.
- If the dialogue is correct, the pair write their initials in both the shaded and unshaded spaces, thus 'claiming' that dialogue (which cannot be used by the other pair). They then roll the die to move to another shaded space and repeat the procedure.

4 Let your students do the activity for about 15 minutes, then tell them to stop and review their answers. The winning pair in each group is the pair with the most *correctly* completed dialogues.

Answer key

1 + 16 (cautious), 2 + 15 (uncomfortable), 3 + 32 (personal), 4 + 25 (hopeful), 8 + 28 (predictable), 10 + 21 (generous), 12 + 30 (pessimistic), 13 + 31 (dramatic), 17 + 36 (adventurous), 19 + 5 (harmless), 22 + 29 (thoughtful), 23 + 7 (sympathetic/thoughtful), 24 + 18 (meaningless), 26 + 14 (unreliable), 27 + 20 (unsociable), 33 + 9 (different), 34 + 6 (unrealistic), 35 + 11 (emotional)

2B Hit or miss

Aim
to practise the use of verb patterns with *-ing* and infinitive

Exam link
none

Activity type
completing sentences with an appropriate verb form in a 'Battleships'-style game of chance

Classroom dynamics
groups of four and pairwork

Time taken
15 minutes

When to use
after Grammar Focus Activity 7 on page 22

Preparation
Make one copy of the activity for each group of four students in your class. Cut it into two sections (Team A and Team B).

Procedure

1 Divide your class into groups of four and ask each group to divide into teams of two. Give each team a Team A or Team B paper.

2 Explain that they are going to complete the sentences on their paper by adding a verb. Allow them a minute or two to read their sentences and think in their teams about (a) what verb might be missing, and (b) what *form* that verb will take: an infinitive on its own; an infinitive + *to*, or an *-ing* form. You should also explain at this stage that they should ignore the words in the grid, as these refer to the *other team's* sentences.

3 Now tell them that the other team has the words they need. The aim of the activity is to complete their sentences as quickly as possible. They will do this as follows:

- Team A gives Team B a grid reference, e.g. C3. Team B reads out the word(s) in that space on their grid. Team A should then decide if the word(s) can be used to complete one of their sentences. If so, they write it in the gap. Note that they should only write the word(s) they hear. For example, if Team B says *work*, Team A should <u>not</u> write *working* or *to work*.

- It is then Team B's turn to do the same. Play then alternates between the two teams until one of them has completed all of their sentences or the allocated time (15 minutes) runs out.
- The winning team is the first team to *correctly* complete all of their sentences or the team with the most correctly completed sentences at the end of the allocated time.

Answer key

Team A

1 take 2 meeting 3 staying 4 talking 5 hitting 6 travelling 7 to do 8 to ring 9 working 10 to get 11 to become 12 remembering

Team B

1 to call 2 seeing 3 going 4 working 5 speak 6 to visit 7 to enter 8 flying 9 to have 10 looking 11 to get 12 to inform

3A True or false?

Aim

to practise *-ed* adjectives + past simple/present perfect

Exam link

Speaking: General, but with more relevance to Part 1

Activity type

giving other students information about yourself (which may or may not be true), and identifying which sentence is true

Classroom dynamics

whole class, with students divided into three groups

Time taken

30–40 minutes

When to use

after Grammar Focus Activity 9 on page 28

Preparation

Make two copies of the activity. Cut into two parts: Part 1 and Part 2.

Procedure

1 Divide your class into two teams, Team A and Team B. Students will need to rearrange themselves so that they are sitting closely together in their teams. Ask each team to choose a captain and give each captain a copy of Part 1 of the activity.

2 Explain that the captain has 14 instructions. They should give each student in their team (including themselves) one of the instructions. That student should then follow their instruction and write three sentences. One of the sentences should be *true*, and the other two should be *false*. Note that they should write complete sentences and their sentences should contain as much information as possible.

3 Allow your students about five minutes to write their sentences, then tell them to stop. Give Part 2 of the activity to the captains.

4 Explain that students are going to read out their three sentences in turn and the other team is going to try to guess which sentence is true. They will do this as follows:
   - Team A begins. One student reads out the instruction they were given, followed by their three answers.
   - Team B decides which sentence is true. The Team B captain then writes that student's name in the answer grid on their Part 2 paper and circles the sentence the team thinks is true. Team B can ask questions to the Team A student to help them decide, e.g. *Hitoshi, you say you're interested in photography. What sort of camera do you have?*
   - A student from Team B then reads out their three sentences to Team A, and so on.

5 Let your class do the activity until all of the students have read out their three sentences. Then review their answers. The teams win 1 point for each true sentence they identified and the winning team is the team with the most points.

3B I couldn't live without …

Aim

to practise writing about something that is important to you and explaining why it is important

Exam link

Writing: Article (Part 2)

Activity type

writing about something that is important, then identifying what other people are talking about while playing a 'Connect 4'-type game

Classroom dynamics

individual and whole class

Time taken

30–40 minutes

When to use

after Writing Focus Activity 8 on page 34

Preparation

Make one copy of the activity for each student in your class. Then make an extra copy and cut this into individual cards along the lines. Make sure that you shuffle these cards well.

Procedure

1 Give each student one card (if you have fewer than 30 students in your class, some students will have more than one card. If you have more than 30 students, some of them will have to share a card. In either case, you must hand out *all* of the cards). They must *not* show their cards to the other students.

2 Tell them to imagine that the object on their card is of great value to them and they could not live without it.

3 Students should write a brief description of their object and why it is important to them, without mentioning the name of the object.

4 When they have written their descriptions, give each student a copy of the whole activity sheet. Allow students a couple of minutes to look up any words that they don't know. Students should then find their own object and draw a large X through it.

5 Explain that they are now going to play a game. The aim is to collect four squares in a row, horizontally, vertically or diagonally. They will do this as follows:

- One student asks another student at random to read out their description (or one description, if they have more than one). That student reads out their description but *should not say what their object is*. Everyone listens, then draws an X through the object they think is being described.
- The student who read out their description then asks *another* student at random to read out one of *their* descriptions. Again, everyone listens carefully and draws an X through the object on their sheet. This is repeated around the class.
- At some point, one student will get four objects in a row crossed out, horizontally, vertically or diagonally. They should then call out 'Four in a row!' The first student to do this is the winner assuming they correctly identified which objects were described. Check with each student that the 'winner's' answers are correct.

  Note that if one student calls out 'Four in a row' early in the game, you can continue playing until other students do likewise.

4A Four stories

Aim

to review and practise narrative forms: past simple, past continuous and past perfect (simple and continuous)

Exam link

Reading and Use of English: Multiple matching (Part 7)

Activity type

completing stories with correct verb forms, then answering questions based on the stories

Classroom dynamics

groups and whole class

Time taken

30 minutes

When to use

after Reading Focus Activity 5 on page 40

Preparation

Make one copy of Part 1 of the activity. Make four copies of Part 2 of the activity on page 165.

Procedure

1 Divide your class into four teams, A, B, C and D. Give each team a copy of the appropriate text from Part 1 of the activity.

2 In their teams, students complete the text with the correct forms of the verbs in brackets (past simple, past continuous, past perfect simple or past perfect continuous).

3 Let them do this for about ten minutes, then tell them to stop and give each team a copy of the Part 2 table. In the table, there are *four* sentences that are true about *their* text. They should try to find these sentences and circle the appropriate text letter in the left-hand column of the table. Let them do this for three minutes.

4 When the three minutes is up, you should call out 'Change!'. The teams then pass their text to another team, who then try to find four sentences in the table that are true about that text. They circle the appropriate text letter in the left-hand column of the table.

5 Step 4 is repeated two more times, so that each team looks at *all* of the texts and gets a chance to match the texts with the sentences in the table. At the end, the texts are then passed back to their original team.

6 You should then review their answers and award them points as follows:
For each correct verb form in their text, award the teams 1 point. (Total: 20 points)
For each sentence in the table that they correctly matched, award them 1 point. (Total: 16 points) The winning team is the team with the most points.

Answer key

Part 1

A: 1 called 2 heard/had heard 3 believed 4 were 5 became/had become 6 was blowing 7 started 8 became/had become 9 began 10 thought 11 had ended/was ending 12 decided 13 had fallen 14 had blown 15 was 16 heard 17 watched 18 lifted 19 came 20 were standing/stood

B: 1 had been flying 2 travelled 3 went 4 was flying 5 entertained 6 decided 7 opened 8 had started 9 was 10 looked 11 was 12 had gone 13 said 14 hit 15 sounded 16 was telling 17 were 18 expected 19 remained 20 smiled

C: 1 almost decided/had almost decided 2 had said 3 went 4 was 5 fell 6 spent 7 had planned/had been planning/were planning 8 decided 9 were packing 10 heard 11 sounded 12 thought 13 shouted 14 looked 15 was pointing 16 were moving 17 knew 18 was 19 stood 20 were running

D: 1 had 2 destroyed 3 introduced 4 warned 5 happened 6 had made 7 had bought 8 had made 9 was celebrating 10 hit 11 lived/were living 12 felt 13 started 14 tried 15 were 16 believed 17 ended/had ended 18 escaped 19 continued 20 looked

Part 2

1 D 2 B 3 A 4 B 5 C 6 A 7 A 8 B 9 C 10 D 11 D 12 B 13 A 14 D 15 C 16 C

4B A good start

Aim
to focus on suitable introductions for Part 1 essays

Exam link
Writing: Essay (Part 1)

Activity type
matching sentences and sentence clauses to form essay introductions

Classroom dynamics
groups of four

Time taken
20 minutes and writing time

When to use
after Writing Focus Activity 7 on page 44

Preparation
Make one copy of the activity for each group of 4 students, and cut into cards. Keep the larger question cards separate from the smaller clause cards. Shuffle the clause cards.

Procedure
1 Divide your class into groups of four and give each group a set of cards. They should place the sixteen small clause cards face down in a single pile on their desk. They should read the four essay question cards, then place them face up on their desk. At this stage, they should not worry about the numbered spaces on these cards.

2 Explain that the smaller cards will build up into introductory paragraphs for the essay questions. Each introduction is divided into two sentences and each sentence is divided into two clauses. The aim of the activity is to pair the clauses to make sentences and to match the sentences with their appropriate essay question. Your students will do this as follows:

- They take it in turns to take a clause card and read it out to the others in their group. They discuss and decide which question that clause might form part of the introduction to, and place the card next to the relevant question card. This will be difficult at first, but will become progressively easier as they work through the clause cards: students can place any clauses they are not sure about aside until they have 'revealed' more of the paragraph.
- The first group in the class to correctly match all of their clause cards with the question cards and put them in the correct order is the winner.

3 Activity follow-on: In Cambridge English: First, Writing Part 1, essay questions are followed by notes, which students have to use in their answer. They are given two notes and must add a third of their own. To follow on from the activity, your students can each take one essay card and work on their own for a few minutes to think of some notes that the question might include. They then share their ideas with the others in their group. The discussion can then be extended to include the whole class, who can choose the best three notes for each question. The students could then write one of

the essays for their homework, using the notes chosen. They can either use the introductions from this activity, or write their own (note that these introductions indicate the opinion the writer will take later in the essay, so might not be appropriate in every case).

Answer key

Essay 1: B, H, M, N

Essay 2: D, F, I, P

Essay 3: A, E, J, L

Essay 4: C, G, K, O

5A Countable and uncountable combinations

Aim
to practise use of countable and uncountable nouns and expressions of quantity

Exam link
none

Activity type
matching expressions of quantity with countable and uncountable nouns in a board game

Classroom dynamics
groups of four, divided into teams of two

Time taken
15–20 minutes

When to use
after Grammar Focus Activity 9 on page 47

Preparation
Make one copy of the activity for each group of four students in your class. Cut the top part of the activity into cards along the dotted lines. You will also need dice (one per group) and counters (two per group).

Procedure
1 Divide your class into groups of four. Ask the groups to divide into two teams of two.

2 Give each group a set of cards (which they should place face down on their desk), a copy of the playing board, a die and two counters (which they should place in the shaded 'Start here' area).

3 Explain that the cards contain words and expressions of quantity and that students are going to match these with the words on the board, then use them to write sentences. The aim is to write as many sentences as possible in a set time limit. They will do this as follows:
- The group turns over one of the quantity cards. In their teams, they look for a word on the board that they think the word/expression on the card can be used with.
- Each team then takes it in turns to roll the die and move their counter towards the word of their choice on the board. They can move horizontally or vertically. They cannot move diagonally and they cannot cross any of the black spaces, but they can cross the 'Start here' space. In order to land on their word of choice, they must throw an exact number but they can move in more than one direction with one throw of their die, e.g. if they throw a five, they can move two spaces left and three up or down.
- As soon as one team lands on their word of choice, they use that word and the quantity word/expression on the card to write a sentence. Once they have done this, the word on the playing grid is crossed out (which means it cannot be used again) and the card is set aside. Both teams' counters remain where they are.
- They turn over the next 'quantity' card, and continue playing.
- When they have used up all of the cards, students put the cards back together as a set again, shuffle them and place them face down. They then play a second round.

4 Let them do the activity for about 15–20 minutes, then tell them to stop and review their answers. The winning team is the team in each group with the most correct sentences.

5B What's the connection?

Aim
to practise the use of 'grammar' words in sentences

Exam link
Reading and Use of English: Open cloze (Part 2)

Activity type
completing sentences with grammar words, then taking letters from these words to reveal two 'mystery' names

Classroom dynamics
pairwork and whole class

Time taken

15 minutes

When to use

after Use of English Focus Activity 6 on page 48

Preparation

Make one copy of the activity and cut into cards.

Procedure

1 On the board, draw the following and ask students to copy it onto a sheet of paper:

1	2	3	4	5

6	7	8	9	10	11

12	13	14	15	16

17	18	19	20	21	22	23

2 Divide your class into pairs and distribute the cards to the pairs as evenly as possible.

3 Explain that their cards contain sentences which each have a missing word. Students are going to find the missing words and use the first letters of these words to reveal the names of two people who have some sort of connection. They will do this as follows:

- One student in the pair with the sentence 1 card reads out the gapped sentence on that card. They should indicate the gap by pausing or knocking on their desk.
- The other student pairs listen and decide (but don't say) which word is missing. They write this down (together with the sentence number) on a separate sheet of paper. The student pair with the sentence 1 card should also write that word down.
- They should then take the *first* letter of that word, and write it down in the appropriate space on the grid they copied from the board, e.g. space 1.
- This is repeated with all of the other cards. When the sentences have all been read out, your students should be left with the names of two people in their grid. They should decide in their pairs what the connection is between the two people. Your students may not know who these people are, so if you have internet access in your classroom, or if your students have smart phones, they can look the people up on the internet.
- The winning pair is the first pair in the class to say what the connection is.

Answer key

1 just 2 are 3 many 4 it 5 every/each 6 over/on 7 last 8 in 9 very 10 each 11 really 12 all 13 little 14 any 15 in 16 no 17 despite 18 until 19 can 20 about 21 so 22 some 23 enough

The two names your students should reveal are *Jamie Oliver* and *Alain Ducasse*. They are both internationally famous chefs. (The word *chefs* is the important connection here. Your students do not need to say that they are famous or celebrities.)

6A Listen carefully

Aim

to practise listening for specific information

Exam link

Listening: Multiple choice (Part 1)

Activity type

listening to situations and using the information heard to choose from a list of possible answers

Classroom dynamics

groups of four

Time taken

20 minutes

When to use

after Listening Focus Activity 4 on page 60

Preparation

Make one copy of the activity for every four students in your class.

Procedure

1 Divide your class into groups of four and ask each group to divide into pairs (Students A and B, and Students C and D). Give each pair in each group a Student A and B paper or a Student C and D paper. They should not show these to the other pair in their group.

2 Tell them to look at Part 1 of the activity. The first box contains the first part of three short conversations (1–3) and the second box contains the second part of those conversations (A–C). Students work in their pairs to match the conversation halves. Monitor and make sure they have matched the halves correctly.

3 When they have done this, they should read out their complete conversations to the other pair in their group. That pair should listen carefully and decide which answer to choose for the questions in Part 2 of the activity.

4 The winning group is the first group to answer all six questions correctly or the group to answer most questions correctly in a fixed time of 15–20 minutes.

Answer key

Students A and B

Part 1: 1 B 2 C 3 A

Part 2: 1 a 2 c 3 b

Students C and D

Part 1: 1 B 2 A 3 C

Part 2: 1 b 2 c 3 a

6B First to 30

Aim

to review tenses used to talk about the future

Exam link

none, but useful for Reading and Use of English Part 2

Activity type

competitive sentence completion

Classroom dynamics

groups of four/pairwork

Time taken

25–30 minutes

When to use

after Grammar Focus Activity 6 on page 64

Preparation

Make one copy of the activity per two students.

Procedure

1 Divide your class into groups of four and ask each group to divide into two teams, Team A and Team B.

2 Give each team a copy of the activity and tell them to look at their section. Explain that each dialogue can be completed with the words from the box. Some words will be used more than once. They should look at their words and dialogues and, in their teams, discuss which words they think they will need for each dialogue. Allow them about five minutes for this. Note that at this stage, they should *not* write anything.

3 Explain that the aim of the activity is to be the first team to complete all their dialogues, while trying to prevent the other team from doing so. They will do this as follows:
   - Team A chooses a numbered gap from Team B's section. Team B then have a maximum of 20 seconds to decide which word from their box goes in that gap (Team A should time them). If they know the missing word, they write it in the gap. If not, they leave it blank. Tell students that they don't have to choose gaps in order, but can choose them at random to make it more difficult for the other team.
   - Team B then does the same for Team A. Play then alternates between the two teams until one team has completed all of their dialogues.

4 The winning team is the first team to complete all of their dialogues or the team to complete the most gaps in their dialogues in a set time of 20 minutes.

Answer key

Team A

1 I'm 2 going 3 to 4 see 5 I'll 6 make 7 you 8 I'm 9 meeting 10 I'll 11 have 12 finished 13 I 14 expect 15 it 16 will 17 rain 18 I'll 19 be 20 sitting 21 Our 22 train 23 leaves 24 I 25 might 26 visit 27 they're 28 going 29 to 30 get

Team B

1 I'm 2 going 3 to 4 study 5 I'll 6 help 7 you 8 I'm 9 seeing 10 I'll 11 have 12 spent 13 I 14 imagine 15 it 16 will 17 be 18 I'll 19 be 20 getting 21 The 22 doors 23 open 24 he 25 may 26 arrive 27 it's 28 going 29 to 30 be

7A It looks like …

Aim
to practise language of description and speculation (including modals of deduction)

Exam link
Speaking: (Part 2)

Activity type
picture matching activity

Classroom dynamics
pairwork

Time taken
15 minutes

When to use
after Speaking Focus Activity 1 on page 71

Preparation
Make one copy of the activity for each pair of students in your class.

Procedure
1 Divide your class into pairs and give each student a Student A or Student B paper. They should not show their pictures to each other.

2 Explain that they have the same pictures, but in a different order. The aim of the activity is to match their pictures with their partner's pictures. They will do this as follows:
   - Student A begins by describing one of his/her pictures to Student B, using the expressions for speculating from the Coursebook. Student B listens and decides which picture Student A is describing. They then both write the number 1 next to their relevant picture on their sheet.
   - It is then Student B's turn to do the same thing, while Student A listens and identifies the picture. They then write the number 2 next to that picture.
   - They then take it in turns to repeat this for their other pictures, numbering them 3–12. The winning pair is the first pair to correctly match all the pictures.

7B Putting it all together

Aim
to practise relative pronouns, language of emphasis (*so*, *such*, *too*, etc.) and language used for adding interest in articles and stories

Exam link
Writing: Article (Part 2)

Activity type
collaborative writing task with a competitive element

Classroom dynamics
groups of three or four

Time taken
30–40 minutes

When to use
after Writing Focus Activity 6 on page 76

Preparation
Make one copy of the activity for each group of three or four students in your class.

Procedure
1 Divide your class into groups of three or four. Explain that they are going to write an article about a memorable event. Write on the board: *Last summer I decided to …*

2 Explain that this incomplete sentence should begin their article. The article should describe something that they did and can relate to any topic, e.g. a trip, an important event, etc. It does not have to be true. Allow the groups a couple of minutes to think of some ideas and complete the sentence.

3 Give each group a copy of the activity. Explain that they are now going to continue their article. The aim is to use as many of the words or expressions in the box as they can in a set time limit. Each sentence must contain one of these words or expressions and should be written on its own line. Students should underline the words and expressions they use. At this stage, they should ignore the 'Points won/lost' column, but advise them that it may be in their best interests to use the expressions with the highest numbers, since these indicate the number of points they could win.

4 Let them work on their article for about 20 minutes.

5 When their 20 minutes are up, tell them to stop and ask each group to read out their article. If their sentences are structurally correct and if they have used the words/expressions appropriately, they win the points indicated by the numbers after them (1 letter = 1 point). If, however, they have made a mistake with the words/expressions, they *lose* these points. The winning group is the group with the most points.

8A You say, we report

Aim
to practise reported speech

Exam link
Reading and Use of English: Key word transformations (Part 4)

Activity type
completing sentences with appropriate reporting verbs and other words

Classroom dynamics
groups of four, divided into teams of two

Time taken
20 minutes

When to use
after Grammar Focus Activity 7 on page 84

Preparation
Make one copy of the activity for each group of four students in your class. Cut into two parts, Team A and Team B.

Procedure
1 Divide your class into groups of four and ask them to divide into teams of two, Team A and Team B. Give each team a Team A or Team B paper. They should not show their paper to the other team.

2 Explain that each team has five direct speech sentences. They also have five gapped, reported speech sentences. The aim of the activity is to complete their gapped sentences using information given to them by the other team. They do this as follows:
- Team A read out their first direct speech sentence. Team B must then change that direct speech sentence to reported speech and complete their first gapped sentence. They must use the correct form of one of the words from their box. They can only use the same number of letters as there are spaces (1 letter = 1 space). Note that no gaps are shown between the words. Team B should spend no more than 90 seconds trying to complete their sentence (timed by Team 1).
- Team B then read out *their* first direct speech sentence and Team A complete their first gapped sentence. Play then alternates between both teams until all of their sentences are complete, or as many as they can do.
- Review their answers. The teams can award themselves one point for each word they wrote in their sentences (maximum: 20 points) and the winning team is the team with the most points.

Answer key
Team A
1 accused me (or *us*) of using
2 asked me (or *us*) to help 3 denied breaking my
4 explained he had been 5 told me to leave my

Team B
1 offered to make me (or *us*) 2 suggested going out
3 reminded me (or *us*) to call
4 advised me (or *us*) to leave 5 asked me how I was

8B Right word crossword

Aim
to practise using correct word forms (especially concrete and abstract nouns) in sentences

Exam link
Reading and Use of English: Word formation (Part 3)

Activity type
identifying incorrect words in sentences, correcting them and using the answers to complete a crossword

Classroom dynamics
groups of four and pairwork

Time taken
15–20 minutes

When to use
after Use of English Focus Activity 4 on page 85

Preparation
Make one copy of the activity for each student pair in your class.

Procedure
1 Divide your class into groups of four and ask each group to divide into pairs (Students A and B, and Students C and D).

2 Give each pair a copy of the Students A and B or Students C and D section of the activity. They should not show their sentences to the other pair. Also give them a copy of the crossword grid, which they should place between them.

3 Explain that each sentence on their paper contains a wrong word form. They are going to identify the wrong word and then write the correct word in the crossword grid. They will do this as follows:

- Students A and B read their first sentence to Students C and D. Students C and D should listen carefully and try to identify the wrong word. They can ask for the sentence to be repeated if necessary. They should then write the correct word in the crossword grid. If they are unable to do this yet, they should pass: they can return to it later.
- Students C and D then do the same with their first sentence. Play then alternates between the two pairs until they have completed the crossword. Note that, apart from reading out their sentences, the student pairs cannot help each other.

4 The first group of four to correctly complete their crossword, or the group with the most words in the crossword after a set time of 15 minutes, is the winner.

Answer key

1 knowing = knowledge 2 employee = employer
3 musical = musician 4 Tourist = Tourism
5 journalist = journalism 6 behaving = behaviour
7 difficult = difficulty 8 application = applicants
9 creativity = creation 10 arriving = arrival
11 advice = advisors 12 permit = permission
13 confident = confidence
14 represent = representatives

9A You're just like me

Aim

to review and practise collocations connected with success

Exam link

none, although the follow-on activity is useful practice for the Speaking Test

Activity type

completing sentences with appropriate words, then matching sentences to form short dialogues

Classroom dynamics

groups of three

Time taken

15–20 minutes

When to use

after Reading Focus Activity 7 on page 89

Preparation

Make one copy of the activity for each group of three students in your class. Cut into two parts (Part 1 and Part 2).

Procedure

1 Divide your class into groups of three and give each group a Part 1 paper.

2 Explain that each sentence on their paper is the *second* part of a short dialogue. They will hear the first part of each dialogue shortly, but first they should complete the sentences with the words in the box. Note that at this stage they should ignore the brackets at the end of the sentences.

3 Allow them five or ten minutes for this, then tell them to stop. Give *one* student in each group a copy of Part 2 and tell them not to show it to the other students in their group. Explain that these sentences (1–12) form the *first* part of each dialogue. Explain that students are going to match the two parts of the dialogues. They will do this as follows:

- The student with the Part 2 sentences reads each sentence out twice, including its number (1–12). The other two students should listen and look for the 'follow-on' sentence on the Part 1 paper. They then write the appropriate number in the space at the end of the sentence.
- Let them do this for about ten minutes, then tell them to stop and review their answers. Award them points as follows:
  For each correct word in the sentences in Part 1, they get 1 point.
  For each correct dialogue number they write, they get 1 point.
  The winning group is the group with the most points.

4 As a follow-on activity, your students could read the dialogue beginnings in Part 2 to one another and should respond using their own ideas.

Answer key

(a) set, 6 (b) aim, 10 (c) be, 9 (d) overcome/face, 2
(e) fulfil, 5 (f) make, 1 (g) cope, 7 (h) let, 4 (i) face, 12
(j) focus, 11 (k) take, 3 (l) give, 8

9B Completely conditional

Aim
to review and practise future, present and past conditionals

Exam link
none

Activity type
writing conditional sentences using prompts provided by other students and using these sentences in a game of risk

Classroom dynamics
whole class, divided into two teams

Time taken
30 minutes

When to use
after Grammar Focus Activity 6 on page 95

Preparation
Make one copy of the activity per two students in your class. Cut into two sections (Team A and Team B).

Procedure
1 Divide your class into two teams and give each student a Team A or Team B paper.

2 Explain that they each have six sentences which they are going to give to the other team. The other team is then going to use those sentences as prompts to write conditional sentences. Begin by giving them this example:

Prompt: *I want to visit my friends at the weekend, but they might not be at home.*

Possible answers: *I'll visit my friends at the weekend if they're at home. Unless my friends are at home this weekend, I won't visit them. If my friends are at home this weekend, I might visit them.*

Explain that they are going to use the conditional sentences they write to collect points. They will do this as follows:

- One student from Team A and one student from Team B come to the front of the class with their activity sheet. The Student from Team A reads their prompt sentence 1 to Team B, and the Student from Team B reads their prompt sentence 1 to Team A.
- With the help of his/her team, the students at the front of the class then write a conditional sentence on the board based on the prompt they have been given. They have 90 seconds to do this (timed by you).
- When each team is happy with their sentence, they write it in the appropriate space in their score card. They then decide as a team how certain they are that they have produced a grammatically correct sentence, and award themselves points (three points if they are *very* sure, two points if they are *quite* sure, one point if they are *not very* sure). They write the appropriate number in the 'Points risked' column of their table.
- The above steps are repeated with the other prompt sentences. For each sentence, a different student should come to the front of the class.
- Review their sentences and tell the teams if they are right or wrong. For each grammatically correct sentence, a team wins the points they awarded themselves for that sentence. However, for each sentence that contains a mistake, they *lose* the points they awarded themselves for the sentence. The winning team is the team with the most points.

Answer key
A large variety of answers are possible for this activity. Here are a few:

Team A

1 If I'd seen Peter, I would have asked him for some advice about language courses.

2 I wouldn't have been late for school if I had taken the bus instead of walking.

3 If I were more confident, I'd become a famous actor.

4 If my parents liked having animals in the house, I'd get a cat.

5 If I don't have too much homework tonight, I'll go to the cinema.

6 I'll do a painting course at my local college if there are any free places.

Team B

1 If the weather's good at the weekend, I'll go to the beach.

2 I'll go to the USA next year if my parents let me.

3 If I had enough money, I'd buy a new computer.

4 If I had the time and money, I'd travel around the world.

5 If I had gone to bed earlier last night, I would have woken up on time this morning.

6 If I hadn't gone for a walk in the rain, I wouldn't have caught a cold.

10A Best friends

Aim

to review expressions relating to friendship, and to practise listening for specific information

Exam link

Listening: Multiple matching (Part 3)

Activity type

matching people with characteristics, then using letters in the expressions they use to reveal a 'hidden' expression

Classroom dynamics

pairwork + and whole class

Time taken

20–25 minutes

When to use

after Vocabulary and Listening Focus Activity 10 on page 99

Preparation

Make one copy of the first page (the cards) and cut it into six cards. Make one copy of the second page (the activity sheet) for each student pair in your class.

Procedure

1 Divide your class into pairs and give each pair a copy of the activity sheet. Hand out the cards at random to individual students in the class (you might want to choose confident students for this, as they are going to be reading the information on the cards out to the rest of the class). These students should look at the cards they are given but they should not show them to their partner.

2 Tell students to look at Part 1 of the activity only. Explain that they are going to hear six people talking about a friendship.

3 Ask the student with card 1 to come to the front of the class and read out his/her card to the class. They should do this twice, then return to their partner. The student pairs write that student's name in the space before sentence 1, then decide which expression in the box can be used to complete it and write this in the space at the end. There are three expressions they will not need.

4 Step 3 is then repeated with the other five cards.

5 When your students have completed all of their sentences, they should follow the instructions in Part 2. The aim is to use the letters they write down to reveal a 'hidden' expression which can be used to complete the sentence at the bottom of their sheet. The first student pair to reveal this expression and complete the sentence is the winner.

Answer key

1 have shared memories 2 do not often see eye to eye
3 are self-confident 4 share the same taste in music
5 have a lot in common
6 enjoy having a laugh together

The letters that your students write down should reveal the expression *sense of humour*.

10B Rejected words

Aim

to practise use of participles (*-ing* and *-ed* forms) in participle clauses and other structures

Exam link

none

Activity type

shortening sentences using *-ing* and *-ed* participles

Classroom dynamics

pairwork + and whole class

Time taken

25 minutes

When to use

after Grammar Focus Activity 7 on page 104

Preparation

Make one copy of the activity and cut into 14 cards.

Procedure

1 Divide your class into pairs and give each pair a card (in any order – the numbers on the cards are for your reference only). If you have fewer than 14 pairs in your class, give more than one card to one pair. If you have more than 28 students in your class, some students will have to work in groups of three instead of in pairs.

2 Explain that the sentence on their card can be reduced by between one and five words *without any change in meaning*. The aim is to rewrite the sentences, removing these words and making any other necessary changes to the sentences. Tell students that in some cases, this may mean changing the form of one of the words or adding

a new word. Each of their new sentences *must* contain a verb ending in *-ed* or *-ing*. They will do this as follows:

- In their pairs, students look at the sentence on their card and write it down on a separate sheet of paper. They then decide how they can reduce it, i.e. which words can be removed and which words, if any, need to be changed.
- They then rewrite their sentence. They should make a separate note of any 'rejected' words. Note that any words which change their form do *not* count as rejected words; students should only make a note of the words they discard completely from the sentence.
- Let them do this for 90 seconds, then call out 'Change'. The cards are passed clockwise around the classroom, and students do the same with their new sentence. This is repeated until all the student pairs have looked at all of the cards.

3 In all, it would be possible to write down 34 rejected words. Review their answers and ask students how many words they managed to reject. The pair with the most is the winner, provided their new sentences are correct.

Answer key

(Rejected words are shown in brackets.)

1. The man selling newspapers in the town square is very friendly. (who)
2. This is just another website claiming to find customers the best deals. (which)
3. My uncle has a long beard reaching down to his chest. (which)
4. My father grows wonderful strawberries bursting with flavour. (which)
5. He was angry with me for leaving without him. (because I had)
6. We live in a world obsessed with celebrity. (which is)
7. I have a sword believed to have been used by Napoleon. (which is)
8. I broke my arm playing football last Saturday. (while I was)
9. He told us about a lost city discovered by explorers in the 18th century. (which had been)
10. Walking to work yesterday, I saw something very strange. (when I was)
11. For my birthday she gave me a cake baked by her mother. (which had been)
12. I had a part-time job last summer taking people on guided tours of my town. (in which I)
13. There weren't enough sandwiches for everyone to have one each, which meant sharing. (we had to)
14. Driving into town the other day, I saw a boy standing in the middle of the road. (while I was, who was)

11A Party on

Aim

to review and practise conditionals (especially mixed, but also future, present and past conditionals)

Exam link

Reading and Use of English: Gapped text (Part 6)

Activity type

'Bingo'-type game involving identifying sentences that can come between two other sentences and putting the verbs in those sentences into their correct form

Classroom dynamics

groups of five or six

Time taken

20 minutes

When to use

after Grammar Focus Activity 6 on page 112

Preparation

Make one copy of the activity for each student in your class. Cut into two parts (Part 1 and Part 2).

Procedure

1 Ask your students to draw a large 2 × 4 grid on a sheet of paper, then give each student a copy of Part 1 of the activity. Tell them to choose *eight* of the sentences from Part 1 and write them into their grid. They should write them down exactly as they see them. Set a time limit of about five minutes for this.

2 Now tell them to put their Part 1 paper where they cannot see it and give them each a copy of Part 2 of the activity. They should now get into groups of five or six.

3 Explain that they are going to play a game of Bingo. They will do this as follows:

- One student in the group looks for a situation in the Part 2 table that can be completed with one of the sentences they wrote in their grid. They should then read out the box number from the Part 2 table to the rest of their group. They should also rewrite the relevant sentence in their grid so that the verb forms are correct.

- At the same time, the other students in their group look at *their* grid to see if they have the same sentence in their grid. If so, they rewrite their sentence as well.
- The situation in the Part 2 table is then crossed out. It cannot be 'called' again.
- Students then take it in turns to choose one of the Part 2 numbers, read it out and rewrite their sentence, while the others check to see if they can do the same.
- The first student to have rewritten all of their eight sentences calls out 'Bingo'. You should check their answers and if they are grammatically correct, that student is the winner.

Answer key

1 If I had left earlier, I wouldn't be so tired this morning.
2 I would have seen my friend Rob if I had stayed a bit longer.
3 I would have gone if I liked parties, but I don't, so I didn't.
4 I would have gone if I liked seafood.
5 If I hadn't had so much of it, I wouldn't have had such a sore stomach this morning.
6 It would be cheaper if I did it all myself.
7 If I had spent more time talking instead, I wouldn't be in such pain this morning.
8 I would be much happier if they had organised a meal out with my friends.
9 If he invites me, I'll probably go.
10 I'll go if we're allowed to bring a guest.
11 If I asked them to throw me a big party, I wonder if they would agree (or: If I ask them to throw me a big party, I wonder if they'll agree).
12 However, if it rains, we'll have to do something else.
13 If we have one illegally, we'll probably get into trouble.
14 I wouldn't have gone if I had known how bored I was going to be.

11B Just supposing

Aim
to practise talking about a specific subject and to practise the use of hypothetical language

Exam link
none, but useful for Part 4 of the Speaking test

Activity type
identifying what people are talking about and using the information heard to form sentences

Classroom dynamics
pairwork + and whole class

Time taken
20–30 minutes

When to use
after Grammar Focus Activity 7 on page 116

Preparation
Make one copy of the activity for each pair of students in your class. You will also need to make one copy of the answer key below which you should cut into individual sentences.

Procedure

1 Before you begin, write on the board: *I wish I had a car.* Then read out the following: *I usually get around by bus and sometimes I use my bike. The problem is that where I live the buses are very unreliable and they cost a lot to use. My bicycle is only good for short distances and I hate cycling when it's raining.*
Elicit that this follows on from the sentence on the board.

2 Divide your class into pairs and give each pair *one* of the sentences from the answer key. They should not show their sentence to anyone else. If you have more than 20 students in your class, some will have to work in groups of three. If you have fewer than ten pairs, you will not need to give out all of the sentences.

3 In their pairs, students write a follow-on paragraph to their sentence, in the same way that you provided a follow-on paragraph to the sentence on the board. Tell them that they are not allowed to use the words in **bold**. Let them do this for about five minutes.

4 Now hand out a copy of the activity sheet to each pair. They will see ten sentences (one of which is their own) but the words have been jumbled up. The aim is to rearrange the words to make hypothetical sentences and to match the sentences with the students talking about them. They will do this as follows:
- One student from one of the student pairs reads out the follow-on paragraph they prepared. The other student pairs then try to identify the prompt sentence on their activity sheet. When they think they have found it, they arrange the words to make the sentence and then write the names of the students who gave them the follow-on paragraph underneath. Alternatively, you could allow your students about ten minutes to rearrange the words in the prompt sentences *before* they start listening.
- This is repeated, with the other pairs in the class taking turns to read out their follow-on paragraphs while the others listen and identify the prompt sentence as before.
- When they have all spoken, review their answers by getting pairs to read out their prompt sentence and follow-on paragraph together. Pairs get one point for each correct sentence and one point for correctly identifying the students who responded to that prompt. The winning pair is the pair with the most points.

Answer key

1. If only I hadn't been so **rude** to my **teacher yesterday**.
2. I feel as though I've just **eaten** enough **food** for **ten**.
3. Suppose **mobile phones** hadn't been **invented**.
4. If only I had enough **money** to **buy** some **new clothes**.
5. I wish my **friends** would **visit** me **more often**.
6. I'd rather you didn't **play** your **music** so **loud**.
7. Suppose we all **refused** to **obey** the **school rules**.
8. I wish I didn't have **so much work** to do this **weekend**.
9. I'd rather **stay** at **home** than go **out tonight**.
10. It's time we all did **more** to **help** the **environment**.

12A All part of the job

Aim
to practise modals of obligation, prohibition and necessity

Exam link
none

Activity type
board game with a productive language element

Classroom dynamics
pairwork

Time taken
15–20 minutes

When to use
after Grammar Focus Activity 5 on page 122

Preparation
Make one copy of the activity for each pair of students in your class. Cut into three sections (the Student A cards, Student B cards and the playing board). You will also need two counters per pair (your students can use coins if you do not have counters).

Procedure
1 Divide your class into pairs and give each student a Student A or Student B card.

2 Tell them to choose ten of the jobs on their card and number them 1–10 in the boxes.

3 Give each pair a playing board and two counters and tell them to place their counters in the 'Start' space at the top of the board. Explain that the aim of the activity is to be the first to get their counter to the 'Finish' space. They will do this as follows:
- Students take it in turns to move their counter *one* space. They can move horizontally or vertically. They cannot move diagonally, and they cannot cross the black spaces.

- Each time they land on a space, they must say a sentence about their chosen jobs using one of the modal verbs in the box. The number in the space refers to the job number on their card and the letter refers to the function of the modal verb. For example, if a student has chosen *pilot* as their number 1 job and they land on a space with 1A in it, they could say: *I must get plenty of sleep before a long flight*. For function E, they will need to think of an imaginary situation in the past, e.g. *I needn't have got up so early because my flight was delayed*.
- Each time they land on a space and say a correct sentence, they must put a tick (✓) in the space. This space is now 'dead' and no player can cross it again.
- Your students may reach a point where they cannot think of a sentence to go with their next space. This is where they may need to change direction, so that they move around or away from that difficult space.

12B Cops and robbers

Aim

to review and practise prepositions and particles, including those used in phrasal verbs (general, from Units 1–12)

Exam link

Reading and Use of English (Part 2)

Activity type

board game requiring students to complete gapped sentences while chasing or being chased by other players

Classroom dynamics

groups of four, divided into teams of two

Time taken

15–20 minutes

When to use

after Use of English Focus Activity 2 on page 127

Preparation

Make one copy of the activity for each group of four students in your class. Also make two or three copies of the answer key below. You will also need one die and four counters per group, two each of a different colour. Alternatively, your student groups could use coins of two different denominations.

Procedure

1 Choose two or three students to be monitors. Divide the rest of the class into groups of four and tell them to divide into pairs. Explain that one pair will be police (the 'cops') and one pair will be robbers. They should decide who is who.

2 Give each group a copy of the activity, a die and four counters. They should place their counters in the appropriate 'Cop start' or 'Robber start' spaces. Give the two monitors a copy of the answers.

3 Explain that the aim of the activity is for the police to try to capture the robbers and for the robbers to try to evade capture by the police. They will do this as follows:
   - The robbers begin by rolling their die and moving one of their counters to one of the spaces on the board. Note that they can only move in one direction on one throw of the die and they can only move horizontally or vertically, *not* diagonally. They then decide which preposition or particle from the box at the top of the activity sheet can be used to complete the sentence, and write this into the sentence.
   - The monitors' job is to check their answers. They should tell the players whether their answers are correct or incorrect, but they should *not* give them the correct answer. The players are only allowed to move on from the space when they give a correct answer. They must remain where they are until they answer it correctly.
   - The cops and robbers then take it in turns to repeat the steps above. The aim is for the cops to land one of their counters on top of one of the robbers' counters, thus 'capturing' it. Note that sentences which have already been answered are 'free' spaces: players can land on one of these without having to answer anything. Also note that players can have both of their counters on the board at the same time.
   - Let students do the activity for about ten minutes. The robbers win the game if they have one or both of their counters still on the board when you tell them to stop. The cops win if they capture both the robbers' counters. They can then play a second game. The students who were monitors the first time can now be replaced with other students, so that everyone gets a chance to play.

Answer key

1 off 2 off 3 over 4 from 5 up 6 across 7 up 8 off 9 to 10 up 11 out 12 away 13 in 14 ahead 15 at 16 about 17 in 18 on 19 of 20 about 21 over 22 of 23 up 24 down 25 after 26 with 27 off 28 up 29 out 30 in 31 out 32 on 33 off 34 away 35 out 36 on 37 over 38 down 39 off 40 off

13A Useful expressions

Aim
to review useful expressions for the Speaking Test

Exam link
Speaking (Parts 3 and 4)

Activity type
matching spoken expressions to their functions and completing them with an appropriate word

Classroom dynamics
groups of three

Time taken
15–20 minutes

When to use
after Speaking Focus Activity 3 on page 133

Preparation
Make one copy of the activity for each group of three students in your class. Cut into three sections (Student A, Student B and Student C).

Procedure
1 Divide your class into groups of three and give each student a Student A, Student B or Student C paper. They should not show these to one another.

2 Explain that Student A has a list of useful expressions. However, these expressions are each missing a word, which Student B has. To make it more challenging, there are ten words on Student B's sheet that do not fit in any of the expressions. Each expression has a function and Student C has a list of these. The aim of the activity is for groups to complete the expressions with the missing words and match the expressions to their functions, without looking at one another's papers. They will do this as follows:
   - Student A reads out the first of their gapped expressions.
   - Student B then suggests a word from their list to complete the sentence.
   - Student C then says which function the sentence is performing. One of the students in the group should write down their answer, e.g. Sentence 1 matches Function E and the missing word is *repeat*. If they are not sure, they should move on to the next one.
   - This is repeated for the other expressions.

3 Let them do the activity for about 10–15 minutes, then tell them to stop and review their answers. The winning group is the group with the most correct matches.

4 As a follow-on activity, your students could write short conversations using five or six of the expressions, then read their conversation out to the rest of the class.

Answer key

1 E repeat 2 H Both 3 O basically 4 K true 5 B kind 6 F while 7 N suppose 8 M view 9 I Anyway 10 G go 11 A meant 12 C see 13 J mean 14 D sorry 15 L point

13B Reflexive revelation

Aim
to review reflexive pronouns

Exam link
none, but useful for Reading and Use of English (Part 2)

Activity type
identifying where reflexive pronouns go in sentences and using them to reveal an idiomatic English expression

Classroom dynamics
pairwork

Time taken
15–20 minutes

When to use
after Grammar Focus Activity 5 on page 137

Preparation
Make one copy of the activity for each pair of students in your class. Cut into three sections.

Procedure

1 On the board, write the following sentence: *I was expecting to be met by one of the President's assistants, but it was the President who was at the airport waiting for me.*

2 Explain that this sentence would benefit from the addition of a reflexive pronoun somewhere in the sentence. Ask your students if they can tell you which pronoun could be added and where it would go in the sentence (*himself*, which would come between *President* and *who*).

3 Divide your class into pairs and give each pair a copy of the grid. Point out that the first line of the grid contains the word *President* from your sample sentence and also the pronoun which follows it. Then explain that they are going to see more sentences that require, or would benefit from, a reflexive pronoun. They are going to use these to complete the grid. The aim is to reveal a 'mystery' expression that is connected in some way with the theme of their Coursebook unit.

4 Give the students in each pair a Student A or Student B paper. They will then do the activity as follows:

- Student A reads out their sentence 1 to Student B. Student B listens carefully and decides which reflexive pronoun can be used and where it should go in the sentence. They then write the word *preceding* the pronoun and the pronoun itself, in the appropriate space in the grid, as in the example.
- Student B then reads out their first sentence to Student A, who listens and then writes the preceding word and pronoun.
- This is repeated until students have completed the grid. They should then use the letters in the shaded spaces to complete the sentence under the grid (one letter for each space). If they have done the exercise correctly, they should reveal an idiomatic English expression which means 'forgets things easily'. The winning pair is the first pair in the class to reveal this expression.

Answer key

0 President himself 1 buy yourselves
2 players themselves 3 make yourself 4 about herself
5 reminded myself 6 studied himself 7 turns itself
8 England herself 9 prepared ourselves
10 introducing themselves
The expression is 'a *memory* like a *sieve*' (your students will find this expression under *sieve* in the Longman Exams Dictionary).

14A Speak up

Aim
to review and practise speaking verbs

Exam link
none

Activity type
completing a crossword using appropriate words and word forms

Classroom dynamics
pairwork

Time taken
25–30 minutes

When to use
after Vocabulary Focus Activity 10 on page 141

Preparation
Make one copy of the activity for each pair of students in your class. Cut into two sections (Part 1 and Part 2).

Procedure

1 Divide your class into pairs and give each pair a copy of Part 1 of the activity. Write the words *say*, *speak*, *talk*, *tell*, *mumble*, *mutter*, *whisper* and *yell* on the board.

2 Explain that you are going to read them some sentences with one of the words on the board missing. After you read each sentence, students should decide which word they think is missing and what *form* the verb should be (infinitive, past simple, etc.). In some cases, more than one answer may be possible, so they should write down as many options as they can, e.g. Number 1 could be *mumbled*, *muttered*, *said* or *whispered*.

3 Read out the sentences in the answer key, but do *not* say the word in **bold**. Indicate the missing word by pausing or tapping on your desk. Read each sentence twice, at normal speed.

4 Now hand out Part 2 (the crossword). In their pairs, your students should now transfer the words they wrote into the crossword grid. In cases where more than one answer is possible, only one of them will fit into the crossword.

5 The first pair to complete their crossword (or the pair with the most words in the crossword after a set time limit) is the winner.

Answer key

1 Sarah **mumbled** something I couldn't hear, and walked away.
2 Can you **tell** the difference between lemon juice and lime juice?
3 She shook my hand and **said** her name was Ann.
4 My sister always **tells** the truth, even if she knows she'll get into trouble.
5 What I liked the most about him was that he always **spoke** his mind.
6 My sister **speaks** five languages fluently.
7 When I was a child, my parents always **told** me a story before I went to bed.
8 'Help me!' she **yelled** in terror.
9 Tom always **mumbles** when he stands up to talk in class, so it's really difficult to hear what he's saying.
10 Generally **speaking**, technology has improved our lives a lot.
11 I don't believe you. You're **talking** rubbish, as usual!
12 He sat in the corner **muttering** something under his breath about people coming late.
13 It **says** on the label that you should take this medicine twice a day.
14 I want to hear your secret. Come here and **whisper** it in my ear.
15 We want someone who works hard and **talks** sense.
16 My brother is always **saying** that he wants to become a famous actor.
17 If someone attacks you in the street, the best thing to do is **yell** at the top of your voice.
18 Stop **whispering**. Talk normally. No one can hear us.
19 Please stop **yelling** like that. I'm not deaf.
20 When I walked into the room, Michael was **telling** a joke about a man and a chicken.

14B Context and meaning

Aim
to practise identifying meaning from context using animal idioms

Exam link
none (but useful for Reading and Use of English Parts 5–7)

Activity type
identifying and matching task

Classroom dynamics
groups of three or four

Time taken
30–35 minutes

When to use
after Reading focus Activity 5 on page 144

Preparation
Make one copy of the activity for each student pair or small group. Cut the numbered and lettered boxes into cards, but keep both sets separate.

Procedure
1 Divide your class into groups of three or four, and give each group a set of cards. They should place the numbered cards face down in a single pile on their desk. They should distribute the lettered cards among themselves. Do not give them the answer key yet.

2 Tell them to take it in turns to read out the sentence on one of their lettered cards. Explain that these sentences each contain an animal idiom or colloquialism in bold. In their groups, they should decide if they know what any of the idioms mean. They should be able to guess some of them but for many, the meaning will not be obvious. Let them do this for about 5–10 minutes, placing each card face up on their desk when they have done so.

3 Explain that they are now going to match the lettered sentences with the numbered sentences on the other pile of cards. Each numbered card contains two sentences, with a gap between each one: the gaps can each be completed with one of the lettered sentences.

4 Working together, the students turn each numbered card over, and try to decide which lettered sentence can complete the gap, pairing the cards up. Then, looking at the three sentences as a whole, they should be able to work out what the idiom means. This is useful practise for the Cambridge English: First Reading and Use of English paper, where it is sometimes necessary to refer to the previous and following sentences in order to work out what a word or phrase means.

5 Let them do this for about 15 minutes, then give each group a copy of the answers. The groups award themselves one point for each correct answer and one point for each meaning they correctly identified.

Answer key

1 I Something that **gets your goat** annoys you.
2 E If you **make a dog's breakfast** of something, you do it really badly
3 M **A dark horse** is someone with a skill, talent or achievement that surprises you when you discover it.
4 A If you **have a bee in your bonnet** about something, especially something that annoys you, you can't stop talking about it.
5 H Someone who **looks like something that the cat dragged in** is very untidy or scruffy.
6 D Someone who **looks like a drowned rat** is very wet.
7 L If you **smell a rat**, you are suspicious about something.
8 B Someone who is or feels **like a fish out of water** is uncomfortable because they feel they do not belong in a place or situation.
9 O Someone who is **the bee's knees** is wonderful.
10 G **A cold fish** is someone who is not very friendly.
11 K If you **do the donkey work**, you do the jobs that are boring and/or difficult.
12 C If you **have bigger fish to fry**, you have more important things to do.
13 N If you **have a whale of a time**, you have a very good time.
14 F Someone who is **like a dog with two tails** is extremely happy.
15 J Someone who **wouldn't say boo to a goose** is very shy and timid.

Why are you studying English?	What could I see or do if I visited your home town?	What sorts of things do you like doing with your friends?
What do you think you'll use your English for in the future?	What subject do/did you enjoy most at school?	What do you like doing in your free time?
What kind of music do you enjoy listening to?	What subject do/did you find most difficult at school?	What are your plans for the weekend?
What was the last film you saw at the cinema or on television?	What do you think you'll be doing in five years' time?	How much television do you usually watch in a week?
What kind of books do you enjoy reading?	What job would you most like to do?	What sorts of things do you use your computer for?
Tell me a bit about your family.	Where do you think you'll go on holiday this year?	Tell me about a favourite website, or websites, that you often visit.
Talk about a family member that you get on well with.	What sorts of things do you enjoy doing when you go on holiday?	Are there any famous people you would really like to meet?
What do you like about the place where you were brought up?	Tell me about your best friend.	Would you like to be famous?

© Pearson Education Limited 2014 Photocopiable

My brother is absolutely mad about music.

1 (A) ....

2 (B) ....

Her favourite phrase is 'Turn that noise down this instant!'.

3 (B) ....

4 (A) ....

He also watches a lot of music channels on television.

5 (A) ....

6 (B) ....

When there's nothing he likes on television, he surfs the internet for new and exciting stuff.

7 (B) ....

8 (A) ....

To tell you the truth, I think there are some he's never even heard all the way through..

9 (A) ....

10 (B) ....

He also loves going to concerts whenever he can, although he can't really afford to go very often these days.

11 (B) ....

12 (A) ....

He really loved meeting his favourite artists whenever possible.

13 (A) ....

14 (B) ....

His big ambition now is to play in his own rock band.

15 (B) ....

16 (A) ....

I can hear him now. He's a terrible musician!

Student A

(Do not show your sentences to Student B)

- As a result, they're always arguing!
- And he would queue for hours to get a ticket to see a band he really liked.
- He listens to part of one, then moves on to the next.
- He would wait outside the theatre after each concert, hoping to meet them.
- In fact, he's practising as I speak.
- He likes *JTV*, which is dedicated to reggae, and *Life!*, which specialises in dance music.
- He's probably got over five thousand songs stored on it.
- He's always listening to it on the radio.

Student B

(Do not show your sentences to Student A)

- However, his favourite one is *Rock Universe*, which shows all the latest rock videos.
- He's probably getting really good at recognising songs from the first few notes!
- Unfortunately, most of them used to ignore him!
- He plays the guitar, and he's learning to play the drums.
- When he finds a song he likes, he downloads it onto his MP3 player.
- My mum is always complaining that he plays it far too loud.
- Of course, he usually ignores her!
- He used to go to a concert once a week, sometimes twice.

© Pearson Education Limited 2014 Photocopiable

Dialogue pairs

adventure caution comfort difference drama emotion generosity harm hope meaning person pessimism prediction realism reliability sociability sympathy thought

1 I've been driving for 20 years and never had an accident.	**2** The chairs in our classroom are really hard.	**3** You're getting rather fat, aren't you?	**4** Do you think it will be a nice day tomorrow?	**5** No, he looks fierce, but he's completely	**6** Do you? I think it's .... to expect such a big promotion so soon.
7 Did she? That wasn't very		**8** Sarah's always doing surprising and unexpected things, isn't she?	**9** Nothing at all. We're completely		**10** I usually give about 10 percent of my salary to local charities.
11 So does mine. She can get quite	**12** I think I failed my exam yesterday.	**13** That was an incredible storm last night.	**14** Well, don't wait for him too long. He's very ...., and will probably forget.	**15** I agree. They're so	**16** I can believe that. You're a very .... driver.
17 Chris is planning to sail around the world next year.	**18** Not at all. It's just a lot of .... noise to me.			**19** Does your dog bite?	**20** Did he? That was a bit ....
21 Do you? That's very .... of you.	**22** It's your birthday today, isn't it? Happy birthday!	**23** When I told Alice my pet rabbit had died, she just laughed.	**24** Do you like listening to classical music?	**25** Well, I'm not very .... The forecast isn't very good.	**26** Michael's promised to come over and help me with my homework at the weekend.
27 At the party, Joe just sat in the corner playing games on his mobile.		**28** I disagree. I think she's always a bit	**29** Thank you. It's very .... of you to remember.		**30** Don't be so .... I'm sure you've done really well.
31 It certainly was. It was really very	**32** Don't be so ....! I've only put on a kilo or two.	**33** Do you and your brother have anything in common?	**34** I'm only a sales assistant, but I reckon that I'll be the manager this time next month.	**35** My sister always cries when she watches sad films.	**36** That's brave of him. Well, he's always been quite ....

© Pearson Education Limited 2014 Photocopiable

Team A

	1	2	3	4	5	6
A	Having	speak	to call	to see	getting	go
B	to go	visit	flying	look	to visit	have
C	See	going	to work	seeing	to speak	call
D	speaking	get	calling	to get	entering	working
E	looking	fly	to have	visiting	to look	to fly
F	informing	to enter	to inform	work	enter	inform

1 My parents always make us .... our shoes off when we come into the house.
2 I really enjoy .... new people.
3 I really regret .... up so late to watch the film last night.
4 I feel nervous about .... to people I don't know very well.
5 There's a big scratch on my car, but I don't remember .... anything.
6 We had a great time .... across the USA by train last year.
7 I want .... a photography course at our local college, but there are no free places.
8 Our teacher expects us .... her if we think we're going to be absent.
9 As soon as the bell rings, everyone stops .... and goes home.
10 I tried .... the book off the top shelf, but it was too high.
11 His first film was a big success, and he went on .... very famous.
12 I hate not .... people's names when I see them.

Team B

	1	2	3	4	5	6
A	Do	to work	meet	talk	ringing	to do
B	talking	take	hitting	ring	to meet	to remember
C	Hit	to get	doing	to take	get	travel
D	to ring	travelling	become	stay	to travel	work
E	meeting	getting	to talk	working	taking	to hit
F	becoming	staying	remember	to become	remembering	to stay

1 She promised .... me as soon as she got home, but I didn't hear from her.
2 After school I suggested .... a film, but everyone said they were too busy.
3 It was a waste of time .... for the interview, as they had already offered the job to someone else.
4 Most of his colleagues retired when they were in their sixties, but he went on .... into his seventies.
5 Our English teacher won't let us .... our own language in her lessons.
6 I would like my friends .... me more often, but they all live so far away.
7 She told me not .... the room without first knocking on the door.
8 I've always been frightened of .... and travel by train when possible.
9 She was very busy, but stopped .... a chat.
10 If you don't know what a word means, try .... it up in a dictionary.
11 Did you remember .... me some stamps when you went to the post office?
12 We regret .... passengers on flight BG241 to Munich that their flight has been delayed until 8 o'clock.

© Pearson Education Limited 2014 Photocopiable

True or false?

Part 1

1 Describe something that you are interested in.
2 Describe something that you find really boring.
3 Describe something that you are frightened of.
4 Describe something that you often feel worried about.
5 Describe something that you get annoyed by.
6 Describe something embarrassing that once happened to you.
7 Describe something really exciting that you once did.
8 Describe something that you have done for a long time.
9 Describe something interesting or unusual that you once did, or which once happened to you.
10 Describe something that you did regularly in the past, but don't do now (e.g., something that you used to do).
11 Describe something that you have never done, but which most people have done.
12 Describe something that you have been doing for some time.
13 Describe something that you haven't done yet, but plan to do in the future.
14 Describe something that you have just done.

Part 2

Student name	Which of their sentences is true?
	first / second / third
	first / second / third
	first / second / third
	first / second / third
	first / second / third
	first / second / third
	first / second / third
	first / second / third
	first / second / third
	first / second / third
	first / second / third
	first / second / third
	first / second / third
	first / second / third

© Pearson Education Limited 2014 Photocopiable

a laptop	a mobile phone	a camera	a teddy bear	a Swiss army knife
a watch	an mp3 player	a bicycle	a sports car	a credit card
sunglasses	trainers	a dictionary	cheese	a bed
a shower	lipstick	a hair dryer	a television	a video games console
a servant	a washing machine	coffee	an alarm clock	friends
a diary	a hot water bottle	an umbrella	a passport	a pet snake

© Pearson Education Limited 2014 Photocopiable

Part 1

Team A

The weatherman on the evening news had sounded very confident. 'Some viewers (1) .... (*call*) me earlier today to say they (2) .... (*hear*) there is a hurricane on its way. Well, don't worry, there isn't.' We all (3) .... (*believe*) him, of course, so we (4) .... (*be*) completely surprised when, a few hours later, the wind (5) .... (*become*) really strong. By midnight, it (6) .... (*blow*) so hard that trees outside (7) .... (*start*) falling over. Sleep (8) .... (*become*) impossible, especially when the wind (9) .... (*begin*) hitting the windows so hard that we (10) .... (*think*) they would break. By 7 o'clock in the morning, it seemed like the storm (11) .... (*end*) so we (12) .... (*decide*) to go outside to see how bad things were in the street. It was a terrible sight. Tiles from the roofs of the buildings (13) .... (*fall*) into the street, and a lot of trees (14) .... (*blow*) over, some of them onto people's cars. All of a sudden, and without warning, there (15) .... (*be*) a terrific blast of wind. We (16) .... (*hear*) a terrible tearing sound, and (17) .... (*watch*) in horror as the roof of our house (18) .... (*lift*) into the air and (19) .... (*come*) crashing down into the street just metres away from where we (20) .... (*stand*).

Team B

Our flight left Sydney at seven o'clock, and by the time we were over Indonesia, we (1) .... (*fly*) for several hours. As the aircraft (2) .... (*travel*) through the night, most of the passengers (3) .... (*go*) to sleep. The friends I (4) .... (*fly*) with (5) .... (*entertain*) themselves in various ways, listening to music, playing cards and watching the in-flight movie. I (6) .... (*decide*) to read for a bit, so I (7) .... (*open*) the book I (8) .... (*start*) a few hours earlier. Suddenly, there (9) .... (*be*) a loud bang, and everyone (10) .... (*look*) around in confusion. It (11) .... (*be*) obvious that something (12) .... (*go*) wrong, but we couldn't work out what it was. A few seconds later, there was an announcement over the speakers. 'Hello everyone,' a quiet, calm voice (13) .... (*say*). 'This is your captain speaking. We have a slight problem. A few moments ago, a bird (14) .... (*hit*) our number 2 engine, which is now out of action, and we need to make an emergency landing.' It was incredible how calm he (15) .... (*sounded*). It was like he (16) .... (*tell*) us dinner would soon be served or something. We (17) .... (*be*) frightened, of course, and I (18) .... (*expect*) everyone to start shouting and screaming. Instead, they (19) .... (*remain*) strangely calm. My friend in the seat next to mine even (20) .... (*smile*) slightly, and just said 'Whoops!'.

Team C

Last summer, my friends and I went camping in the hills above Red Creek. We (1) .... (*almost / decide*) not to go, because the man on the local radio station a few days earlier (2) .... (*say*) that the weather was going to turn bad and people should avoid the hills. We (3) .... (*go*) anyway, and of course the weather (4) .... (*be*) terrible! The rain (5) .... (*fall*) continuously, and as a result, we (6) .... (*spend*) most of the time in our tents reading or sleeping. We (7) .... (*plan*) to spend a week in the hills, but after three days of continuous rain, we (8) .... (*decide*) to give up and go home. We (9) .... (*pack*) up our tents when we (10) .... (*hear*) a loud rumbling noise. It (11) .... (*sound*) like a train, and at first we (12) .... (*think*) there must be a railway line nearby. Suddenly, one of my friends (13) .... (*shout*), 'Look up there!'. We (14) .... (*look*) to where he (15) .... (*point*) and saw that the trees on the slopes above (16) .... (*move*) down the hill towards us. We (17) .... (*know*) immediately that it was a landslide, but there was no feeling of shock or surprise. In fact, it (18) .... (*be*) quite a beautiful sight, and for a few seconds we just (19) .... (*stand*) there watching it. Then the first trees reached our campsite. The next moment, we (20) .... (*run*) down the hill as fast as our legs could carry us.

Team D

The area where I live experiences a lot of earthquakes, and we all accept them as a normal part of everyday life. Most of them are quite small, but in 2003 we (1) .... (*have*) one that (2) .... (*destroy*) some of the older buildings, and shortly after that the local government (3) .... (*introduce*) rules saying that all new buildings must be earthquake-proof. A couple of years ago, scientists (4) .... (*warn*) us that a big earthquake was due soon. As a result, when it finally (5) .... (*happen*), everyone (6) .... (*make*) plans. We (7) .... (*buy*) extra supplies of food and water and we (8) .... (*make*) arrangements for somewhere to go if our homes were damaged or destroyed. I remember the day very well, because I (9) .... (*celebrate*) my 18th birthday with friends and family when the first tremors (10) .... (*hit*) us. At that time, we (11) .... (*live*) on the 18th floor of an apartment block, and that high up we really (12) .... (*feel*) it, so of course we all (13) .... (*start*) panicking! My father (14) .... (*try*) to assure us that we (15) .... (*be*) quite safe in our earthquake-proof apartment block, but none of us (16) .... (*believe*) him. As a result, as soon as the earthquake (17) .... (*end*), everyone (18) .... (*escape*) to the safety of the street. And believe it or not, that's where we (19) .... (*continue*) celebrating my birthday, while all our neighbours (20) .... (*look*) at us in astonishment!

© Pearson Education Limited 2014 Photocopiable

Part 2

1	A / B / C / D …	… are used to natural disasters.
2	A / B / C / D …	… were all doing different things when something happened.
3	A / B / C / D …	… accepted someone's explanation.
4	A / B / C / D …	… didn't know at first what was happening.
5	A / B / C / D …	… ignored someone's advice.
6	A / B / C / D …	… spent the whole night awake.
7	A / B / C / D …	… were shocked at the damage they saw.
8	A / B / C / D …	… were surprised at how someone reacted to a situation.
9	A / B / C / D …	… changed their plans.
10	A / B / C / D …	… were prepared for an emergency.
11	A / B / C / D …	… felt safer outside than inside.
12	A / B / C / D …	… managed not to panic, despite being afraid.
13	A / B / C / D …	… wrongly assumed that something had finished.
14	A / B / C / D …	… carried on doing something that they had started earlier.
15	A / B / C / D …	… mistook one thing for something else.
16	A / B / C / D …	… didn't react as quickly as they should.

© Pearson Education Limited 2014 Photocopiable

Essay 1

In your English class you have been discussing the benefits of living as part of a large family. Now your teacher has asked you to write an essay.

Write an essay using all the points, and give reasons for your point of view. Write 140–190 words.

Is it better to be part of a large or small family group?

Write about:

1

2

3

Essay 2

In your English class, you have had a discussion about fame and the advantages and disadvantages it brings. Now your teacher has asked you to write an essay.

Write an essay using all the points, and give reasons for your point of view. Write 140 –190 words.

Does being famous have more disadvantages than advantages?

Write about:

1

2

3

Essay 3

In your English class, you have been talking about friendship. Now your teacher has asked you to write an essay.

Write an essay using all the points, and give reasons for your point of view. Write 140–190 words.

Is it better to have a lot of friends you know reasonably well, or just a few friends you are very close to?

Write about:

1

2

3

Essay 4

In your English class, you have been talking about personality. Now your teacher has asked you to write an essay.

Write an essay using all the points, and give reasons for your point of view. Write 140–190 words.

Are confident people more likely to be successful than those who are less confident?

Write about:

1

2

3

© Pearson Education Limited 2014 Photocopiable

A While many of us look with envy on people who have a wide circle of acquaintances …	**B** In some countries and cultures, different generations of the same family live together or in close proximity …
C Many say that you need self-assurance and a strong belief in yourself in order to get on in life, …	**D** Most people are under the impression that film stars, sporting personalities and rock musicians lead an enviable lifestyle, …
E … we often tend to forget that friendship means much more than just *knowing* people.	**F** … and would gladly achieve fame for all the privileges it brings.
G … otherwise you will never get anywhere.	**H** … whereas in others they tend to be dispersed across a wide area.
I However, I believe that the reality for them is quite different …	**J** In fact, it could be argued that the more people we know …
K On the other hand, they point out, there is such a thing as over-confidence.	**L** … the less we could call them friends in the proper sense of the word.
M I think it is hard to say which of these situations is better …	**N** … but as one of five children who grew up surrounded by uncles, aunts, grandparents, etc., I would probably argue in favour of the first.
O … and this can be just as harmful, if not more so, than shyness and inhibition.	**P** … with the problems and challenges they face greatly outweighing the perceived benefits.

© Pearson Education Limited 2014 Photocopiable

many	much	a lot of
lots of	some	a few
very few	hardly any	a little (bit of)
very little	any	no

- You *can* move horizontally left or right, or vertically up or down.
- You *cannot* move diagonally.
- You *cannot* cross the black spaces.
- You can move in more than one direction each time (for example, if you roll a five, you can move three spaces left or right, then two spaces up or down).

salad	honey	advice	salt	snack	fat
calorie		vegetable	coffee		
fruit	meat		chicken	knowledge	
child		**START HERE**			egg
	rice	fish		information	cake
		cheese	water		news
luggage	curry	juice	bread	person	chocolate

© Pearson Education Limited 2014 Photocopiable

1 Oh no, I've .... spilt some orange juice down the front of my new shirt!	**2** The restaurants in my town are good, but some of them .... really expensive.	**3** There aren't .... calories in salad, so it's a good thing to eat if you're on a diet.
4 I love chocolate, even though I know .... can be bad for you if you eat too much.	**5** I love seafood, but .... time I eat it, red spots appear on my face.	**6** Who spilt their coffee .... my computer?
7 This restaurant is terrible. It's the .... time I come here!	**8** The waiters stood .... the corner talking and ignoring the customers.	**9** The pizza was tasty, but it wasn't .... well cooked. (*Do <u>not</u> use 'particularly' in this sentence.*)
10 My uncle used to take me and my sister to Burger World, give us £10 .... and tell us to get whatever we wanted.	**11** I .... like eating out, especially if someone else is paying! (*Do <u>not</u> use 'do' in this sentence.*)	**12** People say that fast food is unhealthy, but not .... of it is bad for you.
13 We have very .... money, so I'm afraid we can't eat out.	**14** Are there .... restaurants near here that serve good vegetarian food?	**15** If you're hungry, there's a packet of biscuits .... the cupboard.
16 I'm afraid there's .... coffee left. Would you like tea instead?	**17** I really like this restaurant .... the terrible service.	**18** He waited .... no one was looking, then started putting the sweets into his pocket.
19 I'm not sure exactly what's in this pie, but I .... taste chicken and some sort of herb.	**20** There's an excellent Italian restaurant .... a kilometre away from our house.	**21** It was .... hot in the kitchen that I could hardly breathe.
22 The soup's a bit tasteless, I'm afraid. Try putting .... salt in it.	**23** I had £40 in cash on me, but it wasn't .... to pay for the meal, so I had to use my credit card.	

© Pearson Education Limited 2014 Photocopiable

Students A and B

Part 1

Situation 1

Speaker 1: So, what did you think?

Speaker 2: Disappointed, I guess. There were a few good moments, and I thought that bit at the end with the dog was great. But to tell you the truth, I'm not really sure what was happening most of the time.

Situation 2

Speaker 1: So, what did you think?

Speaker 2: I wasn't impressed. Nothing really happened, did it? And just when you thought something exciting *would* happen, the screen went blank, the credits rolled and the cinema lights went on! And that was it, you know?

Situation 3

Speaker 1: So, what did you think?

Speaker 2: Well, the first seventy minutes or so were great, but then nothing really happened after that. It was just people talking.

Speaker 1: I know. I don't understand why it didn't just end when the man finally found the person he was looking for.

A

Speaker 2: I agree. It certainly went on a bit, didn't it?

Speaker 1: Well, at least it had a happy ending. I love a happy ending.

Speaker 2: Yes, I have to say, it made me smile.

B

Speaker 1: Me neither. I mean, that long scene with the computer near the beginning of the film really confused me. And after that I couldn't follow the story.

Speaker 2: I guess we'll have to read the book to find out.

C

Speaker 1: Right. I was longing for the woman with the red hair to do something dramatic. But all she did was talk! And I had real problems understanding her accent.

Speaker 2: Yes, I'm not sure what the accent was supposed to be, but it was from nowhere I recognised.

Part 2

1 In their first situation, students C and D are talking about
   (a) … a photograph.
   (b) … a painting.
   (c) … a statue.

2 In their second situation, students C and D are talking about
   (a) … a photograph.
   (b) … a painting.
   (c) … a statue.

3 In their third situation, students C and D are talking about
   (a) … a photograph.
   (b) … a painting.
   (c) … a statue.

© Pearson Education Limited 2014 Photocopiable

Students C and D

Part 1

Situation 1
Speaker 1: It's great, isn't it?
Speaker 2: I'm not so sure. To be honest, I could have done a better job myself. And I've only got a cheap camera.
Speaker 1: How?

Situation 2
Speaker 1: It's great, isn't it?
Speaker 2: Yes, it is. I wonder why it's painted.
Speaker 1: People used to do that hundreds of years ago.

Situation 3
Speaker 1: It's great, isn't it?
Speaker 2: I agree. I love the way the artist has just used different shades of blue and yellow. Who's it supposed to be?
Speaker 1: You mean the person in the picture? I don't know. He's standing next to a movie camera. That should be a clue.

A
Speaker 2: But it's only been painted on the front. If you go round to the back, it's just plain stone.
Speaker 1: Yes, that's a bit strange. Still, I like it.
Speaker 2: Me too. Go on, stand next to it, and I'll take your photo.

B
Speaker 2: Well, I would have taken it with the sun behind me, for a start. This has been taken looking into the sun, so you can't see any details.
Speaker 1: That's why I like it. It makes you study it more closely. You have to look closely to see if it's a man or a woman, if it's a real person or something made of wood or stone.

C
Speaker 2: There's a description underneath. OK, it says it's a portrait of film director Tom Carver by the artist Sara Walton.
Speaker 1: Tom Carver? Oh, he's the one who directed *The Dreaming Statues*, isn't he?

Part 2

1 In their first situation, Students A and B
(a) … thought the film was too long.
(b) … didn't understand the film.
(c) … didn't like the way the film ended.

2 In their second situation, Students A and B
(a) … thought the film was too long.
(b) … didn't understand the film.
(c) … didn't like the way the film ended.

3 In their third situation, Students A and B
(a) … thought the film was too long.
(b) … didn't understand the film.
(c) … didn't like the way the film ended.

© Pearson Education Limited 2014 Photocopiable

Team A

be	expect	finished	get	going	have	I	I'll	I'm	it	leaves	make	meeting
might	our	rain	see	sitting	they're	to	train	visit	will	you		

(1) .... (2) .... (3) .... (4) .... my favourite rock group at the weekend.
Lucky you! Where are they performing?

I'm really hungry. I haven't eaten a thing since this morning.
OK, sit down and (5) .... (6) .... (7) .... a sandwich.

(8) .... (9) .... my friends for a meal after school.
Oh, can I come along too?

This time next week, (10) .... (11) .... (12) .... all my exams.
I bet you'll be glad when they're all over.

I hope the weather stays good for our picnic on Saturday.
(13) .... (14) .... (15) .... (16) .... (17) .... It usually does at the weekend.

This time next week, (18) .... (19) .... (20) .... on a beach in the south of Spain.
Good for you. You really deserve a holiday.

We ought to hurry. (21) .... (22) .... (23) .... in half an hour.
Don't worry. The station is only ten minutes' walk away.

Have you got any plans for the weekend?
I'm not sure yet. (24) .... (25) .... (26) .... the new art gallery on West Street.

Tim and Susan seem really happy together.
Did you know (27) .... (28) .... (29) .... (30) .... married in the summer?

Team B

arrive	be	doors	getting	going	have	he	help	I	I'll	I'm
imagine	it	it's	may	open	seeing	spent	study	the	to	will	you

I've decided that (1) .... (2) .... (3) .... (4) .... French and German at university.
Good idea! You've always been good at languages.

I'm having real problems with my homework.
Let me finish mine, then (5) .... (6) .... (7) ....

(8) .... (9) .... Jo and Mike at the weekend.
When you do, please give them my best wishes.

I hear you have a trip planned to London. It's very expensive there, you know.
I do. By the time I get back, (10) .... (11) .... (12) .... all my money.

I'm worried about our English exam next week.
Don't worry. (13) .... (14) .... (15) .... (16) .... (17) .... quite easy.

Are you looking forward to your holiday?
I certainly am! This time tomorrow (18) .... (19) .... (20) .... on a plane to Turkey.

What time does the show begin?
(21) .... (22) .... (23) .... at 8 o'clock, so we should be there by 7.30.

Is Roger coming to the party tonight?
Yes, but he's got to get across the city, so (24) .... (25) .... (26) .... a bit late.

According to the weather forecast, (27) .... (28) .... (29) .... (30) .... a lovely day tomorrow.
I'll believe that when I see it!

© Pearson Education Limited 2014 Photocopiable

Student A

© Pearson Education Limited 2014 Photocopiable

Student B

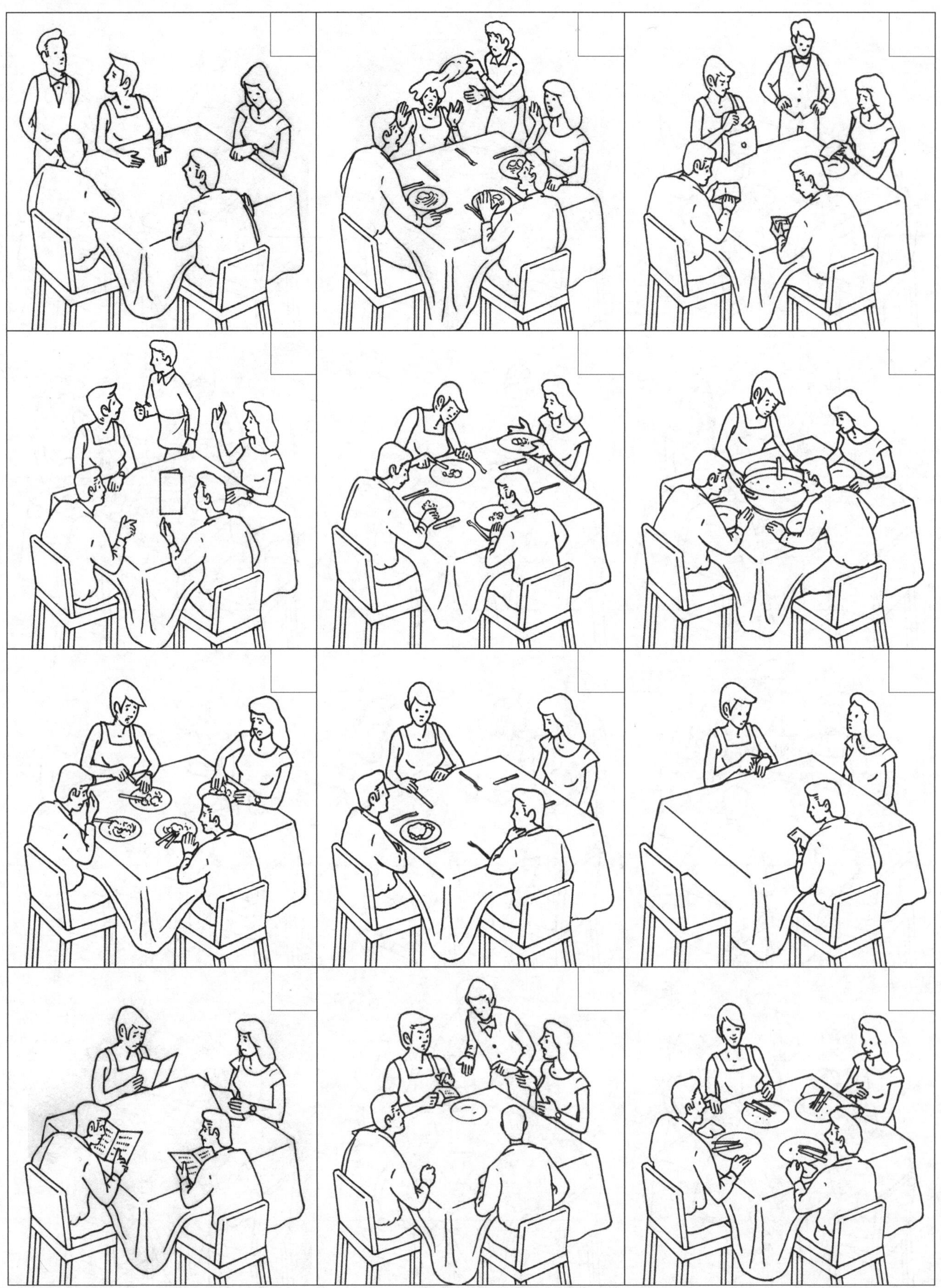

© Pearson Education Limited 2014 Photocopiable

but instead (10)	but unfortunately (16)	enough (6)	imagine how (10)	not only … but also (14)		
on top of that (11)	so (2)	such (4)	to make matters worse (18)	to my amazement (13)	too (3)	
very (4)	what's more (9)	where (5)	which (5)	who (3)	whose (5)	why (3)

Your article or story	**Points won/lost**
Last summer I decided to …	
1	
2	
3	
4	
5	
6	
7	
8	
9	
10	
11	
12	
13	
14	
15	
16	
17	
18	
Total points	

© Pearson Education Limited 2014 Photocopiable

Team A

Here are your sentences to read to Team B:

1 Let me make you something to eat.
2 Let's go out for a meal on Saturday.
3 Don't forget to call your mother.
4 You should leave as early as possible.
5 How are you going to get to London?

Use these verbs in their correct form to complete your own sentences.

accuse	ask	deny	explain	tell

1 He ______________________ his computer without asking him first.

2 He __________________ him.

3 He ______________________ camera.

4 He __________________________ absent on Monday because he had been ill.

5 He _____________________ keys with the receptionist.

Team B

Here are your sentences to read to Team A:

1 You used my computer without asking me first.
2 Could you help me, please?
3 I didn't break your camera.
4 I was absent on Monday because I was ill.
5 Leave your keys with the receptionist.

Use these verbs in their correct form to complete your own sentences.

advise	ask	offer	remind	suggest

1 He _____________________ something to eat.

2 He ________________________ for a meal on Saturday.

3 He ______________________ my mother.

4 He ______________________ as early as possible.

5 He ____________________ going to get to London.

© Pearson Education Limited 2014 Photocopiable

Students A and B

Here are your sentences to read to students C and D.

1 I've often heard people say that if you have knowing, you have power.

2 I don't particularly like my job, but I think my employee pays me quite well.

3 I love playing the piano and would love to be a professional musical one day.

4 Tourist plays an important role in my town, but the current economic crisis means that we are getting far fewer visitors than normal.

5 I've always been interested in a career in journalist, and I would love to work for a national newspaper.

6 I'm afraid I find your behaving completely unacceptable!

7 On the whole my pronunciation is quite good, but I have real difficult pronouncing words that begin with *th*.

Students C and D

Here are your sentences to read to students A and B.

8 Over 20 people were interested in the job, but we felt that none of the application were suitable.

9 A new industrial estate in the suburbs led to the creativity of over 600 new jobs.

10 People attending an interview are requested to report to reception on their arriving.

11 If you need to find accommodation, we suggest arranging a meeting with one of our student advice.

12 Unless a teacher is present, you need to ask for permit to use the computer room.

13 I would love to be an actor, but I lack the confident to perform in front of an audience.

14 Represent from all the main departments held a meeting to discuss plans for the future of the company.

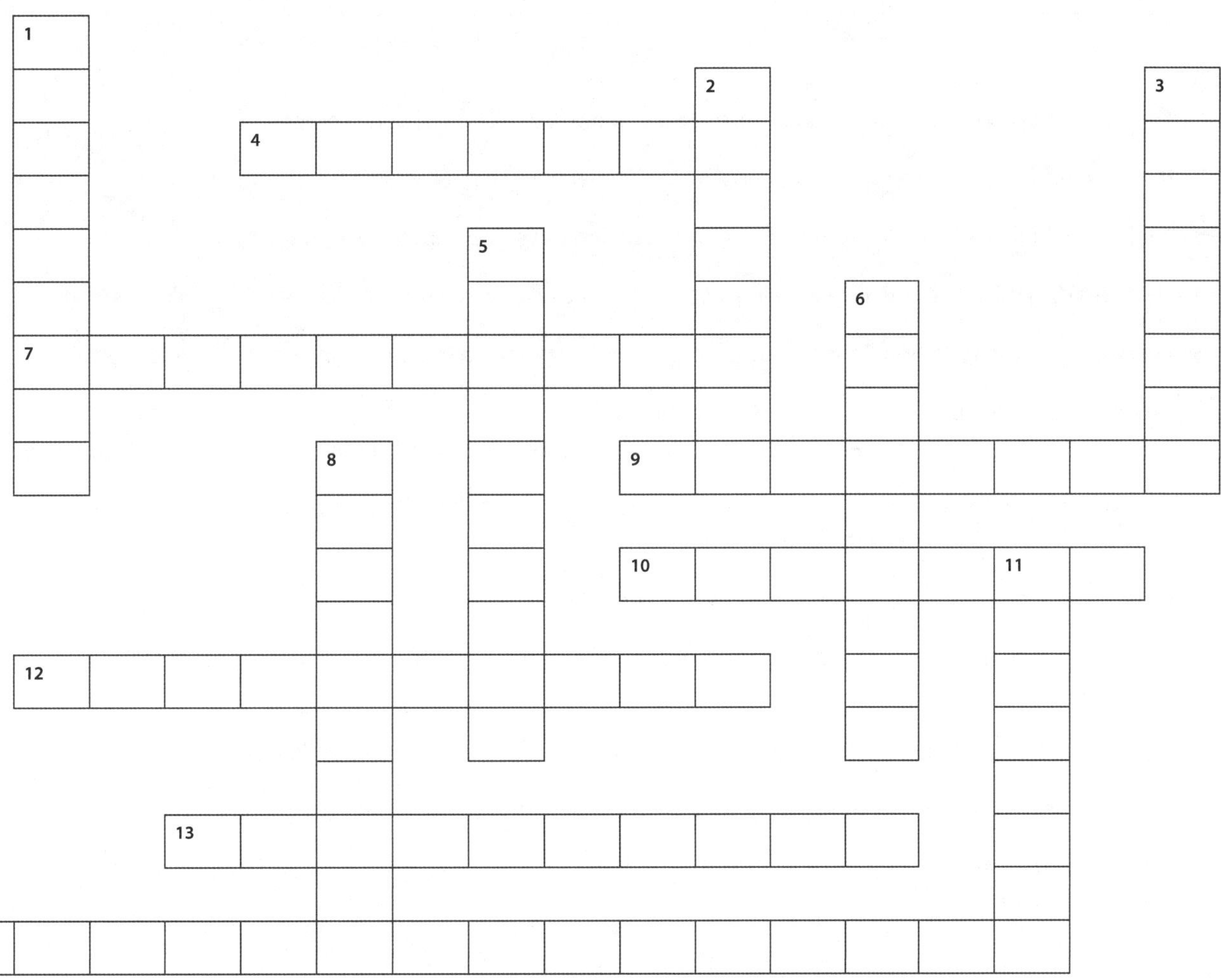

© Pearson Education Limited 2014 Photocopiable

Part 1

aim	be	cope	face	focus	fulfil	give	let	make	overcome	set	take

(a) Same here. It's good to .... yourself a deadline. (..............)

(b) You're just like me. I always .... for the top as well. (..............)

(c) Me too. I need to .... motivated if I'm to get anywhere. (..............)

(d) I've had to .... a lot of setbacks as well. (..............)

(e) I'm the same. Like you, I really don't think I can .... my potential until I've studied more. (..............)

(f) I agree. If you don't .... a go of it, you'll never know. (..............)

(g) I find it hard to .... under pressure as well. (..............)

(h) I agree. It feels bad when you .... your team down. (..............)

(i) Same here. It's better to .... up to problems rather than hide from them. (..............)

(j) Me too. I .... on achieving my goals, and nothing else matters. (..............)

(k) Right. Things get boring if you can't .... on new rivals from time to time. (..............)

(l) Me too. I never .... in to pressure. (..............)

Part 2

1 I think it's important to try anything once, even if you don't think you'll be successful.

2 It wasn't easy becoming a successful tennis player. Earlier in my career, I had a lot of failures.

3 I enjoy playing chess, but I'm getting fed up with playing the same people every day.

4 I hate making mistakes when I'm working, especially if it causes problems for the people I work with.

5 Everyone tells me I'm a good photographer, but I really think I need to learn more. I could do a lot better.

6 When I'm given a job to do, I always make a mental note of when I intend to get it finished, and then stick to it.

7 I'm a good worker when I'm allowed to work at my own pace, but I hate it when people say things like 'Come on, hurry up, we need that work now!'.

8 Once I've started something, I never stop, even if I find it really difficult.

9 I can only get things done if there are people around me who can encourage me and tell me that I'm doing well.

10 Whenever I take part in something, I just have to win, I have to be the best. Nothing else will do.

11 When I have a difficult or demanding job to do, I ignore everything else that is going on around me.

12 Whenever I do something wrong, I don't ignore it. I look at where I've gone wrong and then try not to make the same mistake again.

© Pearson Education Limited 2014 Photocopiable

Team A

Here are your sentences to read to Team B:

1 I want to go to the beach at the weekend, but it depends on the weather.

2 I hope to go to the USA next year, but my parents might not let me.

3 I would like to buy a new computer, but I don't have enough money.

4 I want to travel around the world, but I don't have enough time or money.

5 I went to bed late last night, and as a result I didn't wake up on time this morning.

6 I went for a walk in the rain last week, and as a result I caught a cold.

Answer/score card

3 points: You are *very* sure your answer is grammatically correct.
2 points: You are *quite* sure your answer is grammatically correct.
1 point: You are *not very* sure your answer is correct.

Sentence number	Your conditional sentences	Points risked	Total points
1			
2			
3			
4			
5			
6			

Team B

Here are your sentences to read to Team A:

1 I wanted to ask Peter for some advice about language courses, but I didn't see him.

2 I decided to walk to school instead of taking the bus, and as a result I was late.

3 I want to become a famous actor, but I'm not very confident.

4 I would like a cat, but my parents don't like having animals in the house.

5 I want to go to the cinema tonight, but it depends on the amount of homework I have.

6 I plan to do a painting course at my local college, but there might not be any free places.

Answer/score card

3 points: You are *very* sure your answer is grammatically correct.
2 points: You are *quite* sure your answer is grammatically correct.
1 point: You are *not very* sure your answer is correct.

Sentence number	Your conditional sentences	Points risked	Total points
1			
2			
3			
4			
5			
6			

© Pearson Education Limited 2014 Photocopiable

1
My best friend and I go back a long time. We've known each other since primary school, in fact. It's strange that we're such good friends, because we're very different in so many ways. I'm quite a quiet person, and my friend is one of those people who's always in a crowd talking and laughing. I guess the thing that makes us such good friends is that we've done a lot together over the years. And while we spend a lot of time talking about the good times we've had together in the past, we also talk a lot about the things we want to do in the future.

2
If you asked me what I like about my best friend, it would be very difficult to give you an answer. We aren't interested in the same things, we don't like the same music, we rarely rely on each other for help when we need it, and we disagree on so many things. In fact, when we meet up, we seem to spend a lot of our time arguing! I suppose the reason is that we feel comfortable in each other's company. We feel we can be ourselves, if you know what I mean.

3
I think the thing I like about my best friend is that we share one common feature. We're both very sure of ourselves. Some people walk into a room full of strangers and feel very uncomfortable, or very conscious of everything they say and do. They worry that they might say something stupid. But we're not like that at all. We can go up to strangers, people we've never met, and start a conversation. Or we can stand up in a room full of people and make a speech.

4
I never really expected my best friend to become my best friend. In fact, for years we didn't even like each other very much. There was absolutely nothing we had in common. And then one day, on a school trip, he was listening to something on his MP3 player, and I said 'What are you listening to?', so he passed me one of the earphones and I put it in my ear and, well, it was great. He said it was a band called 'Nuclear Muffin'. Anyway, after that he lent me some of his albums, and I realised that we both liked the same kind of stuff. And since then we've got on really well.

5
People like each other for different reasons, don't they? Sometimes it's because they both find the same things funny, or perhaps it's because they've done a lot of the same things, so you can relate to them a lot. In the case of my best friend and I, I think we get on so well because we like doing the same things, and we have a similar view of the world. For example, we're both concerned about the environment, we're both vegetarians, we're both keen on old black and white films, little things like that.

6
Whenever my best friend and I are together, the time just goes by so quickly! He's great fun to be with. In all the years I've known him, I don't think we've ever had a serious conversation, probably because we don't share any interests. But we tell each other jokes, play tricks on each other, and things like that. And he's always saying and doing the most outrageous things. I promise you that when you meet him, you won't be able to stop smiling. He's also very generous. If he's got something, like a bar of chocolate or a pizza, he'll insist on sharing it with you.

© Pearson Education Limited 2014 Photocopiable

Activity sheet

Part 1

Complete the sentences by writing the name of the speaker and a correct expression from the box. There are three expressions that you do not need.

… share the same taste in music	… are often there for each other	… are self-conscious
… are self-centred	… do not often see eye to eye	… have shared memories
… enjoy having a laugh together	… have a lot in common	… are self-confident

1 .... and his/her best friend ....

2 .... and his/her best friend ....

3 .... and his/her best friend ....

4 .... and his/her best friend ....

5 .... and his/her best friend ....

6 .... and his/her best friend ....

Part 2

Now look at the expressions you wrote in sentences 1–6, and write down the letters indicated below (note that if your expression includes a hyphen (-), you should not count this as a letter).

Sentence 1: write the 5th and 12th letters from the expression. ....

Sentence 2: write the 3rd and 11th letters from the expression. ....

Sentence 3: write the 5th, 9th and 11th letters from the expression. ....

Sentence 4: write the 2nd and 21st letters from the expression. ....

Sentence 5: write the 13th and 15th letters from the expression. ....

Sentence 6: write the 15th letter and the last letter from the expression. ....

Finally, write the letters above in the sentence below in the same order to reveal a hidden expression.

The reason why I get on with my best friend is that we both have the same _ _ _ _ _ _   _ _   _ _ _ _ _ _ _ _.

© Pearson Education Limited 2014 Photocopiable

1 The man who sells newspapers in the town square is very friendly.	**2** This is just another website which claims to find customers the best deals.
3 My uncle has a long beard which reaches down to his chest.	**4** My father grows wonderful strawberries which burst with flavour.
5 He was angry with me because I had left without him.	**6** We live in a world which is obsessed with celebrity.
7 I have a sword which is believed to have been used by Napoleon.	**8** I broke my arm while I was playing football last Saturday.
9 He told us about a lost city which had been discovered by explorers in the 18th century.	**10** When I was walking to work yesterday, I saw something very strange.
11 For my birthday she gave me a cake which had been baked by her mother.	**12** I had a part-time job last summer in which I took people on guided tours of my town.
13 There weren't enough sandwiches for everyone to have one each, which meant we had to share.	**14** While I was driving into town the other day, I saw a boy who was standing in the middle of the road.

© Pearson Education Limited 2014 Photocopiable

Part 1

If he (invite) me, I (probably / go).

If I (not / had) so much of it, I (not/have) such a sore stomach this morning.

I (go) if I (like) seafood.

I (not/go) if I (know) how bored I was going to be.

It (be) cheaper if I (do) it all myself.

If I (ask) them to throw me a big party, I wonder if they (agree).

If we (have) one illegally, we (probably get) into trouble.

However, if it (rain), we (have to) do something else.

I (go) if we (be allowed) to bring a guest.

If I (spend) more time talking instead, I (not/be) in such pain this morning.

I (be) much happier if they (organised) a meal out with my friends.

I (see) my friend Rob if I (stay) a bit longer.

I (go) if I (like) parties, but I don't, so I didn't.

If I (leave) earlier, I (not/be) so tired this morning.

✂---

Part 2

1 I stayed at the party until 2 o'clock this morning. .... I really don't know how I'm going to stay awake in class.	2 I didn't know many people at the party, so I left early. .... Apparently he turned up a few minutes after I had gone.
3 My friends Jo and Tim had a party last night. .... Instead, I stayed at home and watched television.	4 Alice had a dinner party last night in which every course she served was fish. .... Unfortunately, I get terribly ill if I eat it.
5 The food at the party last night was absolutely delicious. .... I don't think I'll be able to eat anything today.	6 I'm thinking of asking a local restaurant to prepare the food for my party at the weekend. .... Unfortunately, I'm not very good in the kitchen.
7 I danced for hours at the party last night. .... My feet and legs are absolutely killing me!	8 My parents say they've planned a party for my next birthday. .... A picnic at the beach would also have been quite nice.
9 Mike is having a party tonight. .... There's nothing I like more than a good party.	10 At the end of the term, the school is going to hold a big party for all the students. .... However, I'm pretty sure the invitation will say 'school students only'.
11 My parents have asked me what I'd like to do on my birthday. .... They might not want a lot of strangers in their house.	12 My friends and I have planned a big beach party at the weekend. .... The weather at this time of year can be so unpredictable.
13 There's a big sign on the beach that says 'No parties'. .... I really don't want to spend my evening at the police station!	14 The party I went to last night was absolutely terrible. .... There was no food, no music, no dancing, and everyone just talked about their jobs!

© Pearson Education Limited 2014 Photocopiable

1 my only I rude hadn't yesterday been If so to teacher

....

Student names: ....

2 feel I as though I've just for enough ten eaten food

....

Student names: ....

3 phones hadn't mobile invented Suppose been

....

Student names: ....

4 I had clothes some enough If to money buy new only

....

Student names: ....

5 friends wish visit my more would often I me

....

Student names: ....

6 didn't I'd play rather music loud you your so

....

Student names: ....

7 school refused we all rules to Suppose the obey

....

Student names: ....

8 work wish I didn't I so weekend much to have do this

....

Student names: ....

9 at tonight rather I'd than go stay out home

....

Student names: ....

10 we all environment more It's to time the help did

....

Student names: ....

© Pearson Education Limited 2014 Photocopiable

Student A

actor ☐ artist ☐ athlete ☐ bank manager ☐ bank robber ☐ call centre worker ☐ chef ☐ doctor ☐
electrician ☐ explorer ☐ farmer ☐ fashion designer ☐ film director ☐ hairdresser ☐ hotel receptionist ☐
journalist ☐ mechanic ☐ model ☐ parent ☐ photographer ☐ pilot ☐ police officer ☐ postman/woman ☐
rock star ☐ shop manager ☐ soldier ☐ student ☐ taxi driver ☐ teacher ☐ television presenter ☐
travel agent ☐ vet ☐ waiter ☐ writer ☐

Student B

actor ☐ artist ☐ athlete ☐ bank manager ☐ bank robber ☐ call centre worker ☐ chef ☐ doctor ☐
electrician ☐ explorer ☐ farmer ☐ fashion designer ☐ film director ☐ hairdresser ☐ hotel receptionist ☐
journalist ☐ mechanic ☐ model ☐ parent ☐ photographer ☐ pilot ☐ police officer ☐ postman/woman ☐
rock star ☐ shop manager ☐ soldier ☐ student ☐ taxi driver ☐ teacher ☐ television presenter ☐
travel agent ☐ vet ☐ waiter ☐ writer ☐

---

don't have to	have to	must	needn't have	not allowed to

A = an obligation you feel is necessary
B = an obligation someone else says is necessary
C = things that aren't permitted
D = a lack of necessity/obligation
E = something that you did but wasn't necessary

⇩ START ⇧						
1A	2C	3B	4C	5A	6E	7D
	8B	9A	10C	1B	2E	
3A	4A	5C	6B	7C	8B	9E
10E		1C	2D	3D		4B
5B	6B	7A	8C	9E	10A	1A
1D	2E		4D		5A	6B
7A	8D	9E	10C	1E	2E	3B
4C	5E	6D		7C	8B	9D
10B	1D	2B	3D	4C	5C	6E
7E	8C		9E		10A	1C
2C	3A	4C	5D	6A	7B	8A
9D		10E	1D	2D		3B
4C	5B	6D	7E	8C	9E	10D
	1D	2A	3B	4E	5B	
6A	7B	8E	9A	10D	1C	2A
FINISH						

© Pearson Education Limited 2014 Photocopiable

Cops and robbers

about	across	after	ahead	at	away	down	from	in	of	off	on	out	over	to	up	with

	Cop 1 Start		**Cop 2 Start**	
1 His acting career really took ...... after he had made his first film.	**2** I used to like coffee, but I've gone ...... it recently.	**3** My father travels all ...... the world selling medical equipment.	**4** My leg injury prevented me ...... taking part in the race.	**5** I'm sorry I forgot your birthday, but I promise to make ...... for it.
6 When I was clearing out the house, I came ...... a box of old photos.	**7** I have always looked ...... to my older brother.	**8** When I left my country to work in Australia, all my friends came to the airport to see me	**9** My brother is also my best friend. He means the world ...... me.	**10** We were only expecting about twenty people, but over a hundred turned ....
11 I must sort ...... my files – they're in a terrible mess.	**12** I need a holiday. I really need to get ...... for a week or two.	**13** I've always been interested ...... history.	**14** I have some good news – we've been told we can go ...... with the project.	**15** She was a creative young artist with the world ...... her feet.
16 You're always complaining ...... the food in the college canteen!	**17** I didn't want to get involved ...... the argument, but unfortunately I did.	**18** This place is a mess. What's been going ......?	**19** I don't mind snakes, but I'm frightened ...... spiders.	**20** Like many other people, I worry ...... the state of the environment.
21 The night before the exam, I went ...... my course notes in detail.	**22** When I passed all my exams, I was on top ...... the world.	**23** I get very worked ...... when people are rude to me for no reason.	**24** I'm afraid I'll have to turn ...... your offer.	**25** I take ...... my mother in many different ways.
26 I was so angry ...... her that several days went by before I could talk to her again.	**27** The pills I took reduced the pain in my knee, but the effect soon wore	**28** I took ...... singing professionally after I had won a talent competition.	**29** I was expecting the evening to be very boring, but it turned ...... to be great fun.	**30** He doesn't notice what's happening around him. He's ...... a world of his own.
31 I can't work ...... why Helen is so angry all the time.	**32** I've never been very keen ...... seafood, but I quite like prawns.	**33** We had to put ...... the start of the race because not all the competitors were present.	**34** We tried to get into the concert, but we were turned	**35** With your new job and new flat, things have worked ...... really well for you, haven't they?
36 He was very friendly at first, but then he suddenly turned ...... me and said I was stupid.	**37** I hope to take ...... my father's business when he retires.	**38** Oh no, the computer system has gone ...... again!	**39** The horrible smell in the restaurant really put me ...... my food.	**40** During the winter, the village becomes completely cut ...... from the outside world.
Robber 1 Start				**Robber 2 Start**

© Pearson Education Limited 2014 Photocopiable

Student A

1 I'm sorry, could you .... that, please?
2 .... of these photos show people on holiday.
3 So .... you're saying most teenagers don't enjoy reading?
4 That's very ....
5 The object in the picture is a .... of camera that sees if people are driving too fast.
6 One picture shows an expensive restaurant, ... the other shows a fast food restaurant.
7 I .... the people in the pictures are either packing to go on holiday or moving house.
8 So, what's your .... on that?
9 ...., I think we've reached a decision on that, haven't we?
10 The most important point, oh, I'm sorry, please .... on.
11 I don't think I explained that very well. What I .... to say was, most students want a good job.
12 OK, let me .... Well, I think that … .
13 I see what you ...., but I see things differently.
14 I'm ...., did you ask me why people like travelling?
15 I agree up to a ...., but there are other things to consider.

✂- -

Student B

all	anyway	apologise	basically	both	continue	correct	go	however	intend	kind	mean
meant	point	repeat	right	say	see	sorry	speak	suppose	true	view	while	wonder

✂- -

Student C

A correcting yourself or making something clearer
B saying something in a different way if you don't know the word
C giving yourself time to think after being asked a question
D checking you understand what someone has said
E asking someone to say something again
F talking about differences
G interrupting someone when you think they have finished speaking
H talking about how two things are similar
I bringing a discussion to an end
J disagreeing with someone
K agreeing with someone
L partly agreeing with someone
M asking someone what they think
N saying what you think people are doing (in a photograph, for example)
O confirming you understand what someone has said by summarising what they've said

© Pearson Education Limited 2014 Photocopiable

0	p	r	e	s	i	d	e	n	t	h	i	m	s	e	l	f
1																
2																
3																
4																
5																

6																
7																
8																
9																
10																

I can never remember anything. I've got a *m*_ _ _ _ _ _ like a _ _ _ _ _ _ !

Student A

Here are your sentences to read to Student B:

1. Here's £5, children. Go to the shop on the corner and buy something nice and cold to drink.
2. There are so many rules for cricket that even professional cricket players are unable to remember all of them.
3. Susan, I'm worried that you'll make ill if you don't start eating properly and getting more exercise.
4. The visiting speaker stood up, said hello and told us a little bit about before explaining what she expected to do during our session.
5. I wasn't looking forward to the exam, but I reminded there was nothing to worry about, as I had done plenty of revision.

Student B

Here are your sentences to read to Student A:

6. Robert studied closely in the mirror and thought, 'I look terrible. I must have a shave and get my hair cut.'
7. You don't need to worry about leaving the computer on because it turns off when it isn't used for more than an hour.
8. We tidied the room so thoroughly before my mother came that you would have thought the Queen of England was coming to visit.
9. The flight from London to Singapore would take thirteen hours, so Alice and I prepared for a long, boring journey.
10. The two men walked into the room without introducing and sat down without asking me for permission.

© Pearson Education Limited 2014 Photocopiable

Part 1

1	2	3	4 ....
5	6	7	8 ....
9	10	11	12 ....
13	14	15	16 ....
17	18	19	20 ....

Part 2

1 2 3 4 5 6 7 8 9 10 11 12 13 14 15 16 17 18 19 20

© Pearson Education Limited 2014 Photocopiable

A She's got a real **bee in her bonnet** about it.	**B** As you can imagine, I felt **like a fish out of water**.	**C** I'm afraid I've **got bigger fish to fry**.
D She stood there in the middle of the room **looking like a drowned rat**.	**E** In fact, I've **made** a complete **dog's breakfast of it**.	**F** She's **like a dog with two tails**.
G A lot of her colleagues think she's a bit of **a cold fish**.	**H** Except Rick, that is, who **looked like something that the cat dragged in**.	**I** That's the one thing about him that really **gets my goat**.
J They get the impression he's the kind of person who **wouldn't say boo to a goose**.	**K** Why do I always have to **do the donkey work**?	**L** However, to be honest, I **smelt a rat**.
M I never realised he was such **a dark horse**.	**N** Everyone had **a whale of a time**!	**O** They all think she's **the bee's knees**.

Answer key

1 I Something that **gets your goat** annoys you.
2 E If you **make a dog's breakfast of** something, you do it really badly
3 M A **dark horse** is someone with a skill, talent or achievement that surprises you when you discover it.
4 A If you have **a bee in your bonnet** about something, especially something that annoys you, you can't stop talking about it.
5 H Someone who **looks like something that the cat dragged in** is very untidy or scruffy.
6 D Someone who **looks like a drowned rat** is very wet.
7 L If you **smell a rat**, you are suspicious about something.
8 B Someone who is or feels **like a fish out of water** is uncomfortable because they feel they do not belong in a place or situation.
9 O Someone who is **the bee's knees** is wonderful.
10 G **A cold fish** is someone who is not very friendly.
11 K If you **do the donkey work**, you do the jobs that are boring and/or difficult.
12 C If you have **bigger fish to fry**, you have more important things to do.
13 N If you have **a whale of a time**, you have a very good time.
14 F Someone who is **like a dog with two tails** is extremely happy.
15 J Someone who **wouldn't say boo to a goose** is very shy and timid.

© Pearson Education Limited 2014 Photocopiable

1 Chris has a lot of good points, but punctuality isn't one of them. But he won't change, I know, even though he knows how I feel about it.	**2** I've just read the essay I wrote last night, and I'm not at all happy. I wonder if I should write it again before I hand it in.	**3** I found out the other day that Tommy can speak ancient Greek and Latin. I wonder what other talents he's hiding from us.
4 Vivienne won't stop going on about the terrible service we got in that restaurant last night. I really wish she'd change the subject.	**5** It was an expensive restaurant, so we all wore our best clothes. Quite frankly, I'm surprised they let him in dressed like that.	**6** Just as the storm ended, the front door flew open and Carol crashed into the room. 'The weather forecast got it wrong again!' she said angrily, dripping all over the floor.
7 Samantha told us that she was late because her car had broken down and she had to take the bus. If that had been the case, I wondered, why was she holding her car keys?	**8** On the first day in my new job, I had no idea what I was supposed to be doing. Eventually, I found someone who was prepared to show me what my duties were.	**9** Everyone in my English class likes our teacher, Mrs Searle. Personally, I don't think she's as good as they think she is.
10 Alison doesn't talk much, and she never socialises after work. Actually, I just think she's a bit shy.	**11** I'm utterly fed up being asked to tidy up everyone's mess. I think someone else should do it for a change.	**12** I won't be going to the office party tonight. The boss wants me to help him organise this year's conference.
13 Your party last Saturday was great fun. I haven't enjoyed myself so much in years.	**14** Jane hasn't stopped smiling since she got her exam results. I haven't seen her this happy since she won the writing competition last year.	**15** A lot of people have the wrong idea about my brother. However, anyone who has seen him lose his temper when he's angry will know that that isn't the case!

© Pearson Education Limited 2014 Photocopiable

Pearson Education Limited
Edinburgh Gate
Harlow
Essex CM20 2JE
England
and Associated Companies throughout the world.

www.pearsonelt.com/exams

© Pearson Education Limited 2014

Teaching notes by Clementine Annabell
Photocopiable activities by Rawdon Wyatt

The right of Clementine Annabell and Rawdon Wyatt to be identified as authors of this Work has been asserted by them in accordance with the Copyright, Designs and Patents Act 1988.

All rights reserved; no part of this publication may be reproduced, stored in a retrieval system, or transmitted in any form or by any means, electronic, mechanical, photocopying, recording, or otherwise without the prior written permission of the Publishers or a licence permitting restricted copying in the United Kingdom issues by the Copyright Licensing Agency Ltd, 90 Tottenham Court Road, London.

Photocopying: The Publisher grants permission for the photocopying of those pages marked 'photocopiable' according to the following conditions. Individual purchasers may make copies for their own use or for use by the classes they teach. Institutional purchasers may make copies for use by their staff and students, but this permission does not extend to additional institutions or branches. Under no circumstances may any part of this book be photocopied for resale.

First edition published 2012
New edition first published 2014
Third impression 2015

ISBN: 978-1-4479-0718-3

Set in Myriad Pro
Printed in Malaysia (CTP-PJB)

Acknowledgements
Illustrated by Oxford Designers & Illustrators